A REMARKABLE MAN

THE STORY OF **GEORGE CHESTERTON**

SHIRE PUBLICATIONS

A REMARKABLE MAN

THE STORY OF **GEORGE CHESTERTON**

Wartime pilot, county cricketer,
public school housemaster, civic figure

With best wishes, and many happy memories.

George

Best wishes, Jock !

Good memories of Brecon trips !

Andy

Andrew Murtagh

Published in Great Britain in 2012 by Shire Publications Ltd,
Midland House, West Way, Botley, Oxford OX2 0PH, United Kingdom.
44-02 23rd Street, Suite 219, Long Island City, NY 11101, USA.

E-mail: shire@shirebooks.co.uk www.shirebooks.co.uk

A CIP catalogue record for this book is available from the British Library.

ISBN-13: 978 1 78096 597 0

Andrew Murtagh has asserted his right under the Copyright, Designs and
Patents Act, 1988, to be identified as the author of this book.

Designed by Myriam Bell Design and typeset in Cochin
Printed in China through Worldprint Ltd
Cover originated by PDQ Media, Bungay, UK

12 13 14 15 16   10 9 8 7 6 5 4 3 2 1

Front cover: George watching the match after finishing his stint with the ball.
Back cover: George, 2011. (Daniel Eglin, Malvern College)

Photographs: All photographs from George Chesterton's personal collection,
unless otherwise credited.

CONTENTS

FOREWORDS

Tom Graveney OBE

I first met George Chesterton when he was 22 yards away. I was playing for Gloucestershire and he was playing for Oxford University. It was 1949. I hadn't been in very long but I was feeling comfortable and confident and I wanted a big score. Then suddenly he bowled me! It was a good ball, doing me through the gate and knocking over my middle stump for three. He was deceptive, bowling in-swingers and little cutters, slightly quicker than he looked. I was his first first-class wicket, something he has never let me forget! He also got me out in the second innings to one of the finest catches I have ever seen. I had scored a hundred, so you could say that I had my revenge.

Our paths crossed rarely for a number of years, certainly not on the field of play. When I moved from Gloucestershire to Worcestershire, George had already retired from playing but he was now on the committee of the club and I met him again. When he was appointed president in 1990, we became firm friends. He brought good sense to the presidency at a time when the club was doing well on the pitch. Everybody found him charming and humorous but he could be strong too and was not afraid to make his feelings known. It was he who recommended that I succeed him as president and I have always been grateful for that and the support he gave me in my term of office. We have remained in close touch ever since and I can truthfully say that there has never been a nicer man in the game. George Chesterton is a gentleman to the core. And he wasn't a bad bowler either!

Tom Graveney

6

Lord MacLaurin of Knebworth

George Chesterton is known to generations of old boys of Malvern College as a master, housemaster and deputy head, and latterly as secretary of the OM Society. He has dedicated his life to the school. We all have our memories of George, which this book will no doubt highlight. I remember him as an inspiration to me when he was master in charge of cricket and he taught me many lessons on the field of play that I have taken with me for the rest of my life. So, GHC or George – however you remember your time with him – there has never been a greater Malvernian.

Ian MacLaurin

PROLOGUE
A TRAIN JOURNEY

I can remember almost exactly the moment when it occurred to me that I would like to write a book about George Chesterton. I had boarded the early morning express to Paddington at Great Malvern railway station, luckily found myself a window seat in a quiet carriage and was settling myself down for a peaceful couple of hours. It was early June 1996 and the weather, if memory serves me right, was balmy and settled and promised a fine day. My destination was in deepest Essex but at least the first stage of my journey, to London, had all the potential for a most welcome snooze. I was a housemaster at a boarding school and sleep is a precious commodity in that job. As the train slowly drew out of the station, I could already feel my eyes beginning to droop.

'Hello, Andy. What a pleasant surprise! Mind if I join you?'

The voice was unmistakeable and familiar to me.

'Of course not, George,' I lied.

He settled himself down alongside me and stretched out his long legs.

'Forgive me for not sitting opposite,' he said, 'The old knees don't take too kindly to being squashed up.'

Now, I yielded to no one in my admiration and affection for my travelling companion but by God I was tired and how much I yearned for the diminishing prospect of a decent nap. It was churlish of me, I know, for George was no tedious bore. On the contrary, you could not but be buoyed up in his company. He was one of those people who made you feel better about the world after just five minutes in his company. But I did so want to get my head down and *sleep*.

'I guess you're off to the funeral too,' he said.

That reminded me, if such a reminder was necessary, of the gloomy purpose of my journey. A boy who had been in my cricket XI at Malvern College (he had been a doughty vice-captain, a solid bat and a more than reasonable off-spinner) had died of cancer at the shockingly young age of 32 and the funeral promised to be an emotional and depressing occasion. Put simply, Simon Creffield was one of the nicest boys you could possibly wish to meet, with an army of friends, many from Malvern, who were bound to be at the church. I wasn't looking forward to it.

Neither was George. He was attending as the secretary of the old boys' association but he would have gone anyway. Simon had been a fixture in the old boys' cricket team and nothing was closer to George's heart than cricket. Especially Malvern College cricket. For a while, we pondered the cruelty of a young life cut short and the randomness of fate. It could well have developed into a most melancholy conversation.

But George doesn't do melancholy. He was soon in the groove, entertaining me with interesting and humorous anecdotes on a wide variety of topics. My tiredness evaporated. I was transfixed as story after story tumbled from his lips. Actually 'tumbled' is an inaccurate term. He has a measured and lugubrious delivery, somewhat circuitous in its narrative, such that you worry at times that he has lost his way. Not a bit of it. He has that knack of bringing all the threads of his discourse together in the nick of time and the *coup de grâce* is always delivered with impeccable timing, accompanied unfailingly with a distinctive low rumble of a chuckle.

Worcester, Pershore, Evesham ... one by one the stations flashed by and still the tales were intricately woven. I knew that he had a reputation as a consummate raconteur but there seemed to be no limit to his fund of stories. Oxford. The carriage was filling up. Time to be British and lapse into silence? Not a bit of it.

'I bet you've never played cricket with a murderer,' he challenged me.

I had to admit that, as far as I could remember, the chances were that I had not. The old lady opposite put down her magazine. The student beside us removed his earphones.

'Well, I have,' he said, warming to his theme, 'When I was up at Oxford, just after the war, I played for Cornwall in the Minor Counties competition during the holidays. This would have been ... let me see ... yes, that's right, 1948.'

'Why Cornwall, George?'

'Oh, my father, who was a vicar, had moved down there and that was the family home. Anyway, in our team was a chap called Miles Giffard. His father was a solicitor in Bodmin and had sent Miles to Rugby. He had got the sack (not sure what for) and was then moved to Blundells, where he fared with equal lack of distinction. The boy was a terrible waster and couldn't settle at any job and as far as I could see spent his time scrounging off his old man. He played one or two games that year, but to be terribly honest, he wasn't a very good player. The story goes that he got involved with a young lady in London of whom his father disapproved. After much pestering for funds, his father threatened to cut Miles off completely if he didn't throw over this girl and settle down to something useful. At their home, Miles spent the day brooding, while consuming a bottle of whisky. When his parents came home, he attacked his father in the garage with an axe, hitting him over the head and killing him. Then he went inside the house and did the same to his mother. He loaded the bodies into a wheelbarrow and tipped them over the cliff edge at the bottom of the garden. Then he got into the family car and drove all the way up to London to rejoin his girlfriend.'

'How long was it before – ?'

'Oh, the police were on to him pretty swiftly. Once the parents' bodies had been discovered at the bottom of the cliff, they felt sure that the son had something to do with it and they traced him to London without difficulty. He had made no efforts to cover his tracks. They arrested him with his girlfriend in a cinema. He admitted it straightaway, so it was a pretty open and shut case.'

'What happened to him?'

'Guilty as charged. The jury took about thirty minutes to reach their verdict.'

'What did he get ... you know, the sentence?'

George put his hand around his neck and stuck out his tongue theatrically.

The old lady gave a little gasp. The student went white.

Of course – the death penalty had not then been abolished.

'I could hardly say that I felt sorry for the fellow,' went on George, 'for he wasn't a very nice chap and what he did was monstrous. And, as I said, he was a very *ordinary* cricketer. But I will say that I thought it was very unfair that he was tried at Bodmin. His parents were very well known locally and the case had stirred up a lot of anger and hostility. He was never going to get an unprejudiced trial. It should have been held over the border in Devon or somewhere well away from the furore. Perhaps it might not have made any difference to the eventual verdict but... Anyway, can you guess what his last words were?'

I shook my head. I had no idea what would be going through my mind as I stood on the gallows.

'Well, I can't be absolutely certain that these were the *very* last words that passed his lips. But he did say shortly before that his only regret was that he would not be able to see the 1953 Australians that summer!'

I joined in with the chuckle. Who wouldn't regret not seeing Lindwall, Miller, Hassett, Davidson, Benaud *et al.* before the trapdoor opened?

10

PROLOGUE: A TRAIN JOURNEY

And so the journey passed swiftly and agreeably. Not all of George's stories were as macabre as that one but it was totally absorbing listening to him talking about his life and some of the fascinating people he had encountered along the way. I had little idea that his career had taken so many turnings, some significant, some merely diverting and amusing. I knew him as a colleague of course, though he was much older than me, we had overlapped as masters at Malvern College by only a couple of years. However, his experiences as a schoolmaster, county cricketer, wartime pilot and civic notable spoke for themselves and it suddenly came to me as the train rattled its way into the capital that here was an interesting story, one worth the telling. Not only would it be an account of one man's life, it would also be, by virtue of its longevity, a chronicle of changing social and historical times.

'When I was at school, seniority was denoted by how many buttons on your waistcoat you were permitted to do up. Today,' he laughed, ' youngsters don't seem to want to do anything up. Even to the extent of exposing their underwear!' And he would shake his head in good-humoured bemusement. Not much has escaped his alert eye over the years but far from turning into a grumpy old man, he has found life's eccentricities and vicissitudes fertile ground for fun. A laugh is rarely far from George's lips.

So, you may ask, why the delay? Why has it taken me 15 years to *suit the action to the word*? I'm not sure really. I have been busy, I could claim, and now I am not, but that does not fully explain the equivocating. The truth is that to tell someone's story is a daunting task. Especially if your subject is still alive, very much so, in George's case, and whose good opinion you crave. All I can say is that I have done my best and my only hope is that I have done the man justice.

George Chesterton is the one to blame, in any event. He should not have kept me awake on that Paddington train, the only journey of my life during which I have slept not a wink.

ACKNOWLEDGEMENTS

It seems platitudinous to make mention of the subject of a biography in a list of author's acknowledgements. After all, had George Chesterton been shot down in flames at the battle of Arnhem (as he firmly believed he would), there would have been no subject for me to write about. Thankfully, he survived that 'cauldron of horror', as he described it, and therefore was able to give me full authorisation for this book about his life. More than that, he was bent on giving me every aid that he possibly could and we spent many, many hours deep in conversation in front of a tape recorder. This spawned the conversational tone in the text that I have sometimes used, retaining my questions, in italics, and his answers, nearly always reproduced verbatim. His memory, for the most part, was sharp and reliable, a fact underlined by the corroborative accounts and stories provided by interviews and correspondence with many people, and supported by my own research. He was ever a willing, nay enthusiastic, participant in what came to be a joint venture. 'Do you know what, Andy,' he said to me once, 'I do *so* much enjoy our weekly discussions.' 'Me too,' I agreed. This book has been nothing less than a labour of love.

The advice, assistance and encouragement provided by the following people have been enormously helpful too, for which I am immensely grateful:

Francis Prichard, Ralph Blumenau, Colin Chesterton, Jack McCready, Jimmy Knighton, Derek Henderson, Ian MacLaurin, Richard Whiley, Pat Hooley, Norman Whiting, Peter Richardson, Tom Graveney, James Stredder, Martin Rogers, Alan Carter, Peter Smith, Quentin Hayes, David Bailey, Tim Forrester, Roger Gillard, Martin Knott, Bruce Burnett, Nigel Stewart, Michael McNevin, Mike Vockins, Duncan Fearnley, Katherine Barber, Vanessa Chesterton, Tamsin Sridharia, Bryan Richardson, Lin Murtagh, Di Charteris, Robin Black, Posy McTurk, Rory McTurk, Philip Clegg, Ian Quickfall, Sarah Broadway, Ruth Sheppard, and of course all those at Shire Publications.

Any mistakes are all mine and I apologise for them.

Andy Murtagh

1
CONNECTIONS

Arnhem, 1944

Market garden. Even Wordsworth might have been hard pressed to come up with a more bucolic phrase, redolent of fruitfulness and tranquillity in an orderly world. One wonders what the bright spark in the War Office can have been thinking of when he dreamt up the codename *Market Garden* for what was to be one of the bloodiest and most controversial military operations of the Second World War. Perhaps he really did believe that Field Marshal Bernard Montgomery's daring plan to seize bridges over the great rivers Meuse, Rhine and Lower Rhine, thereby shortening the war by six months, was going to be a walk in the park. In the event, the operation proved to be a disaster, with enormous loss of life and the extinction of any expectation that the war would be ended in 1944.

Hindsight, however, is a wonderful thing. Military historians are now agreed that the operation was doomed from the outset for a variety of reasons, some that could have been foreseen and some that could not. The arguments over who or what was to blame for the failure do not concern us here; it is enough to reflect that the plan was a bold one and the risks thought worth the taking, considering the prize that was at stake. Among those who were to take part, a mood of optimism generally prevailed once the plans were unfurled. In 190 Squadron of the RAF, based at Fairford in Gloucestershire, there was no talk of defeatism as their role in the forthcoming battle was explained in various briefings. The squadron flew Stirling bombers and their job was to transport the 1st British Airborne Division to Arnhem. Far from questioning the wisdom of their commanders, the mood amongst the aircrews as they prepared themselves for action was one of pride that they should be so heavily involved in what was likely to be a defining moment in the whole war; as well as awe at the sheer scale of the operation – by far the biggest airborne operation in history. But it could be done, and must be done. Of that there was no doubt. The Normandy landings on D-Day had worked, so there was no reason why *Market Garden* could not emulate that success.

Nevertheless, Flying Officer George Chesterton must have had qualms about the operation as he strolled across the tarmac to be greeted by his crew as they joined him by his Stirling, being made ready by the ground crew. The previous day's mission had run into unforeseen difficulties and there must have been a small knot of tension in his stomach as he exchanged friendly conversation with Ginger, a down-to-earth Lancastrian, and all the other familiar faces whose job it was to keep their aircraft serviceable. George was an officer and the five members of his crew were not, but the RAF was not a stuffy establishment, at least, certainly not in wartime, and they all got on well, partly because throughout months of training they had come to trust and respect each other and partly because their skipper possessed a natural air of relaxed authority that inspired confidence and harmony. As they all clambered aboard up the aluminium stepladder, the inside of the enormous aircraft must have been as familiar to them as a classroom when they were at school, the rear gunner turning right for his turret, the others turning left and clambering underneath the large spar that held up the full weight of the wings to take up their respective positions. As captain, George would have been last to reach his seat, the one on the left, with all the controls and instruments for flying the aircraft. Once he had eased himself into the cramped seat (no easy thing for a tall man) and his crew had taken up their respective positions, all essential checks and tests were undertaken. The crew assured him one by one that they were ready for take-off, and George slowly taxied into position on the runway.

On the first day of *Market Garden*, 190 Squadron had been detailed to carry pathfinder troops, whose job was to secure the landing grounds ahead of the main force. The operation had gone according to plan. Fighter escort was effective, only modest flak was encountered, the paratroopers were dropped successfully and the return journey was uneventful. That is, if you did not count the sight of the enormous air armada on its way to the dropping zone. To the onlookers on the ground, it must have been an impressive sight; the airlift took over an hour to pass overhead. On the second day of the operation, 190 Squadron had towed gliders carrying airborne troops. Things did not go quite as smoothly as on the first day; there was more flak but thankfully no sign of enemy fighters (only later did they learn that they had narrowly missed a patrol of Messerschmitt 109s that had had to return to base to refuel). There had been a problem with one of the engines of

George's Stirling, the starboard inner, which had been losing oil pressure and had to be shut down. But they had made it safely home, notwithstanding a tricky landing that had used every inch of the runway.

Up until this point, 190 Squadron had been remarkably lucky, losing only three aircraft throughout the long summer of 1944, including D-Day and what followed, but there was a sense in the mess that all this was about to change and no one truthfully believed that returning to Arnhem was going to be a cakewalk. Indeed, the third day had confirmed the crews' worst fears. Two of the squadron's Stirlings were shot down and those that did get back had been riddled with holes from shrapnel and small-arms fire. George's crew had been rested for that day but his sense of foreboding cannot have been eased by the dreadful news that his flight commander, John Gilliard, a man whom George had come to respect and count as a good friend, was one of the fatalities.

As the aircraft took up their positions on the runway, none of the men in those aircraft could have known that the Allied struggle to secure the bridge at Arnhem had faltered in the face of fierce German resistance and that the dropping zones for re-supply were now firmly in enemy hands. So the previous day's brave efforts had largely been in vain. Nonetheless, all must have been aware that they were in for a hot reception on this, the fourth day of the operation (20th September).

So what were his thoughts as Flying Officer Chesterton opened the throttle and took off, as usual correcting the Stirling's tendency to veer to starboard as it left the ground? Nothing much, he claims – too busy flying the damned thing, especially as visibility was poor, making it difficult to maintain formation. No doubt this is true. In times of great stress and danger, the mind copes best by concentrating on the minutiae of the job in hand, when practice, preparation and training replace all other thoughts. But still … let's pause for a moment. Here was a young man, his life in front of him, flying a bomber over enemy territory, with German fighters on the prowl and anti-aircraft guns lining up their sights as they passed overhead, low and practically defenceless, to drop their loads, fully aware that at any moment, oblivion might engulf him, 'A cauldron of horror' was how he succinctly described it in later years.

Owing to the ferocity of anti-aircraft fire, the pilots found it impossible to keep to formation so they went in as opportunity arose, dropped their supplies and got out of there as fast as they could. Throwing his Stirling into a violent corkscrew dive, he approached the dropping zone at 600 feet and doing about 150 knots. He described running the gauntlet, between lines of quick-firing guns, as a stomach-churning experience, like flying through a shooting gallery.' To his horror, the Stirling next to him, piloted by a well-liked colleague of his, Roderick Matheson, blew up in mid-air. George remembered saying to himself out loud as the plane plummeted to the ground in a ball of fire: 'Thank God it's not me!' Having dropped his cargo and turned to starboard through the wall of flak, he saw so many Stirlings taking evasive action cluttering the sky above that he decided to dive for the ground. At tree height, he raced away at full throttle, not for the first time thankful that his Stirling ('a truly remarkable aircraft') was capable of withstanding such rough treatment. Safely, they made it home. Three aircraft in the squadron were not so lucky. 'And do you know what bugs me to this day?' he told me, 'The sickening thing is that practically everything we dropped went to the Germans!' The British troops on the ground knew that the drop zones were all in enemy hands, but had been unable to get the message back to the UK. The inescapable truth was that by the time George had landed his aircraft, the battle of Arnhem was all but lost.

Malvern College, Remembrance Sunday 2009

The chapel at Malvern College is a beautiful building, set in the heart of the school which itself nestles in the lee of the Malvern Hills. Built in the last decade of the 19th century to reflect the College's burgeoning reputation as one of the leading public schools in the country, it was designed, in the mock-gothic style, to inspire and impress. Whether it inspired and impressed the current generation of pupils as they filed their way in for the service is a moot point; students tend to come to an appreciation of their school buildings, no matter how grand they may be, only later on in their lives. However, Remembrance Sunday is a special day; the ceremony around the statue of St George, the school's war memorial, never fails to affect even the hardest of hearts and lunch isn't too far away. So they always try to look their smartest and listen politely to the address. Their parents, teachers and assorted old boys, some in military uniform, who were filling up the pews at the same time, might have been thinking differently of course, having perhaps a more solemn perspective on proceedings, but whatever the individual motives for being there, the atmosphere is always sober and respectful.

On this occasion, the service was late starting; simply too many people were trying to cram themselves in. No doubt this did little to soothe the nerves of the old gentleman whose task it was to address the school later but, if this was so, he gave little visible sign of it. He sat serenely studying the stained-glass windows opposite as if he had never seen them before. In fact they must have been as familiar to him as the back of his hands, for man and boy he had been at this place for most of his 85 years. At length, the time came for him to deliver his address.

A tall and imposing man, wearing gown and hood, perhaps a little stooped these days (but a stiff back and arthritic knees are the inevitable legacies of a lifetime of opening the bowling), he slowly hauled himself to his feet and made his way to the lectern. The two steps up to the lectern were awkwardly negotiated and then it took him an unconscionable time to unfurl his notes, locate his glasses and get himself ready. One could almost sense the anxiety in his audience as he stared out over the massed ranks of the school for a moment, gathering himself for the difficult task ahead.

Quietly he started. Too quietly perhaps, as his audience strained to hear. But soon he was in his stride, reminding everyone why they were there and how important it was to remember the sacrifice made by so many so that we could worship in chapels such as this in freedom and peace. Gradually, the hypnotic quality of his voice took hold. Those who knew him were familiar with his style of delivery – measured, lucid, captivating, sucking the listener in with all the artful lure of the consummate raconteur – and waited patiently for him, so to speak, to find his length.

Sure enough, he did, and started to tell it like a story:

I would like you to come on an imaginary journey to the Malvern College of 1940. The general framework of Malvern at that time would be entirely recognisable to you, of course. I know there were no girls, nor any study bedrooms, but living was then, as now, in individual Houses, food rationing had not become too severe, so, although we moaned about the food, we really had little cause for complaint. The daily blackout was an inconvenience but scarcely interrupted school life. Games were played, chapel was attended, lectures, plays, concerts all took place; true, there were, for obvious reasons, two corps parades a week. Progress up through the school was as now, culminating in two years in the sixth form and the Higher Certificate, which gave the entrée to universities and other forms of higher education. But here was a dramatic change. For everyone, the choice became very straightforward – the army, navy or air force. And no one knew for how long.

He had his audience rapt. Even bored pupils, hitherto thinking of their lunch, were leaning forward in the pews, intent on his every word:

You have joined me on an imaginary journey into the past; now for a little history. I am going to tell you about five young men whom I thought of today during the two minutes' silence. The first was a member of my college at Oxford. He was born in East Prussia and as a young man won a scholarship to Oxford, later returning to Germany where he became a lawyer in Munich. Although strongly opposed to Hitler, a feeling for his fatherland saw him joining the German Army. He served with distinction in a Panzer regiment, battling through two awful Russian winters. A brass tablet in Brasenose chapel reads: *In memory of Justus Carl von Ruperti, Rhodes Scholar, who died fighting for his country on 19th August 1943.*

There was a collective intake of breath. Not before, in most people's memory anyway, had a German soldier been so commemorated in Malvern College Chapel on Remembrance Sunday. You could say that the reference was a brave one. But not for the first time, the elderly man at the lectern had judged the situation perfectly. In the congregation were a number of young German students; the school was now a truly international institution and the mention of enemy sacrifices struck a fitting and generous note. He pressed on:

I thought too of my flight commander, John Gilliard, who was last seen at the battle for Arnhem, wrestling with the controls of his blazing aircraft, trying to make enough height for members of his crew to bail out. Two of them did.

Those who had their heads down at this point, picturing in their mind's eye the awful scene, were forced to look up, concerned at the long pause that now ensued. At length, the slow, measured delivery was resumed:

Harold Porter was known to many of us as Mercury. The chemists amongst you will understand why: his initials were H. G. I shared a study with him for a year and we became good friends... When he left Malvern, he joined his father's engineering firm. The family had a 30-ft motor cruiser, and two years later they answered the call for small boats to help in the rescue of the British Army from the beaches of Dunkirk. Twelve times Mercury and his crew of four carried men to transports lying offshore. Intending to make one more journey, their little craft received a direct hit from a dive-bomber and sank without trace.

Boxing was quite a popular sport at Malvern in the 1930s. Branny Richards was the school heavyweight and captain of boxing. The climax of the season was a quadrangular match with Clifton, Cheltenham and

Downside. In 1938, this match was held here at Malvern. The result of the whole competition depended on the last fight, that of Branny Richards against a Cliftonian who seemed almost twice his size. Despite being knocked down three times, Richards battled on and scraped victory on points to the tumultuous applause of half the school. Four years later, he was taken prisoner at Tobruk in North Africa. He was transported north through Italy in a cattle truck with the destination a camp in Germany. Richards and a young air force officer managed to scrape away three planks in the floor of their truck and when the train was crawling up a steep gradient, they dropped down onto the track. After weeks travelling south by night, they made their way to within earshot of the Allied lines when Richards stepped on a land mine and was blown to pieces.

Freddie Dunton and I were exact contemporaries and firm friends. Some of you will know the name through the Dunton Music Prize awarded in his memory. He was clever and won a scholarship to Christ's College, Cambridge, to be taken up after the war. He was also a fine musician, his special instrument being the flute. He volunteered for the air force, becoming a Lancaster bomber pilot. We used to exchange occasional letters. In his last one, he said, 'I have put my flute away until after the war and taken up the mouth organ. My crew prefer it and anyway the flute was a bit clumsy in the cockpit of a Lancaster.' In the interval between posting the letter and my receiving it, his Lancaster was blown to pieces over the Baltic.

Another, almost unbearable pause.

Some of these brave men have no known grave but we must remember them, along with the countless others who gave their lives for their homelands and their friends. It is thanks to them that all of us sit in this chapel, from a wide variety of countries and backgrounds, and are able to sit together in security and friendship.

But there is a little more … please, as daily you walk along the terrace and pass St George, remember, but also regenerate, your own faith. That way, we can hope there will be need for no more war memorials.

It seemed that Malvern College Chapel had never known a silence more profound as George Chesterton groped for his stick and made his painful way back to his seat. And, typically, he had not mentioned, not even once, his own story as a bomber pilot.

The University Parks, Oxford, 30th April 1949

Tom Graveney had a point to prove. The stride out to the wicket was casual. He was a tall man and the gait was naturally loose-limbed and graceful. The blue Gloucestershire cap was set at the usual jaunty angle as he took guard. The previous year he had made his first-class debut against this very side and on this very ground. It had been a less than auspicious start to a career for someone who was to become one of the greatest batsmen in the modern era. And what's more, it had been against a bunch of students, which had done nothing to lessen the indignity of the memory over the past twelve months. He may have given every appearance of relaxed composure as he stood there, surveying the field set for him, but there was a score to settle here and even by now, in the infancy of his glittering career, the hard-nosed ruthlessness of the successful cricketer had become apparent. In short, Tom Graveney never forgot and today was no different. 'Caught Travers, bowled Whitcombe ... 0,' he recalled ruefully, some sixty years after the event, 'I wasn't going to let that happen again against this lot.'

'This lot' were Oxford University and lest anyone think that the universities were a soft touch, an opportunity for greedy pros to fill their boots and boost their averages, it should be pointed out that this Oxford side went on to beat four counties that year, as well as the touring New Zealanders. In later years, the standard of university cricket may have sadly declined, eventually losing their first-class status in 2009, but in the immediate post-war years, it could be argued that it was as strong as it ever was. Tom Graveney might have been thirsting for revenge but he certainly didn't underestimate the opposition that day.

However, waiting patiently at the end of his run was a tall young man, unknown on the county circuit. His opening overs had been tidy enough but from the dressing room, it appeared that he had neither startling pace nor excessive movement. Certainly nothing to stir fear in the heart of Gloucestershire's gifted prodigy. The first few balls were played comfortably enough and Graveney set himself for the big score he wanted. 'He was a big, gangling man,' he said of his opponent, 'with a funny run-up of about ten paces. And before I knew it, he had knocked my middle pole out. Went straight through the gate.'

Graveney T. W. bowled Chesterton ... 3.

George Chesterton remembered that ball with equal clarity. 'It was in fact my first first-class wicket. I had the ability – don't ask me how – to get the ball to move into the right-hander, often quite late. On that occasion, it swung in and, Tom having generously left the merest chink of light between bat and pad, it pierced his defences and bowled him.'

Both men, as it happens, have clear memories of what transpired in the second innings. 'I was going quite well,' said Tom (he was on 108 at the time!), 'and George was bowling. I went to chip him over mid-on and their captain, Clive van Ryneveld, who was a bloody fine cricketer, set off from deep mid-off, ran like the wind, dived and caught it one-handed, inches from the turf.' *So Chesterton did you twice in the match?* 'He did indeed,' was the rueful admission, 'Mighty fine bowler, George.' 'It was hardly a chip,' laughed George, 'I remember it as a tremendous blow over mid-on. Van Ryneveld was at long-off. He sprinted across, making … gosh, 30-odd yards before he caught it just above the ground. It was a wonderful catch. I know it says in the scorebook that it was my wicket but in truth I cannot claim any credit for it.'

Maybe not, but the archives record that George Chesterton took nine wickets in the match and you could say that the die was cast as far as his future in the first-class game was concerned. And despite Graveney's inevitable century in the second innings, Gloucestershire's last wicket pair had to hang on grimly for a quarter of an hour to secure a draw against the students.

Malvern College, Friday 2nd May 2003

George Chesterton was at the end of his run. He placed the ball between his first two fingers and thumb, checked the position of the seam, looked up and surveyed his opponent at the crease at the far end. Tom Graveney, strangely capless on this occasion, checked his guard and bent easily over his bat, his bearing watchful, alert, poised. His eyes narrowed as he regarded his old nemesis. He's not going to get me out this time, he said to himself.

Of course, it has to be said that George's run-up was not the usual 10 yards but a mere step up to the popping crease. He had however removed his jacket and rolled up his sleeves. Tom, ever the dapper professional, had not removed his jacket but the easy, relaxed stance was the same as ever.

'Come on, George,' he exhorted, 'Put it on the spot, as you always did.'

George's left arm reached for the sky, his left leg shot out at its usual strange angle, the right arm came over ramrod straight and the ball was propelled towards the batsman. Tom leant forward and brought the bat down in a graceful arc, connecting with the ball with that oh so satisfying thwack that speaks unmistakeably of sweet timing. A Graveney cover drive. Has there ever been a more famous stroke in the history of the game? The purr from the onlookers suggested there was not. A few of us who knew of George's fragile shoulder joint (he'd even recently managed to put it out turning over in bed) let out a sigh of relief to see him donning his jacket again, apparently without mishap. Both men were grinning now, enjoying the moment and acknowledging the smattering of applause.

The occasion was the official opening of the new all-weather nets at Malvern College, which were to be named in George's honour. Would you like me to bring my old friend, Tom Graveney, along to assist with the ceremonies? *Would we indeed, George! Is the Pope a Catholic?* A considerable gathering had been assembled, boys, staff, parents, groundsmen, passers-by, curious to see two famous old Worcestershire team-mates (and presidents of the club in successive years, George reminded us) encouraging the current generation of young cricketers to practise hard in the nets but never to forget the fun to be had when they do it properly. 'Hear hear,' echoed the coaches standing about.

Incidentally, and poignantly, that was the last time that George was to turn his arm over and the last time that Tom picked up a bat. But as they were both now in their mid-80s, there can have been no complaint from either. And none was there. In fact, both agreed that, on balance, honours had been shared.

Malvern College, January 1950, Monday morning, period 1

The moment every teacher dreads had arrived. The new Geography master was about to have his lesson inspected by the headmaster. It doesn't matter whether you are an old hand of thirty years' experience or a callow probationer in your first term, the observed lesson is an ordeal that cannot be described convincingly to anyone who hasn't been there. Standing in front of twenty boys who would rather be anywhere else on the planet than stuck indoors in a classroom at nine o'clock on a Monday morning is bad enough. Standing in front of twenty-one, the extra body being your headmaster, with pen and notebook in hand, is downright terrifying.

This young master was not one to panic easily though. He had been informed in good time that the headmaster would be there. The class were not the brightest but neither were they the most difficult. He felt reasonably confident that they were not out to destroy him and get him the sack. He had prepared the lesson meticulously; he had decided to 'do' ox-bow lakes, and the formation thereof, which was a safe bet, he felt. 'My trusty fall-back lesson,' he admitted good-humouredly. All was ready. All was prepared.

Nonetheless, the young master was not feeling as composed as he looked. His anxiety swelled as the door burst open and Tom Gaunt, the formidable headmaster of Malvern College, swept into the room, wearing his mortarboard with his gown billowing out behind him. Without further ado, George Chesterton was instructed to get on with it. The mystery of ox-bow lakes was about to be disclosed to young minds, hungry for enlightenment.

At this juncture, it might be worth pointing out that George's classroom was directly above the boilers that drove the good ship Malvern College through the hard winters. 'Mighty great leviathans they were,' remembered George, 'Large enough to float the *Queen Mary*!' The chimney ran up alongside the wall of the classroom. When the boilers were going full blast, the room became like an oven, with the walls too hot to touch. Even in the freezing depths of midwinter, the windows had to remain open. 'Boiling in the winter; freezing in the summer. Oddly typical of Malvern,' he said. In those days, the boilers were fired by coke, which necessitated regular visits by the coke lorry. Whoever designed the college building obviously had no regard for poor lorry drivers because the gap between the chapel and the main building is insufficiently wide to allow access by lorry. So the unfortunate driver had to unload fifty or so bags of coke by hand and lug them on his shoulders to the chute placed right outside the classroom window. Whenever a bag was tipped down the chute, a noise resembling the collapse of a mineshaft would rumble around the room, making meaningful teaching impossible.

Luck would have it that period 1 on this particular Monday was the time for the delivery of coke. Gamely, George continued to hold forth on ox-bow lakes above the din of the coke being tipped down the chute. Shutting the window made no difference. It only got hotter and hotter and the noise level remained the same. Somewhat vexed, the headmaster called a halt to the lesson. 'Send a boy out,' he ordered, 'to ask that delivery man to go away and come back an hour later.' A boy was dispatched who duly and politely delivered the message. He was met by such a volley of abuse, clearly heard by the class inside, that he was forced to make an immediate retreat. 'He said that he was very sorry but he was too busy,' he reported back, not wholly verbatim, to his teacher. And the dreadful racket resumed.

'I will move him!' announced the headmaster imperiously, and swept out of the room, gown dutifully following him. The class awaited the outcome with bated breath.

The obscenities that greeted the headmaster if anything exceeded in virulence and inventiveness those directed at the messenger boy. And the delivery of coke was resumed. Everyone, class and master alike, nervously anticipated the headmaster's return.

But of Tom Gaunt there was no sign. Nor did he appear for any subsequent lessons. That term nor any other.

'And in such a way,' acknowledges George Chesterton, 'did Malvern College acquire for itself a very average Geography teacher for the next thirty years.'

Malvern College, 17th December 1982, final assembly of term

The end of the autumn term is always keenly anticipated. It has been a long time since that Indian summer, the nights have been steadily drawing in, and everyone hates those evening lessons. Boys and teachers are similarly tired and the Christmas holidays are beckoning. Big School, the hall where concerts, recitals, lectures, meetings, presentations (oh, and examinations) take place, was packed for the final assembly of term. The atmosphere was animated, excited, febrile even. With scarcely concealed impatience, the usual notices and messages were dutifully listened to, the boys anxious to get away. The tall, slightly stooping figure on the podium, his hands gripping the sides of the lectern, the sleeves of his academic gown falling away from his outstretched arms, stared out impassively at his audience. A sea of expectant faces stared back at him. What was the headmaster going to say by way of a final word? Would the old boy burst out in a verse of Good King Wenceslas? One or two of his colleagues wouldn't have put it past him. George always had a sense of theatre.

Suddenly the headmaster (or, to be strictly accurate, the acting headmaster, for the new headmaster would not arrive until the following term and in the interregnum, the second master had been holding the fort – masterfully) dived down behind the lectern, disappearing from view. What on earth is he up to now, everybody was thinking. Seconds later, George Chesterton straightened up again, a glass in one hand and a bottle of Champagne in the other. Solemnly, he poured, gauging perfectly the tricky upsurge of bubbles and spilling not a drop. It was his last day as a master at Malvern College, he explained, and he wanted to toast the school. With which, he raised his glass to six hundred boys and then put it to his lips. After a stunned moment's silence, Big School erupted into thunderous acclamation, the wooden beams of that venerable old building shaking in protest.

Now, schoolmasters come and go and no teacher is indispensable. But this was different. This was George. It was not so much the length of his service, thirty years, but the manner of its conduct that prompted the ovation. George was a genuinely popular figure, evoking admiration and affection in equal measure. George was just … well, George. No other master was popularly known by his first name alone. In fact, it was a moot point, which was the more central figure on the College campus: St George, the statue on the war memorial, or the other George.

That is why the applause threatened to eat into the holidays and stretch out until Christmas. But the sign was given, the piano crashed out the opening chords of the school song, the boys tore lustily into the obscure Latin refrain and George fled the stage and sought the sanctuary of the headmaster's study.

If, in that moment of solitude, he had shed a little tear, none would have blamed him. Man and boy, he had been at this school and now it was time to bid farewell. What was he going to do with the rest of his life? Plenty, as it happened. But let us go back a little…

2

EARLY DAYS
1922–30

*'It was so much more fun at the vicarage. My family was
like the old Third Programme on the wireless and the
Chestertons were like the Light Programme!'*

Francis Prichard, boyhood friend

There is a glorious tradition in English life, especially in rural areas, which goes back many centuries. The jolly clergyman features in any *dramatis personae* of village life, as much the cornerstone of a community as the squire, the blacksmith, the old gossipmonger and the comely wench. One of the first novels ever written, *Joseph Andrews* by Henry Fielding, has as one of its main characters the popular Parson Abraham Adams, a country curate with 'a head full of learning and a heart full of love.' He wants to do the best for his flock but he is absolutely ignorant of the world, which, in his simplicity, he takes at face value. And then there is the ridiculous Mr Collins in Jane Austen's *Pride and Prejudice*. Dr Primrose in Goldsmith's *The Vicar of Wakefield* is another one. And who can forget the vicar in *Dad's Army* or pretty well any character played by Derek Nimmo (*Oh Brother* and *All Gas and Gaiters*)? And Dawn French in *The Vicar of Dibley* has kept the tradition alive.

By all accounts, Revd Jack Chesterton was cut from the same cloth. The English, by and large, prefer their clerics to have a light touch rather than a heavy hand and Jack, like all good actors, could play many parts. Being a parish priest is a bit like schoolmastering, I reckon. All right, the desired objective of both callings might differ slightly – to get your charges into heaven rather than university – but there is no earthly reason why you should not have a bit of fun on the way. Both jobs demand, variously, a bit of sermonising, lecturing, instructing, encouraging, chiding, comforting, organising, governing, everything really. And there are times when a strong performance is required, a tour de force of playacting, even when the spirit is unwilling. But the crucial quality, for good priests and teachers alike, is humanity. Children, as much as parishioners, can spot a fake a mile off. No wonder George made a success of his chosen career in the teaching profession when he had such an inspirational figurehead as his father in his formative years.

As it happened, Jack was not destined for the life of a country parson. A scholar at St Paul's School, he had the misfortune to suffer from what now would be termed a heart murmur. The accepted wisdom of the day was that he should be taken out of school to build up his strength in the great outdoors. So, at the age of sixteen, he left St Paul's and went to work on a farm. There he learnt a variety of manual skills, chopping wood, building fences, keeping bees, managing poultry, slaughtering pigs. Laughingly, his son admits that none of these aptitudes was passed down the genealogical line. Jack was also a talented artist and, encouraged by his parents, who built him a studio at home, he won a place at the Slade School of Art. There he met his future wife, Mary Long. Her parents, who were very much of the non-conformist persuasion, didn't really approve of their daughter marrying a jobbing artist, so Jack gave up his passion and went to theological college in preparation for entering the Church, a much more respectable profession, though probably equally poorly paid. After a series of curacies following ordination, one as an RAF chaplain in 1918, he took up a post in Chirbury, near Welshpool, north Shropshire, where George Herbert Chesterton was born in 1922. *Why Herbert, George?* 'Come on, Andy! You taught English. You must know who George Herbert was.' *Yes, he was a metaphysical poet. Did your parents want you to write religious poetry?* 'Hmm … never liked his stuff. Bit heavy for me. Anyway, he was born where I was, in Chirbury. And my parents thought … well, there was a certain *ring* about the two names.' Life was hard in the village and with three children to feed (Mary had been born in 1915 and John in 1917), Jack needed to find a better job. This was provided by a move to St Mary's, Tenbury Wells, Worcestershire, when George was two. The annual stipend was £600, which was considered to be quite a step up for the family, both professionally and financially.

Alas, the salary did not keep pace with the steady rise in the cost of living. In fact, it did not rise at all. It was fixed. Nothing could be done about it and that was that. Jack was finding it once again hard to make ends meet. It always rankled with him that the Easter offering, amongst other things, was taxable. The Easter offering was an opportunity for grateful parishioners to show their appreciation for their cash-strapped vicar by means of cash donations. And it was *taxed*! But his friends neatly side-stepped that problem by slipping him money privately, rather than putting it on the plate. Already, a picture of a very popular and unconventional man is beginning to emerge.

The vicarage had a grass tennis court and the love and attention that Revd Jack Chesterton lavished on it matched any bestowed on his parishioners. In short, the court became the passion of his life so much so that it soon rivalled the best in the county, cut and rolled daily, and no doubt blessed with holy water when the weather was dry. The great day would arrive every spring when it had to be measured out and the white lines painted. It seems that Ordnance-Survey precision was demanded in the mathematical calculations and only Jack was allowed to take hold of the paintbrush, having the requisite expertise, patience and dead reckoning eyesight.

Occasionally, beggars and vagrants would appear at the front door, hoping for a bit of charity. Although of a kindly disposition, Jack was no fool, so money would change hands only after some job or other had been performed. To one disreputable down-and-out, the task of rolling the beloved tennis court was entrusted. 'Carry on until I tell you to stop,' he was instructed. This was at about ten o'clock in the morning. When the Reverend returned to the vicarage at about six that evening, he was surprised to hear the familiar sound of the squeaky roller from the garden. He had completely forgotten the tramp and there he still was, steadfastly following instructions. Apparently, that summer the ball flew fast and true off the perfect surface.

Tennis parties were frequent and popular social occasions. George's mother would provide the teas ('unforgettable') and young George was often drawn in to play with his father's friends, even at an early age. One assumes that already a certain ability at games was manifesting itself. There was a stretch of lawn in front of the house, nearly 22 yards long, which George, from the age of six or seven, cut and rolled and prepared a wicket and erected a little net so that he could play until it got too dark. There were no bowling machines in those days, so he had to beg people to bowl at him. 'Anyone – and I mean *anyone* – was dragooned into bowling to me,' he said, 'even my grandmother. She was a prim and starchy old thing, dressed in her black widow's weeds, but she would put in a stint from time to time. Underarm, of course, but straight.' Presumably, this is where his renowned accuracy as a bowler was developed, spending hour after hour bowling at a stump, with no batsman as a distraction.

His father was quite simply nuts about cricket. He was vice-captain of Tenbury Wells Cricket Club for twenty years, most of that time occupying the berth of opening batsman. 'He wasn't very good,' laughed his son at the memory, 'a nudger and nurdler with a limited array of shots. He had no backlift, would shuffle in front of his stumps as the ball was bowled and look to deflect it down to third man or long-leg as his only scoring strokes.' Apparently, he was seldom dismissed for less than 20 but rarely made over 30. About twice a year he would score a 50, which would be the occasion for wild celebrations. In the field, he occupied that rather vague and statuesque position just backward of point, a shrewd hiding place for a man not entirely confident of his catching abilities yet also near enough to the stumps to cede the energetic chasing of the ball to those of a younger age.

One Saturday, a car nosed its way through the gate and into the ground. The driver emerged and shouted hoarsely to the vicar, fielding in his usual position at point, that perhaps it had slipped his mind that he should have been conducting a funeral service that afternoon. In some consternation, the vicar quit the field and donning his vestments, he hurriedly made his way to the church. He was late. Unforgivable really. It is pardonable as the presiding prelate to be late for a wedding or a christening, so it is said, but not a funeral. From that day, Jack Chesterton always wore black socks under his white boots for matches, so he could fling on his cassock over his whites and just about get away with it when required.

Every Saturday in the summer was spent at the cricket club. At the age of twelve, George ceased being a spectator, making his debut as a player. His memory of the occasion is crystal clear. 'It was against Stoke Bliss. I managed to take three wickets, you know!' Stoke Bliss is in Worcestershire and the cricket club is now defunct. That is a shame for it would be fine for one of those blue plaques to be unveiled detailing the spot where George Chesterton took his first wicket.

A word or two about the other great influence in George's childhood would not go amiss at this stage. 'I adored my mother,' he says simply, 'My father was a marvellous man with a tremendous sense of humour. He cared deeply about people but he was a bit of a rogue. Amongst other things, he liked a bit of a flutter on the horses, so we never had any money. It was my mother who kept things together.' She was a pillar of the Church and often gave lectures to such bodies as the Mothers' Union or Women's Institute on a variety of worthy topics and public figures. Her family used to tease her unmercifully about these over-sentimental presentations and one, in particular, sticks in George's mind. It was on Florence Nightingale, and was full of mawkish images of the Lady with the Lamp, flitting up and down gas-lit wards, offering physical and spiritual succour to the brave boys wounded during the Crimean War. The romantic myth could not have had a more helpful makeover than it got that day in St Mary's Church. Back home in the vicarage, the derision was pitiless. But George defended her spiritedly, not because he thought the lecture had been a success ('it was nonsense, in actual fact') but because he had an instinctive compassion for the underdog, a trait that helped to make him such a great schoolmaster in later life, dare I say. And she was his mother and he loved her unconditionally. Perhaps he was her favourite but he wouldn't be the first youngest child to be so favoured.

Mary was a nervous and anxious woman and unsurprisingly she never learned how to drive a car. Her husband, by contrast, delighted in speed when at the wheel (a proclivity that *has* been handed down the male line) and this resulted in some tense journeys. She would watch the speedometer like a hawk and if the needle strayed over 30mph, she would start to twitch. Anything over 50mph would induce violent panic. Now, the vicar of St Mary's only owned two cars in his life and fate would have it that the speedometer in the second was broken. This would result in altogether more harmonious journeys, as she had no idea at what speed her husband was driving. 'Dear thing,' says George, with unalloyed affection.

It is abundantly clear from all that he says that George's childhood was a happy one. 'My parents bestowed on me all the love that I could have wished for. And, above all, it was so much *fun*! I'm not exaggerating here. At least, I don't think I am. I really did have a marvellous relationship with them both.' I felt impelled to probe a little deeper here. After all, we are talking about the 1920s, when parents were meant to be remote figures, strict and unapproachable, distantly benevolent at best. *Was such a warm relationship with one's parents unusual for those times?* 'I have no idea,' he answers with puzzlement in his voice, 'All I know is that it seemed very natural to me.'

As a child, he was thrown very much into his own company. He was not very close to his older brother and sister. Five and seven years' difference is a huge gulf in ages, especially at a young age, and neither of them shared his passion for games. There were no friends in the village of the same background. There were local lads around but he rarely mixed with them; in those days, a vicar's son had a certain social standing and although the family were far from being snobbish, class distinction still held considerable sway. He did strike up a friendship with the doctor's son, despite their differences in temperament. George chuckles at the memory, 'His name was Blethyn Elliott, a Welshman obviously. Of course, by natural osmosis, the name was soon corrupted to Blithering Idiot. We lost contact and the last I heard of him was that he had gone into the army at the outbreak of war. Many years later, I happened to bump into him in Brecon, of all places, where he was stationed with the South Wales Borderers and had reached the giddy heights of second-in-command. I was absolutely delighted to learn that his nickname in the regiment was still Blithering Idiot!'

There may have been a lot of fun and laughter around the vicarage but there was never much money. The annual stipend remained stubbornly fixed at £600 and a succession of slow horses regularly depleted the family's finances. Accordingly, they had to find extra sources of income. One obvious possibility was to take in lodgers. In those days, there was no flying home to families posted overseas for boys at boarding schools; they had to be accommodated with relatives, friends or as paying guests. So one day, when George was about ten, a small boy three years his junior arrived on the doorstep, tear-stained and clutching an oversized valise. His name was Francis Prichard and thus began an extraordinary association that survives to this day. Two lonely boys were thrown together in childhood and a bond was formed that proved to be unbreakable, even into old age.

Francis's father worked in the Civil Service in India as a judge, and for two to three years at a time, the boy never saw his parents. It seems strange to us now but such arrangements were not uncommon between the wars: an empire had to be administered and family life had to be sacrificed on the altar of duty. Francis himself remains stoical about his childhood. He loved his parents but necessarily they remained rather distant figures. 'My mother sent me letters from Assam,' he recalls, 'but I fear I may have left some of them unread. Oh dear.' As it happened, his parents knew the Chestertons and when they heard that they were taking in lodgers, the young Francis was sent to join them at Tenbury Wells for the holidays – summer, Easter and Christmas.

His description of the scene as he stood there in the porch, trembling with fear, is lucid and touching: 'I remember my December arrival at Tenbury Vicarage. It was a spacious house and cold in winter. From a stone-flagged hall there was a curving staircase. There must have been some sort of children's party going on. Certainly there was laughter. George's father was dropping, or trying to drop, golden syrup from the top floor onto a tray in the hall. The Chestertons were so immediately kind to me and took me fully into their family. Those impressionable years were amongst the happiest of my youth. It was a cruel separation in those days for parents living abroad.'

A measure of how readily he was integrated into life at the vicarage was the fact that very soon he was calling George's parents by the names used by everyone in the family – Mums and Dee. Mums was exceptionally attractive and very kind. Dee had a heart of gold and one act of generosity stuck firmly in the memory of Francis. He presented him with a bat signed by all the touring South Africans, which became a prized possession, never to be let out of his sight. In retrospect, the gift was probably even more open-handed than he realised at the time, for it gradually dawned on the young boy that Dee was frequently strapped for cash. 'Money just seemed to slip through his fingers,' Francis recalls, 'He was an inveterate backer of slow horses.' He became aware that there were times when the vicarage was lit by candlelight, presumably when the electricity had been cut off. His own father once asked him about an invoice for petrol that he had received from Dee. Even a cursory calculation of the mileage suggested that Dee had been driving Francis and George the length and breadth of the British Isles night and day for the whole holidays! But the bill was paid without demur. Mr and Mrs Prichard were probably only too aware that the love and care being bestowed on their distant son by the Chestertons was worth an exaggerated petrol claim.

There is one story about Dee that has gone down in family folklore. He used to run up debts, some of them quite substantial, with the local shopkeepers. Eventually, one of them, Mr Walkie, the grocer, came round to the vicarage, his patience exhausted, to remonstrate with Dee about his outstanding account, several hundred pounds, on this occasion, and to demand some sort of interim payment. 'Tell you what, Walkie,' suggested Dee, 'I'll challenge you to a game of ping-pong for the money. Double or quits? What do you say?' Now, as it happened, Mr Walkie was by no means a second-rate table tennis player. He was well known in the local leagues and distinctly fancied his chances, especially as his opponent had referred to the game as 'ping-pong', its rather quaint, dated and unambiguously amateurish tag. The challenge was accepted.

Dee wiped the floor with him. From this outcome we might deduce several things. Dee was an incorrigible gambler. That we know. He was also a more than useful table-tennis player, his skills sharpened by hours of practice on the vicarage's table. And he was a competitor to his bootstraps, a trait inherited by his son. Let no one tell you that George was a generous and sporting opponent on the games field. The avuncular and benevolent demeanour, so conspicuous in everyday life, disappeared once he stepped over the boundary line. You cannot survive, let alone flourish, in the tough arena of professional sport without possessing a ruthless streak. I have heard so many tales of George, hiding behind a tree, puffing away nervously on a fag, while his cricket teams have gone into battle. I once sat with him on the pavilion balcony at Malvern College whilst his old boys' side negotiated the last few runs for victory in the Cricketer Cup competition. He seemed on edge, which was strange because a win was nothing if not a formality, with only three wickets down. 'Do you still get nervous, George?' I asked. 'God, yes,' he replied, 'The tension's unbearable. Makes me want to take up smoking again!' And George was in his mid-eighties at the time.

Take the endless games of cricket in the garden. With Francis Prichard now acting as a surrogate younger brother, the stage was set for Test matches on the tennis court between England and Australia. They lasted for days and were played to a finish. 'I must have been insufferable,' admits George with a rueful shake of the head. 'I was always England, or sometimes, Worcestershire, and poor old Fran was Australia. To be honest, he wasn't as good as I was and of course, he was three years younger. The deal was that he would have two innings and I would have one. He would last a couple of overs and then I, in the form of Jack Hobbs, would bat for hours. There was no suggestion of ever declaring. It must have been miserable for him, toiling away while Hobbs scored yet another century at Lord's.' Actually, Fran remembers those days with nothing but fondness. There was one occasion however when he got his revenge, sort of. George had been bowling and Fran had top-edged an attempted hook into his face, the ball removing two of his front teeth. Dentistry was a little different in those days and the treatment in the surgery later was confined to letting 'nature take its course', so that the teeth 'could knit together in time'. It was only a partial success, as Fran now dryly acknowledges. The reprisal came a few days later. For a change, the game was golf. Fran hit George a fearful blow on the temple with his follow-through with the driver. The wound required stitches, but typically that would not stop him playing in a tennis tournament later that day. While he was being stitched, his mother asked innocently where Fran was. With understandable vexation, George exclaimed, 'I don't give a damn where he is!' In actual fact, the poor boy had remorsefully taken to his room and put himself to bed.

Other games played were tennis and ping-pong (never table tennis!). For both boys, these were magical times. *But what did you do on those days when it rained, George?* He would look at me with astonishment in his eyes, 'But it never rained!' For Fran, a measure of the happiness he enjoyed in the Chesterton household can be gauged by his admission that he was always downcast when it was time to leave. Occasionally, the hospitality would be reciprocated at the Prichard home once they had returned from India but those visits were necessarily shorter and less frequent. 'The sad fact was,' he confesses, 'it was so much more fun at the vicarage. My family was like the old Third Programme on the wireless and the Chestertons were like the Light Programme!'

You might be wondering at this juncture whether I have been in thrall to two old men reminiscing about their childhood through spectacles that are not so much tinted as smeared with rose-coloured paint. I don't think so though. Both men are genuinely grateful for the happy environment in which they spent their formative years. Fran measures the cheerful atmosphere at the vicarage against his own, more detached and formal family. And George is simply bemused at the suggestion that life could have been any different. It is a cliché to say that we are all the product of our upbringing. But anyone who has ever known George and listened to that full-throated chuckle of his cannot possibly believe that there were any demons in his home life. And the stories about his father are too numerous and too entertaining not to contain the substance of truth.

Mr Walkie, the grocer, apparently accepted his defeat on the ping-pong table with good grace and even told the story against himself on many occasions. But he never allowed Dee to run up a tab again. Dee's car was well known around the town. His number plate – CNP 62 – ran off the tongues of the local townsfolk as easily as their own. Chesterton Never Pays the initials stood for. Once, when giving Fran a lift, he pulled the car over and parked in a fairly unsuitable and dangerous spot. It was of course right outside the betting shop. An unimpressed policeman happened upon the illegally parked car and lay in wait for the culprit to return. When Dee got back to the car, he was subjected to a tirade delivered by the policeman. Dee's irritation at being held up was in no way improved by the perceived lack of respect that should have been afforded to a man of the cloth by a very young and callow constable. When he was asked, of all things, how old he was, his patience snapped and off he drove in a squeal of tyres, his parting words being, 'What's that got to do with you? It's none of your business!' Almost in reverential terms, Fran points out that the amazing thing was that he got away with it. Apparently, the constable's senior officer was a parishioner.

'He was an actor, you know,' said Fran, an opinion shared by George. A parish priest has to fulfil many roles and there is no doubt that Dee played them all with gusto and expertise. But he was no charlatan. People are not stupid and his many friends, to say nothing of the wider community in the town, would have spotted any phoniness from a mile off. Especially if it emanated from the pulpit. He was a genuinely kind and generous man and his son clearly reveres his memory, even if he was 'a bit of a rogue'.

There is a sad footnote to his life. He suffered from a dicky heart for much of his later years and eventually died at the age of sixty-nine from a heart attack. Apparently, he had been feeling ill for an hour or two beforehand and, guessing at the nature of the pain, he reached for the phone to summon help. But the line was dead. Not for the first time, it had been disconnected for an unpaid bill.

3

PREP SCHOOL –
THE FAR CLASSROOM
1930–36

'George stands about doing nothing watching other boys doing something.'
Letter home from George's brother whilst at prep school

It was the first day of term. The new boy looked nervously around the dining room, not at all sure where he should sit. Matron beckoned him over. As he was only seven and the youngest boy in the school, he should be seated alongside her, where she could keep an eye on him. Now, broadly speaking, school matrons fall into two categories. You have your motherly types, who may speak brusquely and have a brisk and bracing manner, but whose no-nonsense demeanour belies a kind and compassionate nature. In short, they have a heart of gold. And then you have your dragons. The little lad somehow sensed that the woman who told him to sit next to her belonged in the second category. Desperately he looked around for his elder brother but he was on another table busy chatting to his friends.

Horror of horrors, a bowl of porridge was placed in front of him. He hated porridge, an aversion that would remain with him for the rest of his life. Apologetically, he pushed the bowl away, no doubt hoping that the bacon and eggs, which he could smell wafting from the kitchen, would soon arrive. He was hungry for his breakfast. 'What's the matter with you, boy? Don't you like porridge?' Shyly, the boy had to agree that he didn't. 'Well, you won't get your bacon and eggs until you've finished your porridge.'

The little boy's heart sank. He tried a spoonful but it was no good; he just couldn't take any of it down. He looked pleadingly at Matron but her face was set in stone. And he had to do without his bacon and eggs.

At lunch, he hoped that he might be lucky enough to be assigned a seat somewhere else but Matron had a beady eye and there was no escape. The food was dished out and there in front of him was the bowl of porridge that he had rebuffed at breakfast. 'No lunch for you, my boy, until you've finished your porridge!' There was no way round this; he just had to get the porridge down somehow. But again it was beyond him. He took one spoonful and was very nearly sick. Matron was adamant however and the boy went without his lunch.

Surely she would relent at supper? But no, the bowl of cold porridge was brought and set in front of him. He hadn't eaten a thing all day and he was faint with hunger. In panic and desperation, he plunged his spoon into the gooey, grey mess and forced a mouthful down his throat. He promptly retched and was sick all over Matron's dress.

Funnily enough, there was no sign of the bowl of porridge at breakfast the next day. In fact, the matter was never referred to again.

It would be nice if this were a story of a young boy overcoming an inauspicious start in a tough environment to emerge the happier and the stronger for the experience. Sadly the Dickensian description of the scene was altogether too true. George did not flourish and go on to greater things. He put it succinctly: 'I was miserable.' If his boyhood friend, Francis Prichard, found it hard to be separated from his parents at such a tender age, George found it even harder. Nothing in his home life had prepared him for the rigours, not to say wretchedness, of life in a boarding school in the 1930s. And at seven years of age! 'It was inhuman!' he said, with rare warmth. I delved a little deeper for the reason for a little boy being packed off to a place like that. Was it the accepted practice at that time? Not necessarily, unless the circumstances gave no other choice, as in the case of Fran. Seven was just far too young an age. Were his parents keen to get him off their hands? Hardly. They were devoted to family, and Mary, his mother, worried for him fearfully. The alternative, the local primary school, for some reason, was never considered. In fact, George had never before been to school. His education had until this point been entrusted to a retired schoolmaster, a Mr Hill, who taught him to read and write, a little history and a smattering of French. But by this time, it was becoming increasingly apparent that Mr Hill's value as a teacher was at the end of its usefulness. So off to boarding school he went. Why Wells House Prep School in Malvern? Well, his brother was there and would 'keep an eye' on him. Why his brother had been sent there has been lost in the mists of time.

Most schools, especially small prep schools, stand or fall on the calibre of their headmaster. Mr Frederick, the headmaster at Wells House before George arrived, had been a charismatic and successful figure who fashioned the place in the image of a senior public school, with prefects given a great deal of responsibility and authority. This worked fine when the headmaster was on top of things and exerted a guiding and moderating influence. But it went horribly wrong when Mr Frederick had to retire early on grounds of ill health, to be replaced by a man clearly not up to the task. To put it bluntly, the lunatics took over the asylum. And if you think I'm exaggerating, consider this. If any boy infringed the rules, no matter how trivial, he was sent to the 'far classroom' where a panel of prefects was seated behind a desk, ready to mete out whatever punishment caught their fancy, including a beating. And remember, these 'prefects' were only twelve years old. 'Sinister' was George's terse judgement. One is put in mind of the uninhabited island in *The Lord of the Flies* transposed to the Malvern Hills, a world where boys left to their own devices descend into savagery. George remembers it all with a shudder of fear.

'Chesterton! You're late!'

'Yes. Sorry. Lost track of the time.'

Part of the *laissez-faire* routine was that boys were allowed, encouraged even, to roam the hills at will. In gangs.

'You've got to report to the far classroom.'

George's heart sank. His feelings can only be imagined as he made his way along the corridor to the far classroom. Tradition dictated that onlookers lined the corridor and gathered outside the classroom door to be present at the spectacle. Another image comes into my mind, that of the *tricoteuses*, those women who noisily attended public executions during the French Revolution, jeering at the aristocrats in the tumbrils as they rattled on their way to the guillotine. And between decapitations, they sat there impassively knitting.

George opened the door. On this occasion, only the head boy was present. He beckoned the terrified child into the room. Wordlessly, he produced a slipper and proceeded to give the arm of the chair a few hearty thwacks. Then he splashed some water on George's face and sent him on his way.

Why he had spared him a beating George did not know. Perhaps he felt sorry for him, as the youngest boy in the school. In any event, George felt an immense debt of gratitude to him and indeed Joseph, for that was his name, was particularly kind to him during that first term.

It is not easy to penetrate the mind of a seven year old. At that age there is very little in the way of introspection going on. George probably didn't really understand why he was unhappy, just that he was. And that life at school contrasted bleakly with his life back at the vicarage. All he knew was that he didn't like the regime and wasn't learning anything. Except of course that he would do anything to avoid a visit to the 'far classroom'. One incident underlined how much. The playing fields at Wells House were a long way from the school building, down the path, across the main road and over some steeply sloped fields. Not for the first time, George was finding some solace with a ball in his hand. On this occasion it was a rugby ball. After practice, instead of returning up the hill with the others, he elected to stay behind to hone his kicking skills. Eventually, the gathering gloom persuaded him that he had better get back. On the trek uphill, he realised to his horror that he was probably late and that this would inevitably mean he would have to undergo the walk of shame down the corridor to the far classroom. In desperation, he took a run-up, leapt into the air and landed on his knees, lacerating them bloodily. 'It was the bravest thing I have ever done, I think,' he said. Those of us who have read about his experiences as a pilot in the war might take issue with him over that, but still, it was a crazy thing to do. On his return to the school, he was rushed up to Matron to be cleaned up and bandaged, at once becoming an object of some sympathy, not to say a little hero-worship, amongst his fellows. Of the late return, nothing was said.

At home, his mother was anxious to know how he was faring. I expect young boys were as uncommunicative then as they are now; certainly his brother John was no letter writer, an aversion he maintained until the day of his death at ninety-two. However, Mary did manage to prise one, pricelessly laconic, communication out of her elder son which gave an interesting insight into George's progress at Wells House, even if it did take the provision of a stamped, addressed envelope to obtain it: 'George stands about doing nothing watching other boys doing something.' George still has the letter and chuckles every time he reads it.

Part of the trouble was that the school was very keen on swimming and diving, whereas George preferred ball games. Swimming lessons were a torture. Their standard method of teaching boys to swim was unconventional, to say the least. Matron would take up her station on one side of the pool. The unfortunate boy would be taken to the other side and instructed to jump in and swim across. Most boys got there somehow with a mixture of doggy paddle and desperate thrashing. On being hauled out at the completion of their width, they were considered to be proficient enough in the water and rewarded with a piece of cake from Matron. George reluctantly jumped in and sank like a stone. He had to be fished out before he drowned. And, as a result, he has always hated the water, which had a direct bearing on his choice to go into the RAF during the war. The navy was never in the running.

Eventually, his parents must have sensed his unhappiness and took the only sensible course of action by removing him from the school. George still looks back on his two years at Wells House with horror. It is a source of wonder to those who know him that, on the surface at any rate, he has remained remarkably unscathed by this traumatic period in his life, especially as it occurred at such a young and impressionable age. Perhaps the scars remain deeply hidden. If so, then it is to his credit that no hint of bitterness and resentment has ever surfaced. He rose above it.

He was sent to St Michael's in Tenbury Wells, much closer to home but where he was still enrolled as a boarder – though he did manage to slip home on Sundays for a few hours after church services. One can only imagine the relief of his mother to have her beloved son back in her sight, as it were, and obviously happier. For he was, thankfully, and he looks back on his time there with some affection. The amusing irony was that St Michael's was a choir school and, by his own admission, George does not possess even the merest hint of any musicality in his bones. Thus he was termed a commoner, rather than a chorister and, as he was beginning to shoot up, he was given the job of carrying the cross at daily matins and evensong, a role that he rather enjoyed. Crucially, he made friends with other boys who were equally potty about games. Not only George subsequently made a name for himself on the games field. Christopher Winn later played rugby for Rosslyn Park and England, as well as county cricket for Surrey. He scored the winning try in a famous game against Wales at Twickenham in 1954. He had an older brother, David, who was also a good games player and with whom George struck up a close friendship. He and George were always seeded one and two in the school tennis competition and sure enough, for three years they met in the final. Every time, George lost. On the last occasion, before the match, he took himself off to the church and prayed that he be allowed to win. He does not admit to making anything like a Faustian pact with the Almighty but he does confess to feeling mighty let down when David defeated him yet again. From that moment on, he realised the futility of trying to engage the services of divine intervention in sporting contests and resolved to rely solely on his own endeavours. It was clear, even at this age, that winning on the field of play was very important to him.

For it was important to him that he excelled in something. In this regard, he was surely no different from any child but his confidence had taken a severe knock in his two years of misery at Wells House. He was fortunate to be good at games, which helped enormously, but he also threw himself into all manner of activities in a way that he had not done at Wells House, a sure sign that he was altogether a happier and busier boy. He became a 'senior sixer' in the Cubs, a patrol leader in the Boy Scouts and eventually was appointed head boy. He remembers on one occasion showing off disgracefully in front of his mother. She had come to watch him play cricket, and as he was the captain, he had ample opportunity to put himself forward, irrespective of the team's requirements. In charge of the batting order, of course he went in first. When it came to bowling, naturally he took the new ball and would probably have bowled at both ends if the laws had allowed. Neither history, nor his memory, records the result of the game but as far as he was concerned, he was determined that it should be remembered as 'Chesterton's Match', if only for the sake of his beloved mother.

It may or may not have been a direct result of 'Chesterton's Match' but Dee suddenly decided to present a cup to the school, to be awarded to the best all-round cricketer. This magnanimous gesture tells us three things about the extraordinary Revd Jack Chesterton. One, he had clearly just had a considerable win on the horses. Two, how typical of him that on coming into some money, he might choose to buy something as frivolous as a silver cup instead of paying off a few debts. And three, he should shrewdly present this cup in the full knowledge that his son would be the only realistic candidate to win it. Accordingly, the first inscription on the Chesterton Cup was G. H. Chesterton.

There is a touching footnote to this story. When St Michael's sadly closed many years later, the property and effects were being disposed of and no one was sure what to do with the cup. The problem was solved by the simple and obvious expedient of returning it to the family that bore its name. So, once more, it was presented to George. Rather than let the trophy gather dust on his mantelshelf, he decided to inaugurate a 40-over knock out competition for eight of the leading cricket schools in Worcestershire and round about, the final to be played at New Road, the county headquarters, and the winners to be presented with the Chesterton Cup. One or two strings were pulled and the proposal came to happy fruition. The competition proved to be a huge success and continues to be a firm fixture in the cricket calendar to this day.

Back to the early 1930s. George was happy at St Michael's and quickly gaining in self-confidence: 'I was very pleased with myself with little cause because I didn't measure up academically.' In truth the teaching was pretty poor. George managed to shift for himself because he swiftly worked out what the teachers wanted and was therefore able to secure high marks. A true education demands a bank of knowledge, it goes without saying, but understanding what it is the examiner is asking for, and providing the answer, is half the battle in exam technique. So perhaps George is doing himself a disservice here. Getting along with people and instinctively understanding what makes them tick is a priceless skill in life, one that would stand him in good stead in countless situations in the coming years.

However, he was nothing if not realistic about his chances in the scholarship exam to Marlborough, for which he was eventually entered. To this end, a private tutor was engaged to boost his chances at Common Entrance. This chap rejoiced in the splendidly rustic name of Ned. He was useless, confirmed George, 'He was more interested in chasing my sister than teaching me. This met with my full approval. Not his designs on my sister of course but the wasted hours spent away from our desk. As it happens, he was spectacularly unsuccessful in both his endeavours.'

Before the exam, George and his parents went to Marlborough for an interview with the headmaster. They were ushered into his study and the usual formalities were acted out. But it soon became painfully clear that the headmaster, George Turner, was a bit of a misogynist. He went through the whole audience totally ignoring Mary. Afterwards, Dee was incensed at the snub. 'He didn't even ask your mother to sit down,' he spluttered. 'You're definitely not going there!' George was phlegmatic about the disaster. He knew he had no chance of passing the exam.

As is often the case, and especially so with someone as good-hearted as George, time lends a more charitable perspective to old slights. George Turner, after his time at Marlborough, went on to another headship in South Africa before retiring. Charterhouse at the time were encountering difficulties in appointing a suitable headmaster and George Turner was persuaded to come out of retirement to answer their SOS. During his time at Oxford after the war, George found himself doing a term's teaching practice at Charterhouse under the headmastership of the said George Turner. He discovered him to be a delightful man and very helpful to the inexperienced student. He even offered George a job at the school but George had already accepted a post at Malvern and had to decline. We can all breathe a sigh of relief at that twist of fate. For himself, George puts down the odd behaviour towards his mother as nothing more than crippling shyness.

In any event, Marlborough was completely out of the question. It was time to think about Plan B. Malvern came on the scene as a possibility, for generous terms were on offer for sons of clergymen. Once again, parents and boy entered the study of a headmaster, this time Mr F. S. Preston. If trepidation was their dominant emotion it was justified, for George had performed woefully in his Common Entrance examination. Much rested on the next half-hour or so. Mr Preston was nothing if not a gentleman and busied himself making sure that Mary was comfortably seated. So far, so good. But the elephant in the room, George's poor marks, could not be dismissed. However, providence, hitherto so untrustworthy in Dee's gambles on the horses, suddenly came up with a windfall. The two men recognised each other from a recent burial service, which Dee had conducted, presumably wearing this time a suitable pair of black socks under his cassock. The unfortunate occupant of the coffin had been an unusually tall man of 6 feet 8 inches. When the time had come for the coffin to be lowered into the grave, to everyone's horror, the grave was discovered to be 2 inches too short. With commendable sangfroid, Dee had suggested that everyone retire to the pub while the grave was lengthened.

Amused, Preston remembered the occasion and due to that common ground, together with Dee's well-known powers of persuasion and persistence, George was accepted into Malvern College. 'So I passed Common Entrance,' announced George proudly, 'by 2 inches.'

There is one final story to be told about his prep-school days before he moved on to senior school. 'I was quite a good-looking young boy and I suppose I must have excited the attention of teachers who were, how shall we say, disposed in that direction. But I was terribly naïve, you know, and had no idea of such unorthodox practices.' It was the time of George V's Silver Jubilee and a huge procession through the streets of London had been programmed. One of George's teachers offered to drive him down to London to see the parade and take in some of the sights. Tenbury Wells was a country town and visits to the capital were rare events. Unsurprisingly, George was keen to go. The possibility of nefarious motives would never have occurred to him. Like any sensible parent, Dee checked with the school that it was all above board and was assured that it was. Accordingly, Mr Worthington turned up in his MG and George clambered in, excited at the prospect of a trip to London. He was driven straight to the Dorchester. George had never been in a hotel, let alone one in Park Lane. They were shown up to a very swish room … with a double bed. Even now, the naïve boy did not smell a rat. Mr Worthington seemed a little nervous but George gave it not a second thought. Off they went, to observe the procession from a reserved seat in the Strand, to take in the lights and soak up the atmosphere, followed by a slap-up meal in an expensive restaurant. 'Altogether, it must have cost him a bomb,' said George, with a sad shake of his head. Back to the Dorchester and time for bed. Only then did it dawn on the horrified boy that he was expected to share the double bed with his teacher. He was 12 years old and did not fully understand the ramifications of what was expected to happen but his gut instinct was one of revulsion. He put his foot down and point blank refused to cooperate. Fortunately, Mr Worthington was no seasoned paedophile and accepted the rebuff, 'almost as if he was relieved', said George. On his return home, he mentioned the incident to his father, not out of any sense of reprisal but merely for interest's sake. His father's reaction was not recorded. All George knew was that, three days later, at the beginning of next term, Mr Worthington was nowhere to be seen. And neither, come to mention it, were four other members of staff.

And with that, you might say that George's childhood came to an end.

4

MALVERN COLLEGE
1936–39

'I worked quite hard, so long as it didn't interfere with my games.'
George Chesterton

George Chesterton arrived at Malvern College at the beginning of the academic year in 1936 feeling, by his own admission, pretty smug and pleased with himself. If he thought that being head boy at a minor prep school would cut much ice at public school, he was in for a rude awakening. The senior boys, with their antennae finely tuned to pick up any signs of brashness amongst the new intake, would have spotted George a mile off. And in the time-honoured way of those days, they no doubt quickly made up their minds to teach the cocksure newcomer a lesson.

In more recent times, the word 'fagging' has taken on an almost mythical status, standing for everything that was harmful and unhealthy about public schools. Certainly in these more egalitarian times, the concept of a young boy being forced to act as if he was the personal servant of an older boy seems perplexing at best and downright abusive at worst. But one must guard against applying modern rationality to a bygone era. One might just as well take exception to mediaeval justices of the peace for putting miscreants in the stocks. The fact is that was the way things were done in those days and it ill behoves us, from the safe perspective of the here and now, to be too judgemental. Be that as it may, fagging went on at Malvern in the 1930s as it did in most similar institutions. It either served a purpose or was shamefully abused, depending on the calibre of the prefects administering it. Some first-year boys had a perfectly amicable relationship with their elders. And no doubt an equal number remembered their ill-treatment with a shudder of horror. Most probably just got on with it, regarding it as an unavoidable rite of passage. Nothing much truly changes in human behaviour.

Nevertheless, it is indisputable that prefects wielded considerable power when George arrived in 1936, though it is also true that Preston, the headmaster, had curbed the worst excesses of arbitrary punishment, such as beatings for the slightest misdemeanours. For example, a beating could have been administered for being the last to arrive in response to the call for 'Fag' or 'Boy'. And these beatings could be brutal affairs, delivered with anything from a slipper to a Rackets racket handle to a riding crop. Fortunately, by the time that we are talking about, things had become more systemised and regulated. Details had to be recorded in a punishment book and only a slipper was used. It might sound a little anomalous to our more sensitive ears but in the view of the College's official historian, Ralph Blumenau, 'life at Malvern in the 1930s seems to have been a good deal kinder than before to small boys.'

That is not to say that the lessons taught, and I am referring here to the lessons of life as much as to those in the classroom, were not sometimes short and sharp. It was the tradition that all new boys were given three weeks' grace from fagging and punishment, during which they were expected to learn the ropes. They had to memorise details of the Red Book, the school bible, such as the names, and more importantly, the initials, of masters, the colours of the Houses, the names of the housemasters and the heads of Houses, various school rules and traditions … and so on. In short, the minutiae of life at Malvern. George himself is in no doubt that it was a 'good thing', because in those three weeks you learned 'what made the school tick.' After the three-week period was up, each boy would be subjected to an oral 'exam', which was a formal and formidable occasion, with all the prefects sitting around a table and the head of House asking the questions.

George failed, not for the first time in an exam, nor the last. But on this occasion, he believed that the questions were fixed. He had as much chance of passing as his father picking a winner. He was given a week's grace, as custom dictated, before he was hauled before the prefects again. 'There is no doubt in my mind that the head of House wanted to chop me down. I was undone by several trick questions.' By way of illustration, he was shot this searching enquiry:

'What colour are the slates on the chapel roof?'

'Er … let me see. They're red.'

'Wrong! There are no slates on the chapel roof. They're tiles.'

'Oh yes, I suppose they are. But the colour is red.'

'No matter. You've failed! The statutory punishment is a beating.'

The procedure for the carrying out of this punishment was intimidating and somewhat sinister. It never happened on the spot but the following night. After bedtime, the door of the dormitory would be flung open and a junior prefect would bark, 'Chesterton! Down to your study now – in your pyjamas!' Nervously he would don his dressing gown, sympathetically observed by many eyes as he made his way downstairs to his study. There he would be made to wait until the call came down the passage, 'Chesterton! Come to the Pres' Room now.' The walk along the darkened passage must have reminded him of the summons to the 'far classroom'. The Pres' Room was a blaze of light and the prefects were sitting in their easy chairs. Curtly, he was instructed to remove his dressing gown.

'Chesterton – you know why you're here.'

'Please, yes.'

'Right. Bend over.'

The table had been pushed back and a Windsor chair with a semi-circular back had been drawn up alongside its end.

He duly bent over the back of the chair and placed his head under the table. Then the strokes were administered, 'six, I think', with a slipper.

Then, as tradition dictated, he shook hands with the prefect.

'Thank you, please, David.'

Where the custom had come from of having to insert the word 'please' into any sentence when addressing a senior remained a mystery but it very soon became a habit. And he made his way back to his cubicle where his contemporaries were all agog to know how he had got on and whether he had 'blubbed'.

Extraordinarily, George held no resentment whatsoever for his treatment. In hindsight, he felt he had it coming to him and no doubt deserved it. And he had inadvertently gained for himself something of a reputation, welcome or not. He was the only one of the new boys to have been so punished. One feels that he had already made his mark. Chesterton was not going to stand around doing nothing watching everybody else doing something.

In point of fact, George had stumbled upon a school to which he was perfectly suited. Malvern had a strong reputation as a games-playing school and George relished the opportunities to play a variety of sports. He tried his hand at anything that involved a ball and soon settled down very happily in a climate that not only encouraged the playing of games but actively elevated it to a sort of pre-eminence. The list of illustrious cricketers and footballers churned out by Malvern between the wars is impressive and shows quite clearly where the school's priorities lay. To be fair to Preston, the headmaster at the time, he was well aware of this imbalance between sport and more intellectual pursuits. His own observations on the problem make interesting reading:

If the charge of over-athleticism was true, what should a Headmaster do? The only hope was to restore the balance and to discourage the disease in its worst manifestations… It was, I felt, only possible to wean the average boy from regarding almost with idolatry those who possessed a natural flair for games and treating as VIP the school colours and arouse his interest in other directions and widen his horizon.

By all accounts, he did his best to dispel the aura that surrounded athletic prowess and to raise academic and artistic standards without destroying the ethos of playing games. He was well regarded by masters and boys alike but was a rather remote figure. Certainly, the new boy Chesterton found him so. In those days, the headmaster was also the housemaster of School House, where George was, but his day-to-day involvement in House business was necessarily limited. He would preside on top table at lunch and he would take House prayers in the evening but most of the administration was done by the House tutor, J. S. Rambridge, 'who was courting at the time,' remembers George, 'a very attractive girl called Mary.' So it seems that George's mind was not *wholly* taken up by games, despite his protestations that it was; at thirteen years of age, the next stage in his life had clearly begun. So Preston would not ordinarily have had much to do with the new boy, in spite of the fact that they shared the same house.

But there was one exchange that George remembers very clearly. Preston sent for him and nervously the boy presented himself at his study. 'Chesterton!' he was told, 'You are never to set foot in the Rackets courts again! Your Rackets bill amounts to more than your fees!' With his usual honeyed words, Revd Jack Chesterton had negotiated for his son remarkably low fees, only £30 a term, but still, it was something of an achievement for a boy to run up a bill like that in his first term at the school. It was a shame, because George enjoyed the game and would undoubtedly have been good at it. Many fine cricketers (R. E. Foster, Colin Cowdrey, Roger Tolchard to name but a few) have sharpened their hand–eye coordination and improved their reflexes playing this, the fastest and most difficult of all court games. Who knows by how much G. H. Chesterton's first-class batting average of 8.79 would have been improved had Preston not delivered his injunction? And his word was not to be flouted; George never did set foot on the courts again.

His less than impressive result in the Common Entrance exam meant that he found himself in the bottom form. The form-master was Charles Fiddian-Green, a legendary master at the College, but he was on extended sick leave and his place taken by a part-time teacher. 'He was hopeless,' remarked George, with a guffaw, 'and I soon worked him out. If you handed in your notebook on time, with everything neatly underlined in red, you'd get full marks!' This strategy worked so well that George was awarded the form prize at the end of the year, which just goes to show that charm and a willing disposition can generate surprising benefits. But sadly this success did not herald the flowering of a glittering academic career. The next year, on the strength of his meticulous underlining abilities, he was promoted a form where inevitably he was found out and soon he was struggling in certain subjects. He was good at English but poor at French and hopeless at Latin. He remembers a French oral exam, taken in the Memorial Library, now the staff common room. The examiner asked him to come in and sit down, in French, of course. So far, so *bien*. George could at the very least interpret the hand gestures and he did as he was bidden. Then he was asked what he could see out of the window. This he was able to gather by the jerk of the head and the direction of the look. Obediently, George's eyes turned towards the room's rather splendidly ornate glasswork that gave out onto the Malvern Hills. With a flash of inspiration, he blurted out, '*Les montagnes!*' The examiner was suitably impressed. 'I passed!' George exclaimed gleefully.

He took the School Certificate, the equivalent of today's GCSE, at the end of his third year. All his reports up until that point had been united in their gloomy predictions. He produced one of them, which he had kept, from his desk. They were all fairly damning in their faint praise. One subject in particular caught my eye. It was for Geography: 'I am afraid the syllabus may have proved too much for him.' And this was for a subject that George was later to come back to the school to teach! That observation by his teacher must rank for misguided prescience with Winston Churchill's form-master who wrote in his report: 'He has no ambition.' George, as it happened, confounded the doomsayers by performing creditably in his exams. 'I worked quite hard,' he grudgingly concedes, 'so long as it didn't interfere with my games.' We might deduce two facts from this surprising turn of events. First, George is by nature self-deprecating. It is his stock-in-trade and he has had a lifetime's fun at his own expense. And second, he has always had an innate sense of timing; he is a past master at pulling the rabbit out of the hat at the last moment.

Beyond the classroom, he devoted himself to the playing of games. And the opportunities seemed limitless, even without Rackets. Fives, squash, tennis, football … plus of course cricket. In the cricket term (no self-respecting cricketer ever calls the summer term anything else), he was in the nets every day, if there wasn't a match to be played. The professional at the time was 'Father' Tate, who was not a coach in the modern sense, someone who might refine a bowler's action or curb a batsman's propensity to play across the line. His role was more as a net bowler, who would bowl to order, more often than not serving up a generous helping of juicy half-volleys that the young gentlemen could feast upon.

'Were you ever given advice on how to bowl, George? You know – how to grip the ball and make it swing?' 'No, not really, not as I remember. Probably just as well. I had my own action. No one taught me. I taught myself.'

Just as well indeed. The hours bowling on his own back home at the vicarage, followed by constant practice in the nets at Malvern, taught him one priceless skill – accuracy. Even today, he shakes his head in disbelief at the apparent inability of the modern professional to bowl six balls on the same spot. 'Does no one know how to bowl a maiden any more?' he laments. I asked him whether he was unusually tall for his age, because tall bowlers can make the ball bounce, sometimes disconcertingly, and that, allied to persistent accuracy, can be a potent combination. But George said no, he wasn't particularly tall at that age and he certainly hadn't learned to swing the ball. He bowled off-cutters at medium pace. He took his wickets through a combination of nagging accuracy and by wearing batsmen down. 'I never ran through sides,' he maintains, 'like I felt I could do later on, when conditions were in my favour and the ball was swinging.' That skill came later, 'when I played for the RAF.'

It was a rule that you were not allowed to play in the nets on the Senior Turf unless you were in the XI or it was an official practice. So he was condemned to wheel away in the inferior nets on the Gym Flats. He was indefatigable. There simply weren't enough hours in the day for bowling. Current coaches and various experts in the science of biomechanics would probably throw their hands up in horror if a growing lad in this day and age subjected his body to such a strain. Strict rules are now laid down as to how many overs boys under the age of 19 can bowl a day. George scoffs at the narrow thinking. He believes that constant repetition and long hours of hard toil made him what he was, someone who had the stamina to bowl all day and the strength to remain free of injury. 'Mind you, I had a good action,' he admits, 'It was entirely natural. But it had the beauty of never breaking down.'

It was unusual for a boy in the Remove, the second year at the school, to be selected for the XI, especially as a bowler. In fact it was almost unprecedented. Batsmen who are small of stature can manage at a more senior level, provided they have the talent, but bowlers who are physically immature rarely cope. George was selected for a couple of games that season, but failed, unsurprisingly, to make much of an impression. Nonetheless, he caused a stir amongst his contemporaries. For a start, he was excused fagging, and that was a state of affairs every boy ardently aspired to. Furthermore, it was a tradition that you could then get changed for nets in the pavilion dressing rooms instead of back in the boarding house. And then you were permitted to make your way to the nets *across* the Senior, in full view of the school. The rest of the worker bees had to make a detour via the Senior Bank. As for the older boys, one would have expected that a certain amount of jealousy and resentment would be heading George's way. But not a bit of it. Everyone seemed very pleased for him, though that probably says more for George's naturally amiable and outgoing personality than the generous sentiments of the average adolescent boy. 'Mind you,' he points out, 'I was always very respectful of my elders.'

By 1939, he was in his third year at the school and in the XI for the season. 'It was a remarkable team,' he remembers, 'John Dods was our opening bat and he was a very fine player. He hardly ever failed that summer, scoring 744 runs, which is a lot.' *And how did you fare, George?* 'My three innings that season were 0, 0 not out and 0!' Yet again, the laugh rumbled around the room. Later research revealed that he had also taken 19 wickets and finished on top of the bowling averages!

Malcolm Staniforth was the master in charge of cricket at the time, whom George described as an 'all-time scout', tremendously energetic and enthusiastic and a stickler for the etiquette of the game. He was also a more than useful bowler, 'quite rapid – certainly for schoolboys.' In fact, he was a menace in the nets, George reckoned, because he bowled far too quick and didn't seem to understand that forcing the boys to duck and weave from short-pitched deliveries was not the best way to imbue confidence in their batting. There is one good story about him however. Dee, George's father, was a constant presence on match days. As the clock ticked over to 11.30, Staniforth announced loudly for everyone to hear, 'It's all right, Chesterton. Your father has arrived so we can start now!'

'Father' Tate, the pro, had now retired and his place filled by Bob Beveridge, recently retired from playing for Middlesex. He bowled left-arm and was so accurate he could drop it on a sixpence. And that was his role, to provide the requisite balls for the young batsmen to practise their strokes. You might say that he was the prototype of the modern bowling machine. His subordinate professional and social position was made plain by the accepted custom of having to call the boys 'Sir' at all times. His career at Malvern had an unhappy ending. In the war, he became a PE instructor in the RAF and gained a commission, rising to the rank of flight lieutenant. When he returned to his job at the College, he found that the old traditions remained intact and that he, a former officer in the armed forces, serving his country in time of war, was still expected to address young boys as 'Sir'. Unsurprisingly, he resented this and the rest of his time at Malvern was not happy for him. Towards the end of Beveridge's tenure, fate had decreed that George had returned to his *alma mater*, as a master and in charge of cricket, effectively his boss. 'I got on well with him,' said George, 'but the chip on his shoulder was fairly evident.' When it came for him to retire, he couldn't shake the dust of Malvern College off his shoes quickly enough. He emigrated to New Zealand, a place he believed less steeped in prejudice and hypocrisy. With his customary courteousness, George came to the station to see him off and wish him well. 'Thank God I'll never have to call anyone "Sir" again!' were Beveridge's parting words.

5

EVACUATION TO BLENHEIM
SEPTEMBER 1939–JULY 1940

*'It was said that MI5, who followed us at Blenheim, did more damage
to the Palace in three weeks than we did in three terms!'*

George Chesterton

The gathering storm of war in 1939 did not escape the attention of the boys at Malvern College any more than it did the rest of the country. However, the outbreak of hostilities was to have an immediate effect on the school in a way that no one could possibly have foreseen. That is, with the exception of one man, Tom Gaunt, the headmaster, who had taken over from Preston in 1937, two terms after George's arrival. He was about to be confronted with complications that were going to test all his skills as an administrator and as a leader, and which threatened the very existence of the school at a time when the country itself was in peril.

Throughout the ominous rumblings of 1938–9 on the political scene, Malvern had continued to function as it had always done, not deaf to the worsening situation in Europe, but no doubt, like everyone else, hoping for the best. Lessons still had to be taught, plays had to be acted, concerts had to be performed and matches had to be played – in short, the show had to go on as usual. However, though his outward demeanour betrayed no hint of it, Gaunt was in possession of a dreadful secret.

On Boxing Day 1938, he had received a letter. The significance of this was not that the post was delivered on Boxing Day (yes, the Royal Mail must have been at work on Christmas Day!) but that the letter stood out from late Christmas cards because it was pale bluish-grey in colour and with the rather daunting 'Secret and Confidential' printed on the envelope. Fully expecting an invitation to accept an honour or something from His Majesty, he slit open the flap. Inside was another letter, again marked 'Secret, only to be opened by the Headmaster of Malvern College'. For the contents of this letter, and Gaunt's commentary on subsequent events, I draw heavily on his book, *Two Exiles*.

In it was a letter from Sir Patrick Duff, permanent secretary to the Ministry of Works, informing him that the government 'have had under consideration the question of earmarking a number of large buildings outside London for national purposes in the event of war, and I am afraid it is my ungrateful duty to let you know that Malvern College is one of those earmarked.'

One can imagine Gaunt choking on his toast and marmalade. He was further instructed in the necessity for absolute secrecy and was authorised to inform no one else other than the chairman of the College Council. To Gaunt, the need for secrecy was obvious, for the College as much as it was for the government. After all, he would not have wanted to upset people with the news, especially as the contingency might never arise. He had to think of morale amongst the boys and parents, to say nothing of the danger to prospective recruitment. So the secret remained uncomfortably with him throughout the spring and summer terms of 1939.

That is not to say that he did not attempt to move heaven and earth amongst government departments for assurances about alternative accommodation for the school in the – increasingly likely – event of war. These representations bore little fruit. In desperation, he sought one further interview with Sir Patrick: 'After two hours, we were no nearer a solution, so we prepared to withdraw for the time being. At this point, Sir Patrick almost casually mentioned that he had that very morning received a letter from the Duke of Marlborough, offering Blenheim Palace to the Government if war should break out; and he added, "But I suppose it would not be large enough for what you want!"'

Gaunt was too much of a gentleman to bite off Sir Patrick's hand but we can safely assume that the offer was accepted with alacrity. The next day, he was shown around the palace by the duke and, although there were obviously huge drawbacks in the buildings and accommodation, there was nothing that Gaunt felt was insurmountable. Without further ado, he agreed to the duke's generous proposition.

However, nothing definite could be done. Britain was still at peace. Plans could be drawn up but they could only exist on paper. However, one event was not to be postponed under any circumstances, which coincidentally was to provide Gaunt with some solace and reassurance: 'In June, Lady Sarah Spencer-Churchill, the Duke's eldest daughter, became eighteen and the Duke celebrated the occasion by a Grand Ball to which a thousand guests were invited and which was described by a shrewd commentator as perhaps the last great European Ball. For us, this event had more than historical importance because it gave me assurance that in attempting to cater for 450 boys and staff in the Palace Kitchens and Dining Rooms we were not attempting the impossible.'

Quite apart from Gaunt's masterly stoicism, one has to admire the bullish determination of the English aristocracy to carry on as normal, even in the face of impending doom. Was not the Duke of Wellington similarly distracted on the eve of Waterloo by a grand ball in Brussels?

On 1st September 1939, Germany invaded Poland. Two days later, Neville Chamberlain, in his sombre address to the nation, declared, 'This country is at war with Germany.' I am once again indebted to Ralph Blumenau, the College historian, for his account of what happened next:

That day Ministry of Works officials arrived at the College to prepare it for the Admiralty in case it was compelled by massive bombing to move from London. Gaunt summoned the staff to Malvern. There began the task of packing and labelling the contents of boarding houses and the school, although the College was not yet requisitioned and no one was supposed to know that the school might be moving. On 7th September the requisition order was at last served. It was only now that reconstruction at Blenheim and the move from Malvern could begin.

Back at the vicarage in Tenbury Wells, George Chesterton was blissfully ignorant of these developments, as was the rest of the school. The first he got to hear of the wholesale evacuation was when his parents received a letter three weeks before the beginning of the new term, scheduled for 28th September, informing them that term would start two weeks late. His reaction was all too predictable for a teenager; he couldn't believe his luck that his holiday was going to be extended. For the staff, however, and for the prefects who had been enlisted to help, the rush to move a school – lock, stock and barrel – to another location in such a short space of time was to prove anything but good fun. Quite apart from the logistical nightmare that this entailed, there was considerable confusion and panic, not just in government departments but just about everywhere else in the country as Britain braced itself for the inevitable onslaught. Gaunt once again captures the mood:

Practically all transport at this time was under Government control and consequently the services of the local firms were secured for us by the Ministry of Works. This relieved us of one great anxiety but caused for us another, for although we were spared the trouble and expense of securing vans and labour, we had no control over the movements of the vans or the work of the men. We watched with apprehension the loading up, which was carried out at breakneck speed. At Blenheim we had to be ready at all hours of the day to direct the contents as they arrived at the Palace steps to their proper destination, and the final blow came when on the second day the men announced that they had received orders to dump the vanloads on the steps and return to Malvern with the utmost speed. This meant that the whole of the fifty-five vanloads had to be carried bodily, to the places assigned.

It took them ten days, working feverishly from breakfast until dusk. Another story recounts that all the beds at Malvern were hastily dismantled and loaded up on the lorries for transportation. When they reached their destination, the fixtures and fittings had been jumbled up and it proved to be a nightmare of a job to re-assemble them.

One example of the intrepid spirit that infused the small but committed workforce was the construction of a pipeline from the nearby village of Woodstock to the palace, needed to provide gas for the kitchens. The boilers ran on petrol and as petrol was likely to be severely rationed, a gas outlet was required. Ralph Blumenau writes, 'A gang of Masters began to hack through the limestone to dig a trench for it.' It seems unbelievable to us today from our cosy perspective of peace and plenty that masters – teachers, academics, men of letters – should roll up their sleeves and work like navvies. But they did, such were the times and such was their resolve to get the school ready in time.

Gaunt provided staunch leadership during this period but, by all accounts, the organising genius behind the whole operation was the second master, Major Elliot. His tireless efforts in those chaotic and stressful weeks, described by Ralph Blumenau, was nothing short of 'herculean'. George remembers him well and pays him similar, generous credit for what he did for Malvern in its hour of need. But typically, George adds a wry postscript to the major's career: 'He had to leave, in 1942, I think, because he ran off with his matron in No. 6.' (Unusually, and quirkily, but wholly logically when you think about it, the Houses at Malvern, with the exception of School House, are given numbers, not names.) At last, Malvern College reopened, only two weeks late, in the middle of October. Much was still to be done of course but a great deal had been achieved during those frenetic first weeks. The huts, which were to provide teaching accommodation, would not be finished for another three weeks, during which half the school would go for a walk while the other half sought a corner to be taught wherever they could. George remembers that the living was crude and uncomfortable but, in keeping with the national spirit, there was little complaint and everyone 'just got on with it.' For example, there were not nearly sufficient lavatories in the palace for 450 boys plus staff, so sixty extra ones were built behind the stables, 'a mushroom growth appearing out of the setting concrete with the unabashed functionalism which we are told makes all things beautiful,' wrote Gaunt, with a rare foray into irony. George was less impressed, calling the inconvenient location 'a bloody nuisance.' He also remembered with a laugh that there was a film out at the time, *Sixty Glorious Years*, starring Anna Neagle, which celebrated the long reign of Queen Victoria on the throne of England. With sardonic humour, the temporary facilities were dubbed 'The Sixty Glorious Rears'!

Ten huts were initially built, which usefully matched with the ten Houses and which doubled up as classrooms as well as recreation areas. 'We were hugger mugger, tightly squeezed in with our trunks containing our clothes and personal possessions always kept under our beds. The rows were so close to each other that one bedstead would be practically touching another.' This enforced intimacy had one rewarding, if surprising, consequence: 'Because our heads were only inches away from each other when we were in bed, I struck up a close friendship with a most unlikely fellow. We would converse in whispers into the small hours, about anything and everything. He was a bit, well ... wet, quite frankly. He would go to bed with a hot water bottle, for example. He was hopeless at games and ordinarily you would not have expected us to have anything in common. It was a strange, unlikely friendship but we became very close and confided in each other a lot. Egglestone was his name.'

The teaching was understandably patchy. Some of the younger teachers of course had been called up and it was true that the conditions in which lessons took place were far from ideal. The heating in the huts was poor. Blumenau writes, 'Boys came into morning school wrapped in coats and rugs, to find that icicles had formed under the corrugated iron roofs during the night. As the temperature slowly rose, they melted and dripped onto the forms below. In the summer, with the sun beating down on the roofs, the huts became so hot that the moisture dripped off the boys onto the floor below!' Nonetheless, it has to be said that the standard of teaching did deteriorate. George's form-master, a man called Wilbé-Jones, was the assistant chaplain and taught history. 'He knew his stuff,' admits George, 'and I used to enjoy listening to him because he made it interesting. But he only bothered with the boys who were academic and really wanted to learn. I did not count myself among their number. He couldn't have cared less whether you did any work or not. This suited me down to the ground. He was lazy, I guess. For example, first period in the morning was obviously too early for him – he seldom turned up!' By his own admission, George was not a good pupil. All he wanted to do was get on the games field. He did feel that it was disgraceful that he was allowed to get away with it though. 'I didn't do a stroke at Blenheim,' he says ruefully.

But there were compensations. The spectacular beauty of the leaf colours of the trees in the grounds made an impact on everyone, even notoriously unobservant teenage boys. The South Lawn, in front of the palace, was itself a cricket pitch and still is home to Woodstock Cricket Club. Beyond that was a ha-ha, and thereafter stretched the spacious beauty of the Great Park, which provided excellent football pitches. Tennis courts were already there, though the boys did not have use of them very often. The old stables were converted into a gym and a theatre, where concerts took place. In the Easter term, there was a hard and prolonged frost. The lake froze over and boys were able to skate on it. 'I was no good at ice hockey,' George says regretfully, 'because I couldn't stay upright.' The Ledbury Run, a gruelling cross-country run and a school tradition, was set up around the park. And the baroque magnificence of the palace itself cannot have failed to stir even the most philistine of hearts.

Compensation for George also came in the form of feeding the rabbits; the hutches were behind the stables. *I had no idea that you were an animal lover, George.* 'No, I was not particularly attached to the little furry creatures. Of far more interest to me was the person in charge of feeding them. She was none other than the duke's younger daughter, Caroline. I was quite keen on her and we used to meet up by the rabbit hutches. It meant that I had to get up very early and creep out to see her, as it was all pretty clandestine. I don't think she was at all interested in me romantically – how could she have been with a spotty youth like me?' Perhaps not. But the experience no doubt stood him in good stead when he, in later life, became a housemaster – a case of the poacher turned gamekeeper, you might say. *And just think of it, George, you might have become the duke's son-in-law!* At first, George made no response. Sometimes, the old man is far too wily to rise to the bait like that. But then he did add, *sotto voce,* 'She was no great beauty, you know.' But she obviously had a sense of humour. When George told her about the new, temporary WCs and their nickname of The Sixty Glorious Rears, apparently she laughed like a drain, 'so much so that I thought she would have a heart attack.'

The duke and his family did make appearances from time to time, especially on gala occasions. The duchess was utterly delightful and used to entertain the prefects with her effortless charm. The duke himself was little in evidence on a day-to-day basis, though George did once have an individual audience with him. He had broken a window, one of the priceless bevelled windows dating from the early 18th century, and had to go to the duke to apologise, an undertaking which George no doubt carried off with his usual urbane politeness. 'He was more embarrassed than I was, as it happens, and just didn't know what to say.' One assumes that the small talk did not then extend to the welfare of the family rabbits.

Cricket in the summer term on the South Lawn was 'just marvellous.' Gaunt describes the summer term thus: 'The summer of 1940 was one of the most beautiful I ever remember. Day after day the sun streamed down upon the golden landscape of Oxfordshire, wild flowers and birds abounded in the Park, the gardens and shady nooks of the Palace grounds provided refreshing retreats, and the sound of cricket floated from the great Lawn.'

The spectacular palace, designed by Vanbrugh, provided as magnificent a backdrop as one could imagine. There is a wonderful, large, framed photograph of the scene at the foot of the stairs in the Memorial Library at Malvern College. In the foreground, a row of deckchairs lines the boundary, with blazered young boys in whites paying uneven attention to the match taking place. In the middle, the batsman is about to play forward to the bowler who appears to be a left-arm round merchant. In the background is the imposing palace itself, with tea clearly set out on white linen-covered tables on the steps leading up to the grand entrance. A more quintessential English scene could not be imagined. *Can you remember who's playing, George?* 'Indeed, I can,' he answered. 'It's the Shrewsbury match. "Father" Tate is umpiring and Malcolm Staniforth is the other umpire at square-leg, Peter Houldsworth is bowling. And that statuesque figure at mid-off is me!'

The wicket was as good, if not better, as any that they played on. Traditional rivalries remained intact, for the most part; matches against Shrewsbury, Cheltenham, Rugby and Repton still took place. In addition, Blenheim's proximity to Oxford meant that matches could be arranged against some of the Colleges. And the weather was gorgeous. In an account of the season, Malcolm Staniforth, the master in charge of cricket, makes mention of the strange, almost surreal, contrast between cricket being played on green fields under blue skies and the darkening clouds of war gathering just over the Channel: 'The present season will forever be printed on our memories, not for affairs beyond our control, the rush of arms, the cruel hate of deadly opposites, the crushing of the defenceless, for these things seemed apart from us, and in a sense unreal; much rather when quiet days at Malvern are no longer ours, will we cherish a vision of a smooth wicket, a white marquee and trees as lasting as cricket itself.'

And what of the cricket itself? As for his own contributions, George said that he considered himself 'an insignificant member of the side – perhaps I took a few wickets.' Knowing George's penchant for self-deprecation, I decided to look up the records and see for myself. He took 23 wickets, not prolific but hardly insignificant. It was also noted by Malcolm Staniforth that 'Chesterton in particular began to hit the ball with more confidence, making some excellent shots on the off.' He was now batting at No. 5, which conferred upon him the genuine title of an all-rounder. One match sticks in his mind, not so much for the cricket but for what happened immediately afterwards. It is recorded that in the first week of June, Malvern played against St Edward's School, Oxford. Malvern lost easily, by 6 wickets. Apparently, the boys let themselves down with some shoddy fielding, which was not all that surprising if you remember that this was wartime and they had spent half the night in the cellars during an air raid. Not a memorable match then, but all sides can have off days. But for the next match, two days later, on 7th and 8th of June, a two-innings game against Cheltenham, a 'local' derby if ever there was one, the opening batsman, H. M. Sells, was missing. Injured? Dropped? In detention? No, none of these things. He had left school to join the RAF. Before the term had ended. And the day *before* the Cheltenham match. His call-up could not even be deferred until after the big game. Unusual times indeed.

And of course they were. Momentous, you might say. France fell. The British Expeditionary Force was evacuated from Dunkirk. Churchill, a relation of the Duke of Marlborough and born, as it happened, at Blenheim Palace, became prime minister. And a boy in the 1st XI was called to arms mid-term. Although George maintains that they all took this pretty much in their stride, at the back of everyone's mind must have been the thought that the balmy days of playing cricket, without a care in the world, were probably numbered. They all knew their history. And they had all read about the horrors of trench warfare in a conflict that had devastated the preceding generation.

'The feeling about the war was surprisingly optimistic,' George recalls, 'despite all the bad news. There was no talk of defeat. We were going to win this bloody war, whatever it took.' For the time being, the boys' contribution to the nation's effort comprised twice-weekly Corps exercises. The German airborne forces had been very much to the fore in the invasion of Holland and it was felt by the authorities that the Great Park at Blenheim, on account of its spacious, open, flat terrain, would be ideal landing ground for German paratroopers. Accordingly, a section of the Local Defence Volunteers, later to be renamed the Home Guard, was hastily assembled and the school Corps was entrusted with patrolling the palace grounds. They went out at dusk, slept in the open air during the night and patrolled again at dawn. Then went straight into classes. Imagine what the Ofsted inspectors, entrusted with safeguarding the welfare of schoolchildren, would make of that nowadays. 'But these were desperate times,' George reminds us. 'We really did believe that German paratroopers were going to swoop down disguised as nuns!' Wilbé-Jones was an officer in the Corps – yes, the same Wilbé-Jones who couldn't be bothered to turn up for first lesson. 'He had a revolver – a strange accoutrement for an assistant chaplain, you might think. He was a bit trigger-happy. He used to fire off at any rustle in the bushes. Rabbits, probably.' Not Lady Caroline's pet rabbits, one hopes.

As if to remind them all that this was no game, an armoured division of the Canadian Army suddenly appeared, almost overnight, to set up camp in the grounds. Gaunt describes their impact on the place: 'In twenty-four hours, the Park was festooned with camouflage nets over guns, anti-aircraft batteries, armoured cars, lorries and tanks; while vast spaces were covered with the tents, kitchens, stores and military equipment of six thousand men. For ten days this occupation lasted, during which time we entertained some five hundred men to an open-air concert on the Palace steps... Then one evening, the division began packing up and by early morning the men were gone, leaving behind them hardly a trace of their invasion.' George's description of the visit by the Canadians was more succinct: 'Great fun.'

There was much about that year's exile at Blenheim that was exceptional, bizarre even. *Did you miss the old place back at Malvern, George?* A long pause ensued. 'Not really, now I come to think of it. We were young, you see, and everything was an adventure.' He is in no doubt that, in a curious way, the experience did them all, boys and staff, a lot of good. 'Previously, Malvern was a stuffy, starchy place, suffused with petty privileges and rules. In your first term at the school, as a new boy, you weren't allowed to walk on the path. You had to walk in the gutter! Can you believe it? And all that nonsense about new boys not being allowed to put their hands in their pockets... And in the second year, one hand was allowed in your pocket and only in the third year could you put both hands in. Ridiculous! And you jolly well had to obey the rules! I used to get around all that because I was permanently in my games kit. Overnight, that disappeared at Blenheim. It had to. With us all living so close together, cheek by jowl, there just didn't seem to be any point. And I firmly believe that it was a good thing. Malvern became a much friendlier place as a result.'

Meanwhile, plans to return to Malvern were exercising Gaunt and the College Council. Permission had been granted by the Ministry of Works for the College to re-appropriate some of the buildings of the school, 'provided that in case of an emergency we would be prepared to evacuate them at 48 hours' notice.' Gaunt decided that the risk was worth the taking and accordingly, at the end of term, Malvern said goodbye to Blenheim and its generous host: 'Against the background of total war, the summer term ended with a speech from the Duke of Marlborough, and the saying of many farewells to many we had come to know as real friends during the past year.' In his speech, the duke thanked the boys for not having trashed the place, as teenage boys are carelessly wont to do. 'And it's true – we didn't,' says George. 'Of course all the valuable stuff had been stored and put away but we naturally respected our surroundings. It was popularly rumoured that MI5, who came after us, did more damage to the Palace in three weeks than we did in three terms!'

6

RETURN TO MALVERN
SEPTEMBER 1940–JULY 1941

'Fifty-seven were in my leaving year in 1941; twenty went into the army, fourteen into the RAF and ten into the navy. So we all pretty well knew where we were headed.'

George Chesterton

T he Malvern they returned to in September 1940 was a much-changed place. Gaunt wrote, 'I doubt whether many other towns, outside London, contained so great a variety of men and women of different countries.' The Free French were billeted in No. 5, a naval training centre was centred in Nos. 1 and 2, a contingent of the Belgian Army was in the Abbey Hotel, groups of Poles and Greeks were in town, as well as Canadians, Australians and Americans, and at various times there were visitors from Yugoslavia, Norway and Holland. Into such an environment, the school had to quickly find its feet and settle down to normal life, or as normal as everyone could make it. The buildings that were released by the government were, on the whole, serviceable. Numbers had dropped away, which was hardly surprising, so the school could be accommodated in the living space remaining – by the simple expediency of combining some of the Houses. Gaunt, as the headmaster, returned to School House. 'On entering SH again, the maze of telephones was indeed a subject of astonishment, for there were four in each room, including the private bathroom.' School House had been earmarked as Churchill's private office if the Admiralty had had to move from London and at the time, prior to becoming prime minister, he was first lord of the Admiralty. Gaunt remarked somewhat wryly that of the multitude of phones, none of them worked.

George was now in his final year, at the top of the school and a prefect. Gaunt, in his capacity as housemaster, appointed him head of House, a singular honour and an important position and, in the New Year, made him junior chapel prefect, the Malvern term for deputy head boy. In addition, he was asked to take on the captaincy of the cricket XI. Not bad for a new boy who had scraped into the school 'by two inches'. George believes now, with hindsight, that he was by then feeling pretty pleased with himself and must have been 'insufferably arrogant'. Whatever the truth of that, George was evidently beginning to display those qualities of leadership and strength of character that were to be severely tested in the near future.

The Common Room had greatly changed in a short space of time. Few of the younger masters were left, having volunteered or been enlisted for active service. Their replacements were not always up to scratch. And the older masters probably viewed a rapidly changing world, unravelling in front of them, with dismay and apprehension. Some of the diehards tried desperately to reinstate the obsolete rules and regulations that obtained before the war (indeed, one master had even kept a notebook, jealously guarded, listing all the archaic privileges and traditions), but the will to go back to the old days simply wasn't there. 'They were seen to be what they were,' said George, 'ridiculous and old-fashioned, and they quietly died a death.' On the whole, masters were remote and although relations between Common Room and boys were always respectful, there was no friendliness, as we would expect nowadays. One exception possibly was his new master in charge of cricket, John Rambridge: 'I was his captain and inevitably we would have long discussions about the team and about tactics. I liked him. He was the first person to treat me as an adult, and I greatly appreciated that.'

George's relationship with Gaunt is an interesting one to try to disentangle. You would hardly have expected them to be close. A headmaster is a headmaster and his role is not to befriend boys, even if one of them is his head of House. Nonetheless, there is clearly a deep well of affection and respect that one can sense whenever George talks about Gaunt. His headmaster must have seen something in the young man, some sort of potential, otherwise he wouldn't have made him a prefect. Moreover, he was about to make a significant decision about George's career, the value of which was only dimly appreciated at the time but which was to have an enormous effect on his life: 'He entered me for the Heath Harrison Exhibition at Brasenose College, Oxford. He, with his far-sighted wisdom, could see that I needed to get into Oxford, for my cricket presumably, and that this would open up all sorts of possibilities for me.' Indeed it would, as we shall later discover. It was a shrewd move on Gaunt's part, not least because the award to Brasenose was a closed one and therefore he would not be up against any opposition. And we all know that George's record in the examination room, so far in his life, was not a glittering one. 'Yes,' says George, with a faraway, wistful look in his eye, 'I owed Gaunt a lot.'

His wife, on the other hand, did not inspire much affection. 'Ma Gaunt we used to call her,' he says with an amused grin. As head of House, it fell to George to have to sit next to her on top table every lunchtime, and this tested even his remarkable reserves of affability and ease of manner. There was one occasion when she summoned him into the private sitting room. She announced that it was high time that they had a food committee, and that George should assemble one forthwith, and that they would meet at regular intervals. 'Probably didn't have enough to do' was the predictable but private grumble of the head of House but he did as he was told and accordingly the appointed committee filed dutifully into the sitting room a few days later. 'It was a disaster,' remembered George with a great guffaw, 'She started off by telling everyone that, in her opinion, the food in the House was very good. There was a boy called Cresswell who, admittedly, I did not much like, who announced in response, without any attempt at tact, 'The jam we get is disgusting'! She immediately took offence, the meeting was summarily suspended … and never did reconvene!'

He tells an amusing story his father recalled about Ma Gaunt. On one occasion, she was standing at the top of a grassy slope, welcoming guests to some sort of garden party. She was wearing a new yellow dress in which she firmly believed she looked quite stunning. The reality was somewhat different. She was backlit by a setting sun (in the manner of that famous photo of the young Lady Diana Spencer) and, as the yellow dress was diaphanous it was clearly visible to everyone that she wasn't wearing anything underneath. 'Dear, oh dear,' is George's only comment:'What an *extraordinary* sight that must have been!'

The rest of the staff had less of a lasting impact on George than you might have expected. He freely admits that he wasn't the most assiduous of pupils and did as much work as he felt was necessary to get by and as little as he could get away with. Nevertheless, a faint but unmistakeable note of regret can be detected when he talks about his academic career, which sometimes manifests itself in a wry shake of the head, almost as if he is unwilling to blame anyone other than himself. 'It has to be said that I don't think I was well taught – ever.' Dick Colthurst was now his form-master. George pulls a face at the memory of his lessons, 'All he did was dictate notes. I would carefully copy them down for about ten minutes before my pen would make an ugly squiggle down to the bottom of the page as I fell asleep.'

Ralph Cobb was a brilliant mathematician but his lessons to the less gifted were indescribably boring. In his classroom, a metal bar ran across the ceiling. The boys would entertain themselves by playing a form of ping-pong, the ball having to be knocked over the rod, which acted as a sort of net. Every so often, predictably enough, the ball would be missed and it would bounce over desks and up to the front where Cobb was busy writing up problems on the board. Either he would not notice or, more probably, would affect not to notice. Hilarious of course, but one imagines that not much learning was going on. 'If you were bright and you were particularly interested in the subject, then I'm sure you would have got all the teaching and attention that you needed. But…'

The headmaster, Gaunt, was aware of the deficiencies in the classroom but at a period in the school's history when it was not at all clear whether civilisation as they knew it, let alone Malvern College, would survive, he had to busy himself with more pressing concerns. Indeed, the school was about to be faced by an even bigger challenge than the exile to Blenheim. Within five terms of their return to Malvern in April 1942, government inspectors arrived at the school unannounced and it soon became clear that Gaunt was going to have to deal with a *second* requisition. The vitally important work being done in radar research and development at Swanage on the south coast was believed to be under immediate threat of attack from the air from German-occupied France so the decision was made to move it well away from the range of enemy aircraft and paratroopers. For a variety of reasons, it was felt that Malvern was the ideal location. The decision was all-important and made in the nation's interest and there it was, a fait accompli. It nearly put paid to Malvern College's very existence, for plans were being drawn up to disband the Houses one by one, and surely no school could have survived being broken up and re-formed at some indeterminate date in the future, before Harrow School came to the rescue at the eleventh hour. The story of the second exile at Harrow and the highly secretive work undertaken by the country's top scientists in the College grounds to develop radar is a fascinating one but does not concern us here. George left at the end of the summer term in 1941 and was already training as a pilot at the time of these further travails for the school, but the point to emphasise is that Gaunt had a lot on his plate. So the absence of first-rate teaching for some of his pupils was probably not as high on his list of priorities as it normally would have been. In any event, George harbours no sense of grievance, 'I had a marvellous time at school and in many ways I can be grateful for the education, in the widest sense of the word, that it gave me.'

At Malvern, as the Luftwaffe turned its attention on London, the progress of the war seemed to impinge on the consciousness of the boys more than it did at Blenheim. Everybody used to gather round the wireless each night to listen to the nine o'clock news on the BBC. George remembers one night vividly. He and others were fire-watching from the top of the Preston Science Building and they observed with a mixture of fascination and horror a conflagration in the sky somewhere north-east of them. They firmly believed that Birmingham was ablaze. In fact, it was Coventry.

Rationing was beginning to bite. Some of the school grounds were dug up and a vegetable garden planted. Gardening became a compulsory activity though it had to be admitted that most of the efforts to become more self-sustaining proved to be amateurish at best. The school uniform became expensive in terms of clothes coupons. So Gaunt decided to introduce a new uniform which would cost only 13 coupons instead of 26. But it never caught on. Ralph Blumenau observed, 'The boys cheerfully put up with much during the war, but this was going too far!' Somehow, people would get hold of bits and pieces of the official uniform (there must have been a roaring second-hand trade going on) and in the event, the idea was quietly dropped.

Despite the background of almost continual bad news about the progression of the war, life at Malvern continued day by day, as it had to. As Gaunt wrote, 'And so the months passed, grimly yet gaily, and we felt that our job was to carry on sturdily until final victory in Europe and the Pacific should bring more ease yet greater opportunity.'

It must have been a strange time for the boys, especially those in their final year. In one sense, the bitter conflict seemed a long way away, protected as they were by the bubble of school life and the daily routine of lessons and games. But in another sense, the reality of war must have been in their minds more and more. After all, their immediate future was already mapped out for them. 'We all knew exactly what was in store the moment we left school,' said George, 'Fifty-seven were in my leaving year in 1941; twenty went into the army, fourteen into the RAF and ten into the navy. So we all pretty well knew where we were headed.' *Not much need for a Careers Master then?* 'Indeed not. I was determined from the outset to join the RAF. I'd read all about the horror of the trenches in the First [World] War so the army didn't particularly appeal. And I hated the water – still do, as a matter of fact – couldn't stand swimming lessons. So that cut out the navy. Besides, I always fancied flying.' However, in order to qualify for pilot training, he needed to pass maths. It was a fairly foregone conclusion, in his mind, anyway, that he was not going to get his Higher School Certificate, the equivalent of A Levels, so the decision was made to give up history and concentrate on maths. 'It was probably a shrewd decision,' he says, with a knowing look, 'not least because it gave me a lot of free periods in my last term and cleared the decks for my cricket!'

And it was in the cricket term that the young George Chesterton really came into his own. No longer could even he claim that he was no more than 'an insignificant member of the side.' As captain, opening bowler and No. 4 batsman, he dominated proceedings. He grins at that: 'As I was captain, I made sure I bowled a lot!' The records tell it all. He topped the batting average at 43.50, scoring 435 runs. He was also the leading wicket taker with 45 at an average of 12.89. One match in particular stands out in his memory. The game was a two-day affair, which Malvern won by 68 runs, and was dubbed, this time with good reason, 'Chesterton's Match'. He scored 103 in Malvern's first innings of 277 (no one else managed more than 37). He then bowled 30 overs unchanged, on a blistering hot day, taking 4 wickets, as Cheltenham were dismissed for 137. But they fought back strongly on the second day and it took a captain's knock from Chesterton to steady the ship in the face of some extremely hostile bowling. Malvern were bowled out for 149, Chesterton again top scoring with 59 not out. Cheltenham had given themselves every opportunity of turning the match around, needing to score 289 to win, but Chesterton put paid to any thought of that, taking 6 wickets and the game was won by 68 runs. So he had taken 10 wickets in the match and scored 162 runs, for once out. *You must have been exhausted, George. Still, you had a few free periods the next day to recover.*

'I loved my last term. All that squash and tennis when I wasn't playing cricket. And we had a pretty good season, beating "Teddies", Cheltenham, Rugby and Repton. And we won the House Cricket Cup!' Oddly, he seemed more proud of this achievement than his tour de force against Cheltenham. In fact, those who have experienced life in a boarding house and the passions that House matches can engender will understand perfectly what he means. School House were the acknowledged underdogs; you could say that they were very much a one-man band. The scorecard says it all. Chesterton scored a century (next highest score 22) and took 16 of the 20 wickets to win by just 21 runs. 'Marvellous! That was my swansong. I absolutely loved that last term and was very sad to leave.' No wonder; it all sounds so idyllic, and such a contrast to what was to come in his life. His master in charge of cricket, John Rambridge, was fulsome in his praise of him: 'Chesterton proved himself a first-rate captain. Off the field, he was always cheerful and optimistic, and on the field, he has shown a genuine and mature appreciation of the finer points of captaincy. He has the knack of getting the best out of his men... From early on in the season, the team spirit was strong, and continued to grow... A good captain must study his own men as well as his opponents...'

He has the knack of getting the best out of his men. I shall remind you of this prescient assessment of his character in a later chapter, when he came to command his crew in a Stirling bomber in active service. Clearly the boy had grown up and was about to enter the adult world.

He may indeed have developed the knack of getting the best out of his men but he had not yet mastered the knack of getting the best out of himself in the examination hall. He had to go up to Oxford to sit for the Heath Harrison Exhibition, for which the headmaster had entered him. There he sat, studying with complete bemusement, his Latin unseen paper. 'Honestly, the only words I understood were the instructions. And that was because they were written in English!' A kindly invigilator took pity on his wretchedness and suggested that he put his name to the blank sheet of paper and leave the room. He remembers taking two or three history papers, 'which must have been painful for the examiners to read.' Later, during his interview with the admissions tutors, the history don turned to him and observed, 'It is not at all clear which period of history Mr Chesterton has been studying.' Fortunately, the principal of the college immediately steered the conversation towards more familiar ground – his cricket. 'Anyway, I got the award because it was closed!'

Something else happened during that blissful last term. His father, Dee, was teaching a young lady to drive. The lessons would invariably incorporate a visit to Malvern to watch the cricket. George immediately took a shine to her – unsurprising as photos of the future Mrs Chesterton show her to be a very attractive woman. 'She wasn't very impressed with me to start with, you know.' Her name was Kathleen Dominy but was known by everyone as K (and so remained throughout their married life). He summoned up the courage to ask her what her surname was, so he could write to her. 'I don't see what that's got to do with you' was her unpromising reply. But George was a good enough bowler by now to know that patience and perseverance will assuredly bring their eventual reward, and gradually his persistence paid off: 'Her frosty exterior slowly dissipated and I was able to write to her and the romance blossomed.'

And what of the man who arguably had more influence on him at school than any other? It would be churlish not to include, as a footnote to this story, how Tom Gaunt fared in later years. On his return from Blenheim, he had told his staff, 'Well, we shall never be afraid of a major operation again! But I did not seriously expect that the need for one would occur.' The move to Harrow, where the two schools co-existed side by side; the return to Malvern at the end of the war, in which 258 Old Malvernians had lost their lives; the restoration and redecoration of buildings that the scientists had adapted and changed for their work on radar; the financial problems caused by the continual upheaval; the arrival of new staff and the return of veterans; the adjustment to social change and a new world order ... all these would have tested the mettle of any man. The enduring legacy of the Gaunt years can be encapsulated in one simple phrase: the school survived. And there were times when it seemed that it might not. In 1953, he retired and took holy orders. Ralph Blumenau sums up his stewardship thus: 'No previous headmaster of Malvern College had been faced with such formidable difficulties... All his correspondence shows neither fluster nor self-pity, but a spirit which matched the hour.'

Oh, and he also got George into Oxford.

7

RAF TRAINING
JANUARY 1942–JANUARY 1943

'Of the modest achievements in my life, receiving my pilot's wings was the one that gave me the greatest thrill and satisfaction.'

George Chesterton

On 20th July 1941, George left school. Unlike school leavers today, he did not jump into his father's car and drive down to Newquay to carouse in the bars and on the beaches with his mates on the north Cornish coast. Nor did he hop on a plane to join other school leavers trawling through the fleshpots of Mykonos or Corfu. Nor did he go hiking in the Himalayas or trekking through the Amazonian rainforests. Nor did he embark on a gap year in the Australian outback or go on safari in the African Serengeti. No, his father picked him up from Malvern and drove him straight to Worcester, the nearest recruitment centre, where he signed on for active service in the Royal Air Force. 'By volunteering,' said George, 'you could choose which service to enter. Otherwise I could have found myself down a coal mine or something.' Accordingly, he signed on the dotted line for service in the RAF and was told that his medical would be in one week. Having been passed fit for active service, he was then told there was a backlog in pilot training and that his call up would be deferred for six months. This not only meant that when his service pension was totted up on leaving the RAF, the six months counted – 'The extra ninety quid was very handy when I went up to Oxford in 1946.' – but also enabled him to spend the time at home with his family, something he had not done very much of since he was a child.

'It was blissful. I'd spent most of my boyhood in a boarding school and it was wonderful to be close to my mother again, whom I worshipped.' His father got him a job on a farm where he learned a variety of manual skills – handling a circular saw, making silage, stacking wood, driving a tractor. He also did a paper round, collecting paper for recycling, all part of the war effort. He was paid half-a-crown an hour, which gave him a certain amount of independence. He joined the local branch of the Home Guard, which involved exercises on two evenings a week, plus the occasional weekend: 'It was just like it was portrayed in *Dad's Army*. As probably the youngest and most active of the Tenbury platoon, I was singled out to demonstrate the most effective way of performing the exercises and, in fact, during physical training I had to stand in front so that all the elderly, the farmers and the infirm should follow me.' The image of George as Private Pike demonstrating rifle drill to the Godfreys and the Frazers of the village springs unbidden to my mind.

This idyllic interlude did not pass in total isolation from the war. The battle of the Atlantic seemed to be going badly, Hitler's armies were rampaging across Russia and the bombing of British cities, particularly London, by the Luftwaffe continued unabated. And then in December, the Japanese bombed Pearl Harbor. But George's confidence that it would eventually turn out all right, whatever it took, remained undimmed. 'The only time I ever doubted the outcome of the war was the awful day when the *Repulse* and the *Prince of Wales* were sunk off the coast of Malaya. However, I didn't doubt for long.' One presumes that if he was thinking along theses lines then he was not alone. The spirit of defiance that suffused the country at this time must have been a truly remarkable thing, for it cannot have been at all clear, even to the most patriotic of Englishmen, that ultimate victory was assured.

There was little opportunity for cricket, though one important invitation came his way. He was selected to play in the annual public schools match, traditionally played at Lord's, but of course Lord's had been requisitioned for wartime duties and was currently overshadowed by a barrage balloon. Nonetheless, it was still a considerable honour, even more so when he discovered that he was to captain one of the sides. The opposing captain was none other than T. E. Bailey. The match was played at Honor Oak, in south London. George caught a taxi from Paddington. He gave the address to the taxi driver and settled back in his seat, no doubt contemplating whether to bat or bowl if he won the toss. Not knowing London at all, he had no inkling that the taxi driver was heading in completely the wrong direction. All London cabbies are supposed to pass a stringent exam on London streets, popularly called the 'Knowledge'. Now, this taxi driver's knowledge of the 'Knowledge' was sadly deficient and he got hopelessly lost.

Eventually they arrived at the cricket ground, but late. The match had already started. 'He cleaned me out!' said George, outraged, 'I had to empty my pockets. And then he had the gall to complain when I didn't – couldn't – give him a tip! And I bowled like a drain.'

The six months at home provided ample opportunity for the relationship with K to flourish, 'K was the love of the first part of my life,' he says simply and touchingly. She came to stay at the vicarage several times, 'Our courting was gloriously old-fashioned and simple; we talked for hours, we walked, we played tennis, until we began to find we were miserable when we were not in each other's company.' Very soon they reached what George called 'an understanding'.

All too soon, the six-month hiatus was up and in February 1942 the official letter, addressed to '1578139 AC2 G. H. Chesterton', dropped onto the mat, giving him his joining instructions and enclosing a rail warrant. He was to report to the Air Crew Reception Centre (ACRC or 'Arsie Tarsie' as it was known) in St John's Wood, London. He was joined by twenty-nine others, policemen all, who had been released for aircrew duties. They were, in his estimation, in their mid-twenties and worldly wise; he was still in his teens, not long out of school and wet behind the ears. One imagines that the fun and games started almost immediately. He says that it was a culture shock of the most disagreeable kind and that he spent a miserable time acquainting himself with service life. For example, they took their meals at London Zoo, in the restaurant, he hastens to add, though if they had been having their food with the animals, it would not have been a lot different. On one occasion, a potato was dropped on the floor by one of the WAAFs serving them. Without a blink, she bent down, picked it up and dumped it on George's plate. Egged on by the others, he made a complaint. For his trouble, the following day he was put on two hours' spud-peeling duties. The facilities were basic and inadequate and the accommodation crowded and bare.

The bane of their lives was the 'odious Corporal Jones'. He is a recognisable type in the training of any new recruit, whose sole purpose is to make life as uncomfortable as possible. It was no doubt with some *schadenfreude* that they later heard that he had been court-martialled and reduced to the ranks for certain sharp practices for which he was well known. One day, he marched them for their jabs to the medical centre. They were ordered to strip to the waist and, in long queues, they were attacked on each side by medical orderlies and nurses who plunged needles into their bare arms. There was no pretence that each injection should require a new needle; they were used until they were blunt and could no longer pierce the skin. Actually, George felt fine after this wholesale assault on his immune system but some hours later, the reaction set in and, feeling distinctly worse for wear, he fell off a bus on his way back from the cinema. Onlookers believed that he was a drunk and it was with some difficulty that he staggered back to his quarters where he fell into bed and did not come round for another twelve hours.

While George is sleeping off the effects of the cocktail of drugs which the authorities saw fit to pump into his body, I should like to digress for a moment, the purpose of which should swiftly become apparent. You are in the Away dressing room at Lord's and you are doing up your bootlaces for the tenth time. There is a knock on the door and the dressing room attendant puts his head in and announces, 'Gentlemen, the umpires are on their way!' Your captain leaps to his feet. 'Right lads, let's go. And don't forget – Middlesex say that this is their home. No it's not. It's the Home of Cricket. In other words, it belongs to us as much as to them. So let's not be overawed. Up and at 'em, eh!' 'B*******s!' mutters the bloke next to you, but he is the senior pro and he has been playing for twenty years and he is entitled, you suppose, to be a *tiny* bit cynical. You make your way outside and down the stairs. People always say that cricketers in their spikes clatter down the stairs, but not at Lord's they don't. There is a kind of rubberised quality about the carpet, which muffles the footfall and lends the place a quiet, even reverential, air. You turn right, into the Long Room. You are conscious of the large portraits hanging from the walls and you look up, but the only one you recognise immediately is the familiar, bewhiskered face of W. G. Grace. The members, politely standing aside to give you passage, look at you with vague interest, recognising the famous overseas player in your midst but no one else. Some of the seated members might peer at you over the tops of their *Daily Telegraph*s … or they might not. Nonetheless, and even the hard-bitten pro who changed next to you freely admits that it's always the same, no matter how many times you play there: a shiver runs down your spine as you turn left, pass through the double doors, trot down the steps, through the little white gate, considerately held open by a Marylebone Cricket Club (MCC) flunkey, and step out on to the grass. The first thing you notice is how pronounced (left to right) is the famous Lord's slope. And then you look back at the grand old Victorian pavilion and you say to yourself: *I've just walked through the Long Room … as a player!*

Now consider the same scene on a damp and miserable day in February 1942. George and his compatriots had been marched through the gates of Lord's by the odious Corporal Jones and up into the Long Room. All cricket grounds bear a forlorn aspect in the middle of winter but as George describes: 'The Long Room was stripped bare. The paintings and portraits had been removed, there were no tables and chairs and the whole room was scruffy and dirty. Outside, the pitch was covered with barbed wire and of course there was a barrage balloon anchored above the nursery ground.' A desolate sight indeed. And the irony was that George's first sight of this famous old place should have been the previous summer when he was selected for the Public Schools and he would have had the honour as captain of leading his side down those steps. But what were they doing there that cheerless day in February?

On Corporal Jones's command, they all had to drop their trousers for an FFI inspection. *A what, George?* 'Freedom from infection.' He had no idea what this meant and had to have it explained to him afterwards what had been going on. *Did you pass?* Some questions George seems not to hear. 'The next time I was at Lord's was when I played for the RAF against the army after the war. The crowds were enormous. You see, they had been starved of cricket, or any sort of entertainment, for so many years.'

The following day, he was sent away to Paignton, on the south coast, and Corporal Jones faded from memory. Life at the Initial Training Wing provided a 'joyous contrast'. He was kept busy, for a start, which he liked. There were lectures on navigation, principles of flight, meteorology and the mechanics of engines. He struggled a bit with the theory, especially the mathematical side of things, and never really got to grips with the workings of the internal combustion engine. For exercise, there was much drill and PT. Discipline was tight and they were marched everywhere but George was used to a regimented existence, having been brought up in boarding schools, and he enjoyed the experience. He preferred to take responsibility and organise things and it was not long before he worked his way up to taking command of his particular flight. 'Bit like being a prefect at school,' he reckoned.

One day, all of them were summoned to appear in front of the squadron commander and it soon became clear that he was in a foul temper. He was outraged that a discarded French letter, as condoms were delightfully called in those days, had been discovered on site and he let the recruits know what he thought of this objectionable behaviour. George was mystified; he had no idea what the offending object was, nor its purpose. So naïve was he that he had never even set foot inside a pub. Friends soon set about putting that right.

There were a couple of incidents that put paid to any notion that he might have been back at school. One freezing winter's day, three brave hearts decided to swim round Paignton's pier. They soon got into trouble in the choppy waters and one of them drowned. 'Our first casualty, you might say.' Not long afterwards, the flight was practising Morse code on the beach when one shouted out, 'Three Spitfires coming in fast! My God, they're not Spitfires, they've got black crosses!' They were in fact FW190s and they dropped their bombs in nearby Torquay and Brixham, causing a lot of damage and the deaths of 20 cadets.

Near the end of his twelve-week stay in Paignton, he and K decided that they should get engaged. They managed to persuade a reluctant mother-in-law that it would be a good idea, so long as they both gave their word that they would not actually get married until after the war had ended, whenever that misty outcome would be realised. Accordingly, the announcement was published in the papers. The same squadron commander ushered George into his office to add his personal congratulations. 'But may I point out one significant error,' he stressed, 'It says you are a member of the RAF. Can I bring to your attention that in fact you are a member of the RAF *Volunteer Reserve?*' Once a career officer, always a career officer.

Their initial flying training was to take place in Canada and it was amidst the strictest secrecy that they were assembled in Glasgow and shipped aboard a troop carrier, one of three that was to be escorted across the Atlantic by a US battleship, the *New York*, a veteran of the First World War, and four destroyers. Any communication with family or friends was forbidden but George, with characteristic resourcefulness, managed to smuggle a postcard home, via a friendly railwayman. It simply said: *'We're on our way!'* At first light, the convoy quietly slipped down the Clyde. They were routed well away from the threat of enemy U-boats, thanks to the secret work being done at Bletchley Park to crack the Enigma code, so they were reasonably safe from torpedo attack. But once the heavy Atlantic swell took hold, George fell horribly seasick and was so ill that there were times when he would willingly have accepted a torpedo amidships. Another good reason for joining the RAF and not the navy.

Having made landfall in New York, they were immediately transported north to New Brunswick in Canada. There they were joined by cadets from a host of other countries and all of them found that time dragged as the authorities were clearly encountering logistical problems in feeding them through the system. The air force was crying out for pilots but it takes time and manpower to train them.

To while away the time, the prefect in George decided that it would be a jolly good idea to arrange a 'Test' match between the English and the Australians. Kit was of course hard to come by, so they played in full battledress. The Aussies won, much to George's chagrin. He hates losing.

Eventually, to their relief, they were put on a train across Canada to Alberta, where the serious business of learning to fly began. A routine very soon established itself. Flying took place in the mornings and ground subjects took up the afternoons. The next day, the schedule was reversed. On his first flight, George felt sick and frightened as his instructor threw the aircraft, a Stearman, into a series of stalls and spins, 'for familiarisation purposes'. Later George overheard the instructor saying to his sergeant, 'Don't waste too much time on young Chesterton. He's a total washout!' That sort of comment is tailor-made to stir George's juices and had the effect of making him doubly determined to prove the officer wrong. Need I remind you of the stubborn young boy who wouldn't eat his porridge, as commanded to do so by the dragon of a matron at prep school? Luckily, he was assigned to a brilliant new instructor, a Sergeant Tarry, who was a patient and meticulous teacher and who drilled into George the importance of good airmanship. And George, to his delight, found that he had a natural aptitude for flying, having good hand–eye coordination, and soon he was thoroughly enjoying being at the controls of an aeroplane. Let me quote his description of his maiden solo flight:

> There is no experience in the world like the first solo. I taxied out gently, carefully did all my cockpit drills, turned onto the runway, eased the throttle steadily forward. A little touch of the rudder to keep her straight, watch the speed, 50, 60, 70. Ease back on the stick and lift-off, climbing at full revs to 500 feet, ease back a bit on the throttle, at 800 feet start a gentle, climbing turn to the left until, at 1,000 feet, the runway is at right-angles. Throttle back and level out, turning through 90 degrees to have the port wing running, as it were, along the runway. Do all the cockpit checks for landing, brakes off, mixture rich, fuel level okay, and then another 90-degree turn – looking carefully first, of course – ease the throttle back to let her down to 800 feet; look left and turn to line up on the runway, a little less throttle, keep the nose up – but watch the speed, less throttle and descend steadily to cross the fence at about 10 feet up; close the throttle and then come back slowly on the stick to finish 10 yards down the runway on all three wheels, in a perfect three-point landing. Marvellous!

Lest anyone should believe that they were having a wheeze of a time at a local flying club, a dreadful accident brought them all up short with a jolt. It was remarkable that collisions weren't a frequent occurrence with the air full of inexperienced pilots buzzing around learning complicated manoeuvres but one was more than enough. Two aircraft ran into each other, and the propeller of one sliced through the fuselage of the other, nearly cutting it in half. The pilot, David Brooks, managed to bail out but he was too low for his parachute to be deployed properly and he was killed. A great gloom descended upon the station. No blame was apportioned; it was just one of those things that happened. George was assigned to the rifle party at the military funeral. He remembers the scene as a very moving one as they let off three volleys, more or less in unison, into the vast Canadian sky.

There was no time to sit around and mope. Immediately, it was back to the daily routine of flying and lectures, 'Lots of circuits and bumps.' *Bumps?* 'You'd go up and come in to land. But instead of stopping, you'd take off again, go round and do it again. And again. And again. Great fun!' Soon it was time for his first check, after 25 hours of flying, taken by the chief flying instructor. He was kept waiting. Eventually the officer emerged from the control tower and issued a breezy command: 'OK, Chesterton, let's go.' George grabbed his helmet and followed. As he went to put it on, to his horror, he realised that he had taken the wrong helmet; it was none other than that of the recently killed David Brooks. The dried blood was still visible on the leather skull. Oh dear. Not a good moment. But George was able to put this unfortunate blunder out of his mind and the test went well. That is, until the final approach to land. 'I knew I was 200 feet too high. Biggles then came to my rescue. I remembered in one of those books, that he had let quickly down into a small field by side-slipping. So in desperation, I followed his example… The landing was so gentle that it wouldn't have broken the skin of a rice pudding.' *And the reaction of the chief flying instructor?* 'He said, well done, but he would rather I stuck to the more normal glide approach and landing.' Anyway, he passed him.

Practice and tests in instrument flying, night flying, cross-countries and aerobatics continued apace. George hated aerobatics. It reminded him of PE lessons at Wells House Prep School. The instructor had installed a ladder in the gym and the boys were compelled to do exercises hanging from this ladder upside-down. 'It was my great good fortune that I was assigned to bombers and not fighters. I can't stand being upside-down.'

Soon they moved on from the single-engine Stearman to the twin-engine Oxford, a much more advanced aircraft and in George's opinion, 'probably the best of the twin-engine training aircraft used by the RAF'. His instructor was a quiet man, abnormally so. Before each flight, George would carefully rehearse a topic of conversation, to try to break the ice. Later, he employed the skills he had learnt at Blenheim, only this time to break into, rather than out of, a building. He and a fellow cat burglar entered the instructor's office to rifle through his files to find out how they were doing. Chesterton's report read: 'Flying OK but he talks too much.' George shut up thereafter.

Winter in Alberta was something that just had to be endured. On one occasion, they secured a weekend leave and took the train to Calgary. On the way back, the train struck a horse that had strayed onto the line and frozen to death. It had to be hacked away with axes. One week, relentless blizzards swept through the station and to all intents and purposes everything shut down and all simply concentrated on survival. By contrast, the Canadian hospitality was warm and welcoming. Off duty, they made many friends and people would often go miles out of their way to provide lifts. Of course there was no rationing and no blackout so the comparison with home was poignantly obvious.

George had set his heart on gaining a commission as an officer. Only the top third in the group at the end of the course would go on to be officers; the rest would be sergeants. It was now clear that the moment of truth, for all of them, was rapidly approaching. George's logbook makes interesting reading at this pivotal moment in his life. It records somewhat blandly:

Proficiency of Pilot: Above Average.

This pupil has shown aptitude as a Pilot/Navigator: Yes.

Awarded Flying Badge 22/1/43.

And it was signed by the Officer Commanding 36 Service Flying School. *The RAF certainly enjoy their capital letters.* 'Never mind the capital letters. I came seventh. And the first eleven got their colours… I beg your pardon, their commission.'

The Wings Parade took place in a heated hangar and one by one they stepped forward to have their wings pinned on by the group captain. 'Of the modest achievements in my life, this was the one that gave me the greatest thrill and satisfaction.' *And all to prove to that idiot of an instructor that you were not a total washout.* 'No. I wanted to gain a commission for my mother, to make her proud of me. And she undoubtedly was. But in truth, it was of no consequence to her. All she was worried about was whether I was safe and well.' It should be remembered that she was, as George said, an excessively nervous woman, forever suffering torments about the possibility of accident or injury. But it was to her eternal credit, so says her son, she never, not once, uttered a fretful comment in his hearing from the day that he signed up for the RAF, 'even though she must have been worried sick.'

What does a young man do to celebrate the passing of an exam? He seeks out the city and the bright lights, that's what. Together with a friend, George decided to blow what little funds they had on a trip to New York. All right, New York is a mighty long way from Alberta but they were all to travel east anyway for the next stage of their training and they had been granted three weeks' leave. The Battle of Britain had been fought two years previously but the exploits of the RAF had already passed into folklore, even in America. Subsequently, anyone wearing the light-blue uniform was treated like a god – 'a bit like wearing your colours blazer at school' – and far from quickly spending all their back pay, they barely had to put their hands in their pockets. The generosity of the Americans never failed to astonish them. Free drinks, free meals, free theatre tickets, free entry to clubs and dances and music halls – you can imagine that they had a whale of a time. On one occasion, George was swept onto the dance floor by Katharine Hepburn. *Not the film star?* George grinned. 'Indeed. The very same. She asked me what VR stood for on my uniform. "Volunteer Reserve," I replied. "Oh, how disappointing," she said. "I thought it might stand for Very Romantic."' It might very well have, because after swirling around the dance floor with him for ten minutes or so, she handed him over to another beautiful woman, who just happened to be Gipsy Rose Lee, the most famous stripper of her era. History does not record, and neither is George telling, the direction that their conversation took. All that needs to be said is that the young man who had had no idea what a French letter was had evidently come a long way in a short space of time.

Sadly, the pleasant, almost surreal, interlude in New York came to an o'er hasty end and it was back to New Brunswick and the serious business of preparing for war. Newly qualified pilots, wireless operators and navigators were being assembled and formed into crews. The process of forming a crew, to the outsider, no doubt appeared extraordinarily casual and *ad hoc*, but it seemed to work. Everyone was herded into a large room and you … well, you simply went up to anyone you liked and asked him whether he fancied being in your crew. A bit like picking football teams in the schoolyard, if you like. George took a glance at the list on the board and noted the name Knighton. Knighton was a village near his home in Tenbury, so he looked out for a sergeant named Knighton and asked him whether he would like to join him in his crew. 'Sure thing,' he answered in the unmistakeable tones of a Canadian. George then asked him whether he knew any navigators. Jimmy Knighton recommended his roommate, Harry Whiting, and when approached, he readily agreed. Hey presto! A fighting unit was formed which survived intact until the end of the war. 'And never did I have cause to regret the choice we made.'

They were now practising formation flying and low level cross-country in Venturas, low-level fighter-bombers. The Ventura was not an easy aircraft to fly. It was a development of the Hudson, a reliable workhorse of Coastal Command, which had been fitted with bigger engines, in order to beef up its speed. It certainly went faster but at the expense of balance and manoeuvrability. So it was clumsy and difficult to handle and, even worse, it couldn't stay in the air on one engine. Nonetheless, flying practice continued, with the purpose of eventually going into action striking at shipping and supporting troops on the ground. One incident became the talking point of the station. One of the Venturas had an engine failure and as it couldn't be flown on one engine, the pilot put it down, with considerable skill, on a fortuitously located, nearby, frozen lake. No one was hurt and on his return to base, the pilot was highly commended for his flying skill and coolness under pressure. But the story does not end there. The lake was too small for the aircraft to take off again once the engine was repaired, so tracks, cranes and transporters were employed to lift the aircraft out. Suddenly, great cracks were heard as the ice began to split and everyone scarpered in the direction of the shore, to watch in horror as the ice finally gave way and a lot of very expensive equipment gently sank to the bottom of the lake. Unfortunately for the poor pilot, whose resourcefulness had been so highly praised, an enquiry had to be held and he was left to kick his heels for three months whilst everyone else moved on.

Meanwhile, George was getting on like a house on fire with his crew, a testament to his natural geniality as well as the relaxed style of leadership that seemed to come naturally to him. I asked him about the relationship between officers and the lower ranks, conscious that no organisation is more jealous of hierarchy than the armed services. His reply was interesting. He admitted that he might, on occasions, have been a bit stuffy about rank. And the regular officers, as opposed to the Volunteer Reserve, were obviously more strict and old-fashioned in their dealings with their men. However, the RAF was the youngest of the services and as such probably the least hidebound about the nuances of authority. Furthermore, this was war and old class barriers were breaking down. He and his crew used to socialise easily and perfectly naturally off camp, usually in the pub. But on site, the barriers of rank remained; George would go to the officers' mess and the others would go to their own quarters. On board, he was the pilot and obviously in charge (he was called 'Skipper') but they all had their jobs to do, and training and experience gave them total confidence in each other. As his cricket master at Malvern said of George, the captain of the 1st XI, 'He has the knack of getting the best out of his men.' Enough said.

Finally, after a year away, it was time to go home. Not back to the vicarage of course and his mother's roast dinners, because he was at the beck and call of his masters in London and would have to go wherever he was sent, but at least it was a return to England and the opportunity to do what they had been so exhaustively training for – to have a crack at the enemy. They sailed from Halifax in the *Louis Pasteur*, a former luxury liner. No escort of warships this time; the ship relied on its speed to evade the U-boats. A week later, they docked in Liverpool and were sent down to Bournemouth, just missing a raid by FW190s, which wreaked severe damage and killed 100 people. *Did you manage to have any contact with your parents? With K?* He shook his head. But the good news was that the unreliable Venturas had been withdrawn from service, following a disastrous raid on Brest, from which only one aircraft had returned. The reason given was that they were too slow, carried too small a bomb load and were not airworthy on one engine. 'Hmm, we could have told them that ages ago,' was George's terse comment.

There now ensued a long wait to be reassigned to another aircraft. Whilst the Air Ministry were deciding what to do with this newly trained batch of pilots and their crews, George had some time on his hands. K came down to Bournemouth, taking some leave from her job as an operations clerk in the WAAF, and they were reunited, not without some understandable butterflies, in the town park. No need to eavesdrop as they talked and wondered whether it was still going to work after all that time apart. It didn't take George long to make up his mind. 'Let's get married!' he exclaimed, completely forgetting his promise to her mother that no declaration would come before the war had ended. George has always been of the 'strike while the iron is hot' persuasion. K took little convincing, and that was that. The banns were published and her mother, still in blissful ignorance, nearly fell out of her pew in astonishment and fury when she heard the details being read out in church. How the silver-tongued RAF officer managed to talk his way out of that one is a mystery but eventually she came round and sportingly gave way. The wedding, taken by Dee, was a low-key affair and the bride and groom dashed off to the Norfolk Hotel in Bournemouth for an all-too-brief honeymoon of only three days. That is all the leave she was granted. George had fourteen days, so he went back home to Tenbury. He was barely 21.

After what seemed an interminable delay, they learned that their new aircraft was to be the North American Mitchell, a superlative light bomber, according to those who flew it, with no vices and equipped with all the latest mod cons, including ashtrays! 'Not that I ever allowed smoking in any of my aircraft,' said George, a little piously. Knowing that he was a smoker, I rather impishly asked whether he had picked up the habit, like most people, at school. 'No, I started when I was training in Canada. But I did give it up when I was at school; as a master that is. I suddenly realised that I needed to pause for breath outside the cricket pavilion on my way to class. Not a good feeling. So I stopped.'

Exercises in the new Mitchell were an endless round of bombing, formation flying, single-engine practice and the usual circuits and bumps. At this time, they were joined by a new member of the crew, Tiny Shaw, a gunner, 'one of the most even-tempered men I have ever met … he was a joy and we were very lucky to have him.' Talking of luck… About this time, George had a lucky escape. He had secured for himself a motorbike and having persuaded the garage owner that he was more than competent on two wheels (he had never ridden one before), he set off with a wobble and decided to put the machine through its paces. Inevitably, he came off further down the road, skidding along the tarmac on his backside while the bike ended up in a ditch a hundred yards further on. He was unhurt and you could say, perhaps a little unkindly, that he didn't learn his lesson. George, whether on two wheels or four, has always enjoyed speed. I have it on good account from numerous of his friends, including no less an authority than his son Colin, that fuel conservation has never been uppermost in his mind whenever he switches on the ignition. 'I don't put my foot down any more, like I used to,' George reassured me. In his ninetieth year, I should think not.

Before we switch on the ignition of George's active service, a little bit of background history is required. It was clear to the War Office from early in the conflict that airborne forces were going to play an increasingly influential role. To transport them, gliders and aircraft to tow the gliders would be necesary. According to George, from the outset not enough attention had been paid to the crucial task of towing these gliders. Various planes were tried and abandoned. Then some bright spark in the Air Ministry remembered that there were 50-odd Venturas, which could fit the bill, and not only that, the crews to fly them were trained and ready. So, in November 1943, 38 Group was formed for this specific purpose. Of course, any one of those trained and ready crews could have told the brass hats that the Ventura was peculiarly *unsuitable* for the role and it must have been with a hollow laugh that they heard the unsurprising news that the idea had been scrapped. What next? The Stirling bomber had originally been an integral component of 'Bomber' Harris's huge bomber force but it had to be withdrawn because casualties sustained in his Stirling squadrons had become unacceptable. Basically the Stirling could not fly as high as the later Halifax and Lancaster, and so was particularly vulnerable to anti-aircraft fire and fighter attack. However, it could do the job of towing gliders and was subsequently made available to 38 Group. It wasn't ideal but with certain modifications, such as stripping out the mid-upper gun turret, it would do. The Stirling's wingspan was designed to be 109 feet. But the hangars built to house them were only 99 feet wide. Quite incredibly, instead of building wider hangars, a few feet had to be chopped off the wingspan! Nonetheless, despite its modifications, George thought that the Stirling was a remarkable aircraft and he had good cause to give thanks for its resilience and airworthiness in the months to come.

One last entertaining anecdote before training finished and operations started. They were out on night-flying training, yet another run of circuits and bumps. When they had finished, they needed the flares, old-fashioned gooseneck ones, to indicate the landing strip. But the wind was shifting and the control tower informed them that the flares could be moved to illuminate the other strip, more favourably situated for the wind, but that it would take an hour. An hour pootling around in the night sky waiting to land did not fill anyone with much enthusiasm so the decision was made by the control tower to allow the landing to go ahead, provided they did it at once. As George made his approach, he realised that the wind was right behind them, and instead of being a few feet off the ground, he was at least 50 feet higher. Desperately he tried to get the great aircraft down, which he did eventually but there was only 200 yards left of runway. Not enough. There was a grassy overshoot of 200 yards for such an eventuality ... still not enough! On ploughed the Stirling, through two earth banks as if they were not there. A road crossed their path. A bus trundled past, oblivious to the fact that it just missed a collision with a heavy bomber by about ten seconds, George reckoned. On the Stirling scythed, demolishing two large chicken coops, eventually coming to rest in a storm of feathers, alongside, and towering above, the farmer's house, 'accompanied by the indignant squawks from a thousand frightened hens.' In George's ears came the voice of the control tower, instructing him that he was clear to back track. George made no response; he was spitting feathers.

Miraculously, no one was hurt. Even more miraculous was that the sturdy Stirling was undamaged. Its pilot suffered no disciplinary repercussions (though the officer in charge of night flying in the control tower might well have got his knuckles rapped) and the whole thing was put down to inexperience. They were flying again the next night. However, in the officers' mess, George did not, as you might imagine, escape unscathed. 'How many eggs for breakfast, George?' became one of the more printable wisecracks that met him each morning. And of course the episode went into Chesterton family folklore, oft repeated to successive generations down the years. More than half a century later, George revisited the spot, in Tilstock, Shropshire, and was a little disappointed that there remained no trace of the crash, nor the earthen banks, nor the chicken farm. The farmer's house had disappeared too. As he withdrew from the spot, now not at all sure that he had even got the right place, he went to a nearby house and asked the occupant whether there had been a chicken farm and a house there. The man was a bit vague but he said he thought there had been once but that it had been 'moved by the MoD because a bomber had run into it.'

8

RAF ACTIVE SERVICE
JANUARY 1943–SEPTEMBER 1946

'At last, in the full-moon period of April 1944, we went to war.'

George Chesterton

It is an extraordinary fact that George took to the air on 332 separate occasions before he flew his first mission against the enemy. He left school in July 1941 and immediately joined up, yet it was not until April 1944 that he was on operational duties over enemy soil. Nearly three years. Other pilots, in Bomber Command, for example, were on operations six months after completing their training. For a variety of reasons, he became the victim – you could argue that it was a blessing in disguise – of hold-up after delay. It seemed the top brass couldn't make up their minds how best to employ these newly trained pilots and of course there were problems deciding on the most appropriate aircraft to give them. Every day you don't get shot at is a day nearer the end of the conflict and personal survival but these young men, highly trained, were no doubt anxious to get on with the job. The periods of just hanging around must have been intensely frustrating for all of them.

Eventually, 190 Squadron was formed to tow gliders, provide support for airborne troops on the ground and to drop supplies for SOE forces – Special Operations Executive. The cloak and dagger boys. Churchill loved the idea of taking the war to the enemy and the Secret Service dirty tricks brigade, trained to wreak havoc behind enemy lines, greatly appealed to his appetite for derring-do. Indeed, when a war correspondent during the Boer War, Churchill was captured behind enemy lines with a scouting expedition and would have been shot as a spy had he not escaped. In any event, the agents, couriers and wireless operators needed constant supplies and the Stirling proved to be the ideal aircraft for this role, able to carry 24 containers and four large panniers. During the full-moon period each month, 'there must have been dozens of Stirlings flying at low level all over the continent.'

So, dropping supplies at designated zones, including the odd operative himself, and towing gliders laden with airborne troops was George's fate in the final chapters of the war. Needless to say, both tasks carried considerable risk but it is typical of George to make light of this. His admiration was reserved for the 'quite staggeringly courageous' SOE agents who disappeared through the hatch of the Stirling into the cold night air and the 'hardened regulars' of the 1st Airborne Division as they lined up to board their gliders.

Both tasks required considerable skill and airmanship so there was plenty of practice to be got through. Imagine taking off towing a glider. 'It was a bit like towing a caravan. Violent movements had to be avoided and the rope had to be kept taut at all times.' With aircraft taking to the skies in a continuous stream, the potential for accident, and disaster, was always present. For re-supply missions, large numbers of aircraft would rendezvous at a designated point, form into streams and then converge in proper order on the dropping zones. These operations, performed at low level, could only be carried out at full moon so there was always the fear of running into enemy fighters. 'Sometimes we felt very vulnerable.'

It wasn't always the enemy that engendered a feeling of vulnerability. One shocking accident reminded them all of the perils of what they were doing. The nylon tow-ropes for the gliders were valuable pieces of equipment; after exercises, a special dropping zone for the ropes was designated. Two Stirlings from 620 Squadron collided when undertaking this manoeuvre. George remembers 'the two hideous black columns of smoke which billowed into the air only half a mile from the airfield.' The image haunts him to this day. Later, he was accosted in the mess by a white-faced, breathless friend who said, 'My God, George, I was just told that you were flying one of those aircraft.'

To accommodate 38 Group, which comprised 190 and 620 squadrons, both dividing into two flights with twelve aircraft in each flight, a new airfield had to be found, and quickly. Many new airfields were being built all over the place, under the control of Sir Robert McAlpine, and in no time at all, by the middle of March 1944, a field in Fairford, Gloucestershire, was made operational. Well, it may have been for the aircraft, noted George grimly, but it certainly wasn't for the airmen. Conditions were basic. He remembers it being damp in the winter and plagued by spiders in the summer. But he had been to boarding school and was used to getting on with things. And there was a large number of Australian, New Zealand and Canadian airmen and they were a pretty cheerful and resourceful bunch.

'At last, in the full-moon period of April 1944, we went to war.' It was nearly one o'clock in the morning of the 10th that they took off on their maiden operations flight. They were detailed to drop 24 containers and three panniers somewhere over France between Argentan and Alençon. They headed out over the Channel at 1,000 feet and, as there was little cloud cover, the drop zones were expected to be visible. The agreed recognition letter was flashed, which was immediately returned. Then torches were lit, sometimes bonfires, indicating the drop zone. The panniers were dropped and the containers released from the bomb bays. The return was uneventful, apart from 'a little lazy flak' over the coast. How something as potentially deadly as anti-aircraft fire can be described as lazy is a moot point, but there we are. Back over home soil, they encountered heavy fog, so they were re-routed to Boscombe Down, 'which was one of the most secret airfields in the service.' He was closely interrogated by an intelligence officer, who naturally wanted to know his business, but, following strict instructions, George said nothing apart from the standard 'Operation Successfully Completed.' A few days later, a message came through thanking Pilot Officer Chesterton and his crew for 'goods received'. Their satisfaction knew no bounds.

Not all SOE operations were equally satisfying. Their next trip, for example, was 'boringly unsuccessful.' Over Limoges, where the drop zone was scheduled, there was no reception. They flew round about four times and seeing nothing, they returned home with their full load still on board. On top of this, 'there was a battery leak, which resulted in the aircraft being filled with noxious fumes.' On this occasion, their satisfaction knew every bound.

It happened. Sometimes there was no obvious reason. Perhaps there had been a breakdown in communications. Perhaps the Germans were particularly vigilant that night. Perhaps the drop zone had been betrayed to the enemy. If the flashed recognition letter was not flashed back to them, they simply had to fly back home without dropping anything. On one occasion, the reception party was ambushed as they were about to unload. A firefight ensued, which was visible to them, and they had to return home, with their load, and then pass on the distressing news that the Resistance party would have stood little chance. Frustrating yes, but the dangerous trip, over enemy territory, had to be done, successful drop or no.

It wasn't only in the air that danger lurked. After one such night operation, George was given the next day off so he jumped into his car, called 'The Flier' for one or two obvious reasons, and set off for a rare meeting with K, who was also off-duty from her job as a WAAF in Middle Wallop in Hampshire. At some stage in the journey, he fell asleep at the wheel. This will come as no shock to George's friends who chuckle at his propensity to fall asleep in a car, often before they have swung out of the drive. 'The Flier' somersaulted and landed on its roof. 'Two old dears looked over a fence and said quite casually, "He must be dead." As calmly as I could, I said, "I am not dead. Can you find someone to lift the car?" As it happens, I was unhurt.' He was given 48 hours' sick leave, however, on the insistence of the squadron's medical officer. It was his first hat-trick, as it were. George had now managed an accident on two wheels (the motorbike), on three wheels (the visit in his Stirling to a chicken farm) and now on four. Honestly, I don't know why the Germans bothered to shoot at George. Had the war gone on much longer than it did, he would surely have done a number on himself.

There were other light-hearted moments besides. Having had his weekly, relaxing bath, he was enjoying a whisky or two in the mess. His commanding officer rang to ask him to do an air test on an aircraft that had just had its engine changed. As it was a bit of an emergency, and as he got on well with Squadron Leader John Gilliard, George agreed, perhaps against his better judgement. Once in the air, he realised that the two whiskies had impaired his vision more than was comfortable. Basically, he wasn't fit to fly. The engineer, a young chap named Jack McCready, advised him to turn on his oxygen and, lo and behold, his vision cleared instantaneously. Back on the ground, he went to see Gilliard. 'Young McCready – he's one in a million. Can I have him on my crew? My engineer is going on a course and leaving us.' I don't know whether Gilliard raised an amused eyebrow at the grizzled old veteran, Chesterton, all of 21 years, describing the engineer as a 'young chap' but he readily assented and Jack McCready became the latest, and the last, recruit to George's team. 'He was outstanding, a calm, shrewd Scot, whose judgement was always sound and he never, ever, let us down.'

George had immense respect for John Gilliard, and got on well with him, 'probably because I was always willing to do little jobs for him,' said George, ever the helpful prefect. He also had an excellent relationship with Wing Commander Graeme Harrison, the station commander, who had recently been awarded the Distinguished Flying Cross 'for high skill, fortitude and gallantry'. The two senior men obviously saw the potential of the young pilot, both in the air and on the ground, and were prepared to give him his head. 'But I never overstepped the mark. I was always respectful, because they were my superiors and they were regular officers of long standing. But I liked to consider them my personal friends and that was why it was such a devastating blow when they were both killed in quick succession not long afterwards.'

There is an interesting and poignant sequel to this narrative. The wives of Gilliard and Harrison were close and went on holidays together. George would fly one or other of his senior officers down to Cornwall where the wives were and pick them up later. The whole exercise would be put down under the heading of 'training'. As it happened, both women had babies within weeks of each other. Gilliard's son John was born just before he was killed and Harrison's daughter Tessa was born just after he was killed. George went to both christenings and still keeps in touch with both of them.

By now it was clear to everyone that the big mission, D-Day, was in the offing. A steady flow of hundreds of thousands of troops, as well as artillery, tanks and other military materiel were clogging the lanes and by-ways of the south coast. Operation *Overlord*, the biggest military invasion in history, was close at hand. On 4th June 1944, all RAF stations were sealed off and remained so until the invasion was underway. No phone calls, no communication whatsoever with the outside world; in effect, everyone was confined to camp. George remembers a pep talk delivered to them by a senior staff officer in the operations room at Fairford. It was clumsily delivered. They were told that a casualty rate of over 50 per cent was to be expected: 'His talk was not well received.'

The job of 190 and 620 squadrons was to drop paratroopers from the 6th Airborne Division, Fifth Parachute Brigade, onto the eastern banks of the River Orne. This was two hours in advance of the seaborne troops; their object was to secure the Allies' left flank. Bad weather intervened and the invasion was postponed for 24 hours ... time to get in a game of cricket. Another 'Test' match was organised against the Australian airmen, on the tarmac. Same result, so the Aussies were now two-nil up in the series. 'Regrettable,' winces George.

Finally, Eisenhower put his trust in a more favourable forecast and the order was given for the invasion to go ahead on Tuesday, 6th June. No one was in any doubt of the momentous nature of what was about to happen. Churchill spoke to Franklin Roosevelt, the US president: 'My dear friend, this is much the greatest thing we have ever attempted.' In his order of the day, Montgomery told his troops: 'In the better days that lie ahead, men will speak with pride of our doings.' And Eisenhower in his capacity as supreme allied commander had told everyone in the invasion force: 'You are about to embark on the Great Crusade toward which we have striven these many months. The eyes of the world are upon you.' George said that they were all tense and nervous, but they had trained exhaustively for this moment and they all had the fullest confidence in each other. As the captain of his crew, he had to give every impression of being calm and in control; after all, he was the only officer on board and that was what officers were expected to do.

Though it was eleven o'clock at night when the paratroopers were driven to their allotted aircraft, it wasn't yet dark as the country was on what was called Double Summer Time. The Stirling engines were started up to warm up then shut down to allow the paratroopers on board. George's load was eighteen, including two officers and a sergeant-major; his impression was amazement at the amount of kit they carried and admiration for a group of fine-looking young men. Others were struck by the fatalism shown by the paras as they climbed aboard, often giving away prized possessions such as pens or watches, with some grim comment about no longer needing them. For a while, everything was deathly quiet. Then the signal was given and the Bristol Hercules engines, 'splendid and always easy to start', roared into life. At 11.15pm, the first aircraft of 190 Squadron, led by Wing Commander Harrison, took off from Fairford and climbed into the rapidly darkening sky. The rest followed at ten-second intervals. George's aircraft, newly painted with its special D-Day stripes, roared down the runway at 120 knots and set course for France, crossing the Channel at only 1,000 feet.

Many Stirlings ran into anti-aircraft fire and paratroopers in several aircraft received shrapnel wounds. George was luckier. As they crossed the enemy coast after a rapid climb to about 9,000 feet, he encountered some 'desultory' flak but little else as he descended to 800 feet over the drop zone. The door was opened, the red light went on and the paratroopers disappeared in quick succession. Tiny Shaw, the rear gunner, reported that they were all safely away and that he thought he saw the first of them reach the ground.

The return flight was uneventful, according to George. 'But we did have the spectacular sight of the invasion fleet making its way to the Normandy coast. Ships of every type, size and description stretched across the Channel – only just visible as it was half past midnight.' Onlookers were equally stirred. 'I saw aircraft above and below,' wrote one, 'and down in the Channel this amazing sight … a naval and air show of an immense armada, heading for the French coast.' Another observed: 'A column of ships stretched from the English to the French coast and it just looked as if you could have walked across the Channel on their decks.'

All 190 Squadron Stirlings returned safely to base. But three Stirlings from 620 Squadron were shot down with no survivors from two of the planes. One of 190 Squadron returned with their load of eighteen paratroopers still on board, having failed to locate the drop zone. All the rest had dropped their loads without mishap. However, twenty-seven of the Stirlings were reported unserviceable on inspection, having been damaged by flak, light cannon, machine-gun and small-arms fire. George's Stirling was untouched; his luck was holding.

Well, perhaps not entirely. Though the enemy had failed to cause him any injury, on returning to the operations room after leaving his plane, he ran into a coil of barbed wire that someone had put there (he swears) while he had been away. With blood pouring from his hand, he delivered his report to the debriefing officer, who was sufficiently concerned to send him straight to the medical officer. Both he and Squadron Leader Gilliard were hugely entertained by the incident and though George was disappointingly not recommended for an immediate VC, he was given the next day off, as clearly he was unable to fly.

Unable to fly, no doubt, but driving 'The Flier' was no problem so off he went to see K. As the invasion had started, the ban on anyone leaving the camp had been lifted. On seeing him with his enormous bandage, K laughed long and loud. Nonetheless, as a newly married couple living a life of enforced separation, and with George on dangerous active service, these snatched meetings must have been highly precious. In fact, the powers that be recognised that regular leave was essential for those on front-line duty, to maintain morale and the efficient discharge of their duties. George was more fortunate than most, for K was at least within striking distance and he was able to get out to see her at every available opportunity. For the rest of them, who were unmarried or not attached, there was the comforting sanctuary of the mess. From George's description, the mess was like any common room, dressing room, work canteen or smoking den where young men gather to seek solace in each other's company, especially when they are involved in difficult and stressful work. And then the high jinks would set in, as would only be natural with all that emotional energy pulsing around. There were stories of building up the furniture like a tower so that footprints could be left up the wall, across the ceiling and down again. There were mess parties when the moon was on the wane. This had nothing to do with any druidical tendencies in the RAF but because operations over enemy territory did not take place at those times. Ties of the less wary would be in danger of being snipped off by scissors. Before the move to Fairford, following a ball with a party of Wrens, the much-derided Venturas came into their own as perfect destinations for clandestine rendezvous – it is gratifying to report that the dear old Venturas were not, in the end, a total waste of money.

George's bloodstained debriefing was not, as it happens, much different from normal. You would gather at one of the small tables in the operations room with your crew and an intelligence officer and run through the mission. Usually it took about five minutes but could take longer, depending on how the mission had gone, or whether the flak had been 'lazy' or a little more energetic. Cups of steaming coffee were on hand with a tot of rum. A plateful of ham and eggs was always on offer in the mess, a great treat. And then back to the Nissen huts, to try to compose an agitated mind for some sleep. Breakfast was usually bacon and eggs. No matter what the day had in store, George always managed to get his breakfast down, 'even before the Australian match!' *Which Australian match, George? The one on the tarmac or the one at Worcester?* No response needed. None given. Normally he would meet his crew at 9.00am in the crew room where they would be briefed on the day's operation. Aside from flying, officers were given supplementary tasks; one of George's was to be responsible for safety equipment. Scissors for some reason seemed to go missing on a regular basis. Otherwise, they were given a great deal of freedom, which suited George, as he would have wanted to slope off to see K whenever he could.

The injury to his hand did not keep him long out of the cockpit. Two days later, he was over France again, dropping supplies for the ground forces, the only problem encountered being a sniper on a church spire. George swung round so that his tail gunner could deal with him and everything went quiet very quickly. Thereafter, it was a busy period supplying the Resistance, who were hard at work behind enemy lines, attempting to distract the Germans as much as they could from their defence of the Cherbourg Peninsula against the invaders. The SAS in particular had achieved some notable successes in sabotaging railway lines and attacking road transport. So it was felt that keeping these forces properly supplied was essential to the initially hesitant progress of the invasion. Any failure to drop through bad weather proved of huge frustration to George and his fellow pilots. One operation, code-named *Grog*, involved five Stirlings, including George's, which set off for the Brest area. One Stirling dropped troops, the rest the usual 24 containers each. Their problems started on their way home. US warships were anchored offshore and rumour had it that the Yanks tended to be a little trigger-happy. Sure enough, the Stirlings came under fire. George takes up the story: 'There was a shattering explosion, which at first I felt was a direct hit on the tail; the aircraft was thrown out of control but only momentarily... Jimmy Knighton was instructed to send out a mayday call but happily it was possible to cancel this as full control of the aircraft soon became possible.'

Another perspective can be offered by Tiny Shaw, the rear gunner: 'The skipper had great difficulty flying the aircraft. We had met heavy ack-ack, presumably from the Americans, despite firing the colours of the day... One blew in the lower escape hatch. The Skipper warned us to be prepared to bail out. My chute was strapped to the rear of the aircraft in the fuselage behind the gun turret ... I found that the doors had jammed. With the help of Jimmy Knighton, the wireless operator, we managed to free them. Happily, we did not have to jump. I decided to fly with the turret doors left open – in case they jammed again. I found it very cold and draughty.' The next morning, Ginger, the flight crew sergeant, called them all to the hangar where the aircraft was having some much-needed repair work done on it. He showed them that the rear turret had only been held together by one bolt. The others had been blasted off by an American shell. With typical magnanimity, George said, 'In fairness to them, we were possibly out of position.'

On 23rd July, one Stirling from 190 Squadron crashed in France in bad weather, flying straight into high ground. On board were SAS paratroopers. There were no survivors. Flying low in bad weather is always hazardous, even without enemy searchlights and anti-aircraft batteries looking out for you. Once, George was caught in the harsh glare of one of these searchlights. It was a very uncomfortable experience. 'I remembered Biggles's advice – never look out of the cockpit at a searchlight, it will blind you. Tiny Shaw opened up with his guns and out went the lights. We all gave him credit for his sharp shooting.'

Early in September, planning and preparation for Operation *Market Garden* commenced in earnest, a short interlude before what George called 'the horrors of Arnhem'. All Stirlings had been withdrawn from operational flights because they had to be at maximum serviceability, so only air tests took place. On 7th September, Fairford was sealed off from the rest of the world. On 16th September, all crews attended briefings. These were not as detailed as those given for D-Day; that simply would not have been possible. Operation *Overlord* had been months, years, in the planning; Operation *Market Garden* had all the signs of being a rushed job, made up on the hoof. 'It was sprung on us really,' said George. 'Monty's idea of seizing the Rhine with airborne troops in an attempt to win the war before winter set in was a bold one. But it was badly thought through.' However, at the time, as the plan was outlined to them, there was no lack of enthusiasm in the squadron for the task that had been allotted to them. Everyone could see the possibilities for a significant, perhaps crucial, breakthrough into Germany.

The sheer scale of what was about to unfurl was quite staggering. Twenty squadrons were involved in the airlift supported by twenty-seven fighter squadrons. Twenty thousand paratroopers were to be dropped in addition to 14,000 soldiers carried in gliders. On the first day, the air armada took 65 minutes to pass overhead. The role of 190 Squadron was to carry the first wave of paratroopers, whose job it was to secure the ground and to clear it of any defensive obstacles so that the second wave, of gliders, could land safely.

On 17th September, all serviceable aircraft from 190 Squadron – twenty-five of them – took off, one by one, from Fairford and assembled at the rendezvous point somewhere over Hatfield in Hertfordshire. They formed into three parallel streams, 1½ miles apart, crossing the Suffolk coast at 2,500 feet, over the Channel and making landfall over the Dutch coast and on towards Arnhem. There were no enemy fighters in sight. It seemed that Allied air superiority was complete. There was a little flak but the paratroopers were dropped without problem and they turned for home. 'It was a piece of cake really,' said George. 'So why didn't we go again straight away? It was clear we had caught the Germans napping. But we had to wait until the next day to deliver the second wave and by that time, of course, the Germans had woken up and were lying in wait for us. I never understood the delay. It proved to be costly, probably decisive.'

The following day, 18th September, the plan was for them to tow Horsa gliders laden with troops from the Dorset Regiment. Bad weather delayed proceedings so they did not take off until the evening. This time, the reception was a great deal hotter. About 5 to 10 miles short of the drop zone, one of George's engines developed an oil leak and he was encouraged by his flight engineer, Jack McCready, to shut it down straightaway. This presented George with an uncomfortable dilemma. Towing a heavily laden glider on just three engines was not a realistic proposition. There were only a few miles to go. Yet the engine could blow at any time. He decided to press on and thankfully was able to cast off the glider from the towrope over the drop zone, which was seen to circle and land safely by Tiny Shaw. A calm but insistent voice came over the intercom. 'Skipper, you must feather the starboard inner immediately.'

Returning on three engines was a sluggish affair but they made it home safely, though the landing was just about the worst he had ever made in his flying career. A watching John Gilliard gave him a much-deserved rocket. Within twenty-four hours, Gilliard was dead.

The next day, 19th September, was scheduled for re-supply mission, though as it happened, George and his crew were being rested. By now, of course, the Germans had reacted to the danger and mounted a fierce counter-attack. It was the Allies' misfortune that, unknown to them, two crack Panzer divisions had been resting nearby from front-line duty so the lightly armed paratroopers suffered reversal after reversal and, unsurprisingly, the drop zones that had been arranged in the planning stage had either not been secured or had fallen back into enemy hands. Take off for the Stirlings from 190 was delayed for bad weather and thick fog over Belgium had grounded all the fighter escorts. The Germans were able to put all their fighters into the air and by the time the Stirlings dropped down over Holland to make their approaches, as the ground batteries opened up unopposed, they were sitting ducks. Two were shot down in the midst of intense flak, including that of Squadron Leader Gilliard. He remained at the controls of his aircraft, desperately trying to keep it level so that as many of the crew as possible could bail out, before it crashed in flames. The Stirlings that made it home were all badly holed by shrapnel and gunfire. And the galling thing was that most of the supplies dropped went to the Germans. One of the great problems about the whole enterprise was the poor quality of the radio sets used by the Allied troops. As a result, there was inadequate, sometimes no, communication between the forces on the ground and between them and headquarters. So although the men on the ground were bitterly aware that the pre-arranged drop zones were invariably in enemy hands, the message never made it through.

The mood in the mess back at Fairford was unavoidably grim that evening. After all, they had lost one of their flight commanders. Trained combatants are schooled, by bitter experience if nothing else, to put private anxiety and grief to one side and to concentrate on the job in hand. George may well have appeared as calm and as phlegmatic as usual as he met his crew the next morning, strolling over to the flights to discuss the technical preparedness of his aircraft with Ginger and the ground crew, but misgivings were gnawing away at his stomach. *Did you think of Gilliard, your friend and commander, at any time?* 'Not then. Too busy. It wouldn't have helped. That would come later.'

On this day, the fourth day of the operation, the weather was again bad. It was difficult to keep in formation so they flew loosely in pairs. There was no sign of enemy fighters but, to their relief, they met up with their own fighter escort. The ground batteries however opened up with a vengeance and the Stirlings had to drop down and steady out amidst a curtain of heavy flak. The scene must have been

George's father, Revd Jack Chesterton, posing in front of the scoreboard which records his maiden (and only) century. 'Dee' was a fanatical cricketer 'but not a terribly good player,' George told me. Note the grip on the handle of the bat – perfect for 'nudging and nurdling', as his son described his batting style.

George's father (far left) at the dedication of an RAF chapel on the Isle of Dogs, presided over by the Archbishop of Canterbury, William Temple. George is always amused that his father is staring straight at the archbishop instead of lowering his eyes respectfully, like the others. Perhaps his mind was wandering to the 3.30 at Kempton.

George and his older brother on the steps of the homemade family caravan, built on the chassis of a trailer and the handiwork of a local cabinet maker, one of Dee's parishioners. 'My mother hated it!' said George, 'Mind you, it does look a bit dangerous.'

Christmas at the vicarage. George is lolling on the back of the sofa with his father. His mother is on the far right. Black tie for dinner, you will notice.

A flat tyre on the way to George's sister's wedding in 1941. Note the number plate CNP 62 (Chesterton Never Pays). The Revd Jack Chesterton had a fondness for backing a succession of slow horses, which gained for him an unenviable reputation in the neighbourhood for not paying his debts.

In 1940, the buildings of Malvern College were requisitioned by the War Office, which necessitated an evacuation to Blenheim Palace. George was sent on one occasion to the duke to apologise for breaking a priceless bevelled window. 'The poor fellow was more embarrassed than me,' said George.

Malvern v Shrewsbury at Blenheim Palace, 1940. The summer of 1940 was one of the most beautiful in living memory. 'Cricket on the South Lawn, in front of the spectacular palace, was simply marvellous,' reminisced George. Note the blazered young boys in their whites, paying uneven attention to the match from their deckchairs, and tea set out on white linened tables on the steps leading up to the grand entrance. 'And the statuesque figure at mid-off is me!' he chortled.

Until the huts were constructed in the grounds of Blenheim Palace, lessons took place in the makeshift dormitories. 'It looks very orderly,' said George, 'with masters patrolling up and down. Of course, the photo was staged. It wasn't always like that.'

A lovely informal shot of George and K outside the vicarage in Tenbury in August 1941 before they were married. Both look so happy and relaxed yet war was raging and he was about to be called up for the RAF.

Malvern College XI, 1941. George as captain is seated in the middle of the front row. Unusually, they are not wearing their blazers. 'My idea,' said George, 'I wanted to be different, I suppose. How insufferably arrogant!'

Prefect, Malvern College 1941. George is sitting on the master's left. A poignant photo of poised and confident young men, all of who were destined for armed service in time of war. Note the elegantly crossed legs sheathed in voluminous grey flannel.

Flying Officer G. H. Chesterton, portrait by William Dring RA. Dring was a well-known portrait artist, and a friend of K's family. The portrait of George is in pastels and was a wedding present to the couple from the artist. Dring became an official war artist and many of his paintings hang in the Imperial War Museum. The sitting for George took only two hours. He remembers it being a hot afternoon and feeling distinctly uncomfortable in the heavy serge uniform.

George at RAF Tilstock in 1943, at the scene of the famous overshot landing that ended up in a chicken farm. Note the pilot nonchalantly holding a cigarette as if a crash landing were all in a day's work. 'Goodness, it was wet,' remembered George, 'sloshing around in all that mud.'

Battle of Arnhem, 18th September 1944. George's Stirling towing a Horsa glider, laden with airborne troops from the Dorset Regiment. The painting is by Steven Warwick Fleming, a seventieth birthday present to George from son Colin and daughter Posy. 'All I can remember,' said George when it was presented, 'is the noise and the smell.'

George and his crew at RAF Tilstock in early 1944. Left to right: Harry Whiting; Jimmy Knighton; Johnny Ecart; George; Tiny Shaw; Doug Smith. 'It was a happy crew,' said George, 'We got on well and relied on each other.' Note the ever-present cigarettes.

Flight Lieutenant G. H. Chesterton as a proud father. The occasion is Posy's christening in 1945. His beloved mother is on his right. His grandmother, on the far left in her black widow's weeds, used to bowl to George when he was a boy. 'Underarm, but accurate,' George noted approvingly.

George and K with daughter Posy outside the rectory at Leonard Stanley in Gloucestershire in 1945. At this time, George was in Transport Command. He only changed a nappy once in his life. He couldn't understand why Posy wouldn't stop crying afterwards. Further investigation revealed that he had put the pin through the poor girl's stomach.

Oxford v Cambridge at Lord's 1949; the Oxford team. Standing left to right: Murray Hofmeyr; Robin Rudd; George; Mike Wrigley; Ian Campbell; Brian Boobyer. Sitting left to right: Philip Whitcombe; Christopher Wynn; Clive van Ryneveld (captain); Harfeez Kardar; Donald Carr. Van Ryneveld (SA), Kardar (India), and after Partition, Pakistan) and Carr (Eng) all played Test cricket. 'Note I have no badge on my blazer,' said George, 'Couldn't afford it.'

Worcestershire CCC 1950. Standing left to right: Hamish Anton; Peter Jackson; Don Kenyon; Roly Jenkins; Tom Wells; Hugo Yarnold. Sitting left to right: Reg Perks; Ronnie Bird; Bob Wyatt (captain); George; Dick Howarth. Just down from Oxford and the newcomer has secured for himself a place on the front bench!

On board the luxury liner, Empress of France on the way to Canada for the MCC Tour in 1951. Walter Robins, the captain, is at the foot of the steps. 'Not a lovable man,' confided George. John Warr of Middlesex is sixth up from the bottom. George is at the top, right at the back. On his left is Mickey Walford, who opened the batting for Somerset. 'Listen fellas,' George overheard him say to his teammates, 'I know this chap Chesterton. All you've got to do is get your front foot well down the wicket and he'll never get you LBW.' He fell cheaply to Chesterton twice in the match – LBW on both occasions!

Worcestershire v Australia at New Road, 1953. George straightens up, having delivered the ball, Ken MacKay has lunged forward and edged it, to be caught by George Dews at 2nd slip. It was a full house as you can see by the packed temporary stands. The ancient cathedral looks on approvingly.

Worcestershire v Middlesex at Lord's, 1954. Standing left to right: Don Kenyon; Louis Devereux; Bob Broadbent; 12th man: Jack Flavell; George Dews; Laddie Outschoorn. Sitting left to right: George; Reg Perks; Ronnie Bird (captain); Peter Richardson; Hugo Yarnold. George looks very smart in his MCC blazer.

unimaginable. I shall leave it to George to describe, in his usual understated way, what happened:

It was very, very unpleasant. The last few miles as we approached the drop zone were lethal. The flak bursts, some from 88s, some from Bofors-type quick-firing guns, punctuated the whole sky. It was almost impossible to retain the loose formation of pairs; I threw our Stirling into a violent corkscrew pattern and although shrapnel could be heard hitting the fabric of the aircraft, we received no direct hits. Approaching the drop zone at a height of 600 feet and at a speed of 150 knots, through lines of quick-firing guns, was a stomach-churning experience.

Beside him, Roderick Matheson's aircraft simply exploded following a direct hit and plummeted to the ground in a ball of fire. George dropped his load and then, deviating from accustomed practice, he did not climb, as the skies above seemed too cluttered and chaotic, but screamed away at tree-top level, somehow avoiding being hit. Although they were not to know it, by the time the survivors had made it home, the situation on the ground had deteriorated so badly that the battle of Arnhem was already lost.

The next day's operation was the most disastrous in 190 Squadron's short existence. George didn't go; by now, the squadron was short of aircraft so some of the crews were rested. If ever in the years to come, his many friends and family were to make light-hearted reference to the legendary Chesterton luck, then they would have cause to remember this day and give thanks. To put it bluntly, had George been on flying duty on 21st September 1944, I wouldn't have written this book. Their fighter escort was grounded through bad weather. Ten Stirlings from 190, and eleven from 620, went in unescorted. Approaching the drop zone, they encountered fierce and accurate flak and, even more deadly, enemy fighters. Of the ten from 190, only three returned and they were all badly damaged. One of the casualties was Wing Commander Harrison, the squadron's commanding officer. His aircraft was hit by flak and crashed with no survivors. 'Gradually, as time wore on,' said George, 'it became clear that one after another of my friends were not coming back.' He had been busying himself during the day cycling across to the local pub to make arrangements for a skittles match that evening. As the enormity of the tragedy that had engulfed the squadron slowly unfurled, he went to the nearest telephone to ring the pub. 'My message was simple: No skittles tonight.'

As he was recounting this, he fell unusually quiet. The silence lasted a minute or two. A sudden squall outside the French windows whipped up a swirl of dead leaves, throwing themselves against the panes of glass. There was no awkwardness in this hiatus, though he was obviously wrestling with his memories. I know I was but a bystander to his distress yet in a sense it was something of a privilege to be sharing it with him. After all, my generation owes his, at the very least, the occasional moment of recollection and gratitude.

In due course, he stirred. 'Yes. That was a very, very bad day.' *Your worst of the war?* He nodded. And then he put his hand up, as if he was having second thoughts. 'Actually, no. The next day was the worst. That is to say the *anticipation* of the next day was worse. In the event, the reality proved not to be so bad.'

As it happened, the next day, the 22nd, dawned in thick fog, which failed to lift, so all operations were postponed. But they knew it would only be a temporary respite. 'We had to go back. Of that there was not the slightest doubt.' By now it was clear that the ground forces were suffering severe losses, which only meant that re-supplying them had become even more vital. So there was no suggestion of holding back; they just had to go again. 'I didn't see how I could possibly survive another venture into that cauldron of horror,' George said. Before D-Day, when they had been warned to expect at least 50 per cent casualties, in common with many others, George had availed himself of a service which would deliver letters to loved ones in the event of their death. He had written one to K which remained 'on file' as it were and which he destroyed when he left 190 Squadron. Now he felt compelled to write one to his parents, with instructions to a dear friend of his to post it 'in the event that I didn't return.' There was little doubt in his mind that he wouldn't return. One can imagine its contents. He loved his parents deeply and has always been immensely grateful for the happy and secure environment in which he had been lucky enough to grow up.

The next day, the 23rd, 190 and 620 squadrons were briefed about their re-supply mission. No one was under any illusions about what was in store for them. There was an agonising delay for the weather to improve and then, at 2.10pm, the first Stirling, this time piloted by the 620 Squadron commanding officer, Wing Commander Lee, rumbled down the runway. The fog had lifted and there was now no more than a light mist and to their immense relief, they were met by their 'little friends' the fighter escort. Of the enemy fighters nothing was seen. The flak however was as intense as ever. Wing Commander Lee was shot down but survived and many others were hit and badly damaged. 'It was still an intensely unpleasant experience,' said George. Yet again, after dropping his load, he dived for the ground with all guns blazing and hurtled away at treetop level.

Back in England, the weather had taken a turn for the worse and they were unable to land at Fairford so were diverted elsewhere. Later, they discovered once again to their intense chagrin that the drop zones had been entirely in enemy hands.

Unfortunately, his friend had posted the letter. George hadn't returned so he had taken George's words literally and popped it into the letterbox. This was premature; George hadn't returned because he had been diverted, not because he had been shot down. When he discovered the mistake, he rang his father at once. He had received the letter but with commendable circumspection had chosen not to show it to his wife. He was not at all sure, at that early stage, that there was anything necessarily sinister in George's failure to return to base. If there had been, he believed that he would have received that dreaded knock on the door from a man in uniform. Only when he had the news of his son's safe return, did he give the letter to his wife. He did mention the matter again to George, but only in passing. He merely thanked him for it and said no more. There was no need. What George had wanted to express to his parents had been said and there is little doubt that it was appreciated.

190 Squadron was scheduled to make another visit to Arnhem the next day but by then the British forces, what was left of them, had retreated back across the Rhine so the need had gone and further operations were cancelled. Operation *Market Garden* had been an unmitigated disaster and soon the recriminations started. The war would not be ending anytime soon, not by a long chalk. In the bitter aftermath of the loss of the battle of Arnhem, it might well have seemed to those who had taken part that the end was nowhere in sight and that the struggle would be prolonged for a good while yet. As for George, and many others, the whole experience had left a dreadful scar on his memory. 'I continued to have nightmares about it for the rest of my life. It is only now, when I am well into my eighties that they have started to go away. I still have them occasionally but not so severe.' That is about the limit of his willingness to expose his inner demons and who can blame him for that? On speaking to the members of George's crew who are still alive, Jimmy Knighton and Jack McCready (Harry Whiting also still survives apparently but no one knows where he is), they too have remained reticent about their memories, claiming that the passage of time has dulled their powers of recall. And this is wholly understandable and naturally one is hardly disposed to press them. Which of us doesn't want to consign unpleasant experiences to the dustbin of our subconscious? Jimmy Knighton says that he can remember the awful flak and always gives thanks for their good fortune never to have run into enemy fighters. 'We were just a bunch of kids really,' he said, 'and

as kids we didn't take it all too seriously. Of course we were frightened sometimes but we all had our jobs to do and we all had total confidence in our skipper, who seemed to have the knack of knowing what to do in any situation.' Jack McCready took the same line. 'George was an excellent skipper. He never panicked and never lost his temper. We always felt that whatever happened we could depend on our skipper to get us home… I am sorry but my memory of events of that time has faded and I find it difficult to recall details.' It is of no matter. Sometimes what is left unsaid echoes from the rooftops.

Have you ever been back? 'To Arnhem? Yes, three times. And I hope to go once more. You know, it never fails to astonish me the way the Dutch welcome us with open arms. After all, it was the Allies who reduced their town to rubble. It was a lovely town, full of trees and nice houses. And we blew it to pieces. And they look upon us as their liberators!' He vividly recalls one such visit. He was in RAF uniform, which he was entitled to wear as a serving officer in the RAF section of Malvern College CCF, and the ceremony of remembrance took place in the beautifully maintained military cemetery. There was a sermon given, in English. Then another one was given in Dutch. George was struggling not to give in to his usual impulse to nod off as the speech droned on in a foreign language. He remembers the mayor repeatedly referring to bloomin' this or bloomin' that, but he gave it little further thought. And then a signal was given and a thousand schoolchildren stepped forward and each placed a bunch of flowers on an individual grave of the fallen. 'Of course! *Bloemen* is Dutch for flower. Everyone else knew what was about to happen but we didn't. It was very hard to keep one's emotions in check at that moment.' And to cap the drama of the scene, there was a flypast by the RAF, and SAS paratroopers descended from the sky, their parachutes billowing in the breeze.

'I always go to pay my respects at the graves of John Gilliard and Graeme Harrison. Gilliard's son, also called John, goes every year without fail. He too became a pilot, a commercial pilot. It seems impossible but he is now retired! In some ways, Arnhem seems like yesterday. But of course it was such a long time ago.' And once again he fell silent. I reminded him of the terse but telling entry in his logbook: '14 aircraft lost in this period.' He nodded. 'So many of my friends, senior pilots who had come into the squadron with me, one by one they…'

But there was no time to dwell on things. There was still work to be done. Once the offensive had stalled with the failure of *Market Garden*, the Allies would be unable to cross the Rhine for another six months. The winter that year was an abnormally cold and harsh one. Hopes the war would be over before the bitter weather set in, which had been surprisingly widespread, were dashed when the Germans launched their unexpected counter-offensive through the mountains and forests of the Ardennes, in what came to be known as the Battle of the Bulge. So, for 190 Squadron, SOE operations began again in earnest. By now, much of the airspace over Europe had been cleared of enemy fighter activity but the drops, at night, remained hazardous. Another airborne venture, this time in Yugoslavia to assist Marshal Tito's forces, which were fighting the Germans in the Balkans, was planned. This necessitated towing Horsa gliders vast distances across Europe and proved to be a logistical triumph if nothing else. Its strategic effectiveness however was less obvious; the operation was cancelled and within days, all the glider pilots had returned to England. What happened to the abandoned gliders never became clear. With a snort, George suggested they ended up as chicken coops! He did entertain himself by making a detour to have a look at Mount Vesuvius, which was erupting at the time. He soon changed his mind. As he flew closer, nature's reception proved to be even hotter than the anti-aircraft batteries at Arnhem, so he cut his losses and retreated. The short stop at Naples, now liberated from the Germans, gave him the opportunity to take in a bit of culture. He went to see *Tosca* at the Grand Opera House. I wonder if he nodded off during the third act. He normally does.

Back home, another SOE operation, this time in Norway, turned out to be particularly dicey. It involved flying hundreds of miles over the North Sea, out of range of radar aids. Harry Whiting was a good navigator and on this trip he employed his little-used skills plotting a course by the stars. So precise were his calculations that they made landfall near Oslo only a quarter of a mile from their destination. As they made the drop, a vivid flash lit up the night sky. It was a 620 Squadron Stirling that had been caught by enemy fighters and destroyed. This served as a reminder to them all, if they really needed one, that what they were doing was still highly dangerous.

Not long into the new year of 1945, he was informed that he had completed his first tour of operations. George had assumed you had to carry out thirty operations before finishing a tour but he was told that six months also counted, whichever came the sooner. He was also told by his commanding officer that he was being recommended to join a new transport squadron, which was carrying out important work in the Far East. This put George in a quandary. It meant of course that he and his crew, who all got on so well, would be split up. And also he would miss the third great campaign of the war in Europe, the crossing of the Rhine and the final push into the German heartlands. Having taken part in the D-Day and Arnhem operations, 'it would have been nice to have all three under my belt.' Hmm. I'm not sure his family and friends would have agreed with that. Who knows how long his luck would have held out? K was certainly keen for him to accept the new posting and as she was five months pregnant, a move for George away from the front line, so to speak, would relieve her of some anxiety. And if he was honest with himself, after Arnhem, a change was what he probably needed. So many of his friends had died in that fiasco that the squadron was now, necessarily, a quite different place. So he accepted and it was time to say goodbye to his loyal crew.

Their friendship had been forged in the white heat of battle and in desperate circumstances like that affection does not survive unless total respect and sincerity are earned. It would seem that George was held in the highest regard by his crew, a fact endorsed in my communications with Jimmy Knighton and Jack McCready. For his own part, George is quick to praise the close-knit partnership that they all formed and has the utmost respect for every one of them, both on a personal and professional level. It says it all that he did his very best, and continues to do so, to keep in touch with them and to take an interest in their lives once the war was over.

When George joined 242 Squadron, Transport Command, the war in Europe was in its last throes so attention was turned to the conflict in the East and his role was to work on a strategic transport system to India and beyond. Initially they were equipped with Stirlings but later they were given the Avro Yorks, the transport equivalent of the Avro Lancaster bomber and 'powered by the same beautiful Merlin engines … a fine aircraft and a joy to fly.' First, however, there was an important domestic duty to fulfil. Back home on 18th April, Posy, their first child, was born. And George was there. 'Well, not actually *there*, as seems to be obligatory these days. But I was nearby, in the garden.'

In Transport Command, leave seemed to come in 'liberal chunks' because the trips to India and beyond and back again were long shifts. On one of these operations, to Ceylon, news filtered through that the second atomic bomb had been dropped on Nagasaki and that the Japanese had shortly afterwards surrendered. The war in the East was over. There is a naïve belief amongst some of the succeeding generations that everyone would simply put down their weapons and go home once the guns fell silent. Of course it was not like that. Demobilisation of a huge number of fighting men, to say nothing of the vast support services, obviously had to be planned very carefully and phased in gradually. George's release was scheduled for February 1946 but then he was made aware that it had been deferred for another six months – they were short of experienced pilots. He was due to start term at Oxford in October, so the delay, to say nothing of the extra pay, would suit him down to the ground. As it transpired, it would suit him down to the ground, all right. One might even say, *on* the ground. A cricket ground, that is.

The squadron was moved to Oakington, near Cambridge, and one day George noticed a request for cricketers posted on the board. Of course, he signed up immediately and there began an astonishingly quick rise up the ladder of RAF cricket. In one sense it was astonishing, for he had not been a noted cricketer before the war whose name would have been on everyone's lips (after all, he was only 18 when he joined up) but in another sense, perhaps it was not such a surprise after all. He had shown exceptional promise as a schoolboy and he had been picked for the Public Schools before the country's attention had been turned aside by more pressing matters. Soon he was having trials for the full RAF side. He went straight into the squad and hardly flew again. It was a lovely time as the world slowly adjusted to peacetime and re-learnt the pleasures of recreation. For George, to have a ball in his hand again was blissful. There was a succession of internal competitions to play in with the Fighter, Bomber, Coastal and Training commands. He remembers playing against Coastal Command at the Oval in the final: 'a drab game, which was drawn.' He played regularly for the Adastrians (RAF officers), which had a full fixture list. And at weekends, he played for the local club, Fenstanton.

Then there was the three-cornered fight between the RAF, army and navy for bragging rights in the services. These were played at Lord's. You can imagine George's feelings as he entered the pavilion and made his way through the Long Room. Remember the last time he had been here, he had been instructed by the odious Corporal Jones to drop his trousers. 'The ground looked in wonderful condition and a great contrast to the barrage balloons and barbed wire that I remembered.' The crowds for these matches were astonishing; they flocked in their thousands through the gates. 'People, you see, had been starved of any entertainment through nearly six years of war.' The standard of cricket was high. Among those playing for the RAF were Leo Harrison (Hampshire), Bernie Constable (Surrey) and Alan Shirreff (Kent). In the navy side was John Dewes (Middlesex and England) and in the army side were Dick Pollard (Lancashire and England) and Donald Carr (Derbyshire and England). The matches couldn't have been anything other than fiercely contested.

George also was asked to go on a short tour with the RAF Officers to Berlin. *Berlin? You mean the capital of the Third Reich that had only recently been reduced to rubble by Allied bombing and Russian artillery? That must have been an eye-opener?* 'Yes, I suppose it was.' I must have raised a quizzical eyebrow because he quickly gave an embarrassed chuckle. 'I must in all honesty point out that it was a very alcoholic trip!' It was great fun playing for the RAF all that summer, with only minimal duties to distract him. But considering what he had just gone through, who could begrudge him the gentle readjustment to normal peacetime life?

Did he ever contemplate a career in the RAF? Yes he did, as it happened. He was now a flight lieutenant and was encouraged to seek a permanent commission and he applied, but the trouble was that the selection board couldn't make up their minds about the future strategy of recruitment. So all the applicants were stalled for six months. Still in the RAF, he went up to Oxford in October 1946 and of course had to join the University Air Squadron. After the six months were up, he was offered a permanent commission. He could stay at Oxford and complete his degree and the years would count as seniority in service. *Were you tempted?* 'I was. It prompted a lot of soul-searching. For three weeks, I walked around with two letters in my pocket, one to accept and one to decline.' He then posted the No letter. There were no regrets. He admits that he wasn't totally dedicated to flying. He enjoyed it but it didn't stir his soul in the way that cricket did. Furthermore, K didn't fancy the life of a peripatetic service wife and they had a young daughter. And what might have clinched it was another illicit peek at his personal file in which his squadron leader had described him as 'a large but not over-intelligent officer.' George roars with laughter at the memory. 'You see, it would have been a huge mistake.'

If he did not go up to Oxford with an overwhelming endorsement from his senior officer, he did go with an ill-fitting demob suit and 'nice little dollops of money' from the RAF. He had the six months' pay, plus the £15 per month gratuity for the length of his service. He was delighted to discover that the six months that he had spent on the farm after he had joined up also counted for this gratuity as it was regarded as 'deferred service'. And he had the full student's grant as a married man with a child. 'I was rich! Comparatively speaking. And it was tax-free! Marvellous!' It is interesting to point out that the full grant was £450 per annum – the same as his first salary at Malvern College, three years later, 'which of course was taxed,' he added with a shake of the head.

9

OXFORD

1946–49

'We're one short for today's match. Quick – go and fish George out of the Geography department.'

Clive van Ryneveld, Oxford captain

'Don't be silly – George doesn't know where the Geography department is. You'll find him in The Mitre.'

A team-mate

What is the point of going to university? It is a question I was frequently asked as a schoolmaster and indeed it was one that I often asked of myself before, during and after my undergraduate days. This is not a moral conundrum, nor even a rhetorical question; clearly there *is* a point, else so many would not strive to go. The point of a university education can of course be many different things to many different people. But if we had to answer the question sensibly, most of us would say, surely, that it is an unparalleled opportunity to extend the boundaries of our hinterland: intellectually; academically; socially; politically; recreationally. We go there to develop, to evolve as people, to grow up really. I know that the antics of many students might give the lie to any suggestion that they are becoming more grown up but that in essence is what is, or should be, happening. Undergraduates are immature, undeveloped, attempting to find their feet in the adult world. Not yet the finished article, you might say.

That is why Oxford, Cambridge and other academic institutions must have been particularly unusual places in 1946, the year George went up to Brasenose College. Ex-servicemen were flooding back into the country, anxious to take up their places at university that had been denied them by the outbreak of war. George was now twenty-four, not eighteen as he would have been had he gone straight from school. He was, in every sense, already 'grown up'. The freshmen he met on his first day that October were mostly men who had seen active service; the school leavers were very much in the minority. George remembers that morning sitting next to 'a DSO and Bar'. In front of him was a fellow wearing an RAF greatcoat. Behind him was a Spitfire pilot. Not your average bunch of freshers then. But still the question has to be asked. If we accept the earlier definition of the point of a university education, did George develop as a man for the experience? The answer will probably be in the telling.

You will remember that George had been awarded the Heath Harrison scholarship to Brasenose, mainly because it was closed and no one else from Malvern had been put up for it. In reality, the award was in the gift of Tom Gaunt, the headmaster, and he had seen fit, with remarkable perspicacity, to give it to George. That gave him a place at Brasenose, but not at the university. For that, he had to pass what was known as the London Matric, the equivalent of the School Certificate. This he had failed to do, the Latin paper being the stumbling block. He had sat the exam again and again but on each occasion he got a worse mark than before. But fortune shines on the righteous and George, not for the first time, was in receipt of a large slice of luck. The Department of Education made the decision that servicemen returning from the war could be excused one subject. George's Latin could therefore be heaved through the bomb bay to disappear into the night sky. He was in!

The principal of Brasenose was Professor Stallybrass, whose real name was Sonnenschein but which he had changed for obvious reasons. Notwithstanding, he was known by all as 'Sonners'. George remembers two things about him. He was passionate about cricket, which probably had something to do with George being accepted at Brasenose in the first place. And he was hopeless with women. The fact that George was married completely threw him and he simply didn't know what to say in K's presence. It was agreed with K and the family that George would spend the first term living in college, the better to find his feet and to make friends. Imagine his surprise and delight to discover, on the same staircase, in the room next door, his old childhood friend Francis Prichard. 'It was the most extraordinary coincidence,' said Fran, 'and a most delightful one too.' Needless to say, their close association was renewed, 'as if those lovely days at the vicarage had only been a few months earlier', and they have remained firm friends ever since.

Another companion on the same staircase was Robert Runcie, a future archbishop of Canterbury. He was no callow youth either. He had been in the

Scots Guards in the war and as a tank commander, he had gained the Military Cross for two acts of exceptional heroism while fighting in Normandy in 1945. So, uniquely amongst modern archbishops of Canterbury, he had killed fellow human beings. Never mind killing Germans in Normandy, he nearly killed fellow undergraduates at Brasenose. 'He was a menace with anything electrical,' remembers George. 'He was always blowing the fuses. Dangerous fellow.'

There was no Geography don in college ('probably never heard of the subject'), so George had to go outside for tutorials. His tutor was 'a decent sort of fellow, very sympathetic to us games players' which was just as well as George had decided pretty early on in his university career that games would be his main subject. In common with all undergraduates, he was assigned a moral tutor, whose job it was to look after the interests and wellbeing of his tutees. 'He was about 100!' Apparently, at his first meeting with George, he said, 'I understand, Mr Chesterton, that you are already married. So I don't see much purpose in having to look after you.' And that was the last George ever saw of him.

The atmosphere in college was very much like an ex-servicemen's club. They had a 'scout', a sort of batman, who looked after them, trying to keep the rooms reasonably tidy and always looking after their interests, such as making sure they all had gowns when required and seeing they were properly attired for formal occasions. His name was Ernest and though terribly old-fashioned, he was a thoroughly 'decent chap', as George remembers. Many of the petty rules and distinctions had been waived for returning servicemen but the college doors were still banged shut and locked at midnight. The younger undergraduates, who were very much in the minority, no doubt felt left out of things. How could it be otherwise? They must have looked on these older undergraduates as if they had been parachuted in from another planet – George had danced with Katharine Hepburn, for heaven's sake.

That winter was a savage one, the coldest of the century. Snowfall was heavy and covered Britain from late January to mid-March. George's first term had passed pleasantly enough but, as had been agreed, he moved out of college after Christmas and took rooms in a large Victorian building with K and daughter Posy. In one way, he rather regretted it, for he felt that the advantages of living in college were many and that somehow he missed out. Still, he looked forward to the warmth of family life. Or he might have done had it not been so infernally cold. The water froze in the pipes and they had to go to the nearby house of a former Malvern housemaster, appropriately named H. H. House, for their baths. George was now 'specialising' in climatology and meteorology with a don called Professor Kendrew. One morning, the students, under the sharp eye of their don, were busy taking weather readings from the instruments outside the School of Geography and no doubt not quite believing the evidence of their eyes at the levels of the thermometer. But George was nowhere to be seen. Eventually he arrived, a little flustered and full of apologies. 'I'm so sorry, Professor, but the car wouldn't start in this frightfully cold weather.' Professor Kendrew was underwhelmed. 'Mr Chesterton,' he said, 'I live further away than you. I came on my bicycle. And I was on time.'

It has to be said that studying was never at the forefront of George's priorities. He admits, a little sadly, that he wasted his time at Oxford. Later on, he realised what a shame it was that he had not done more work and made better use of the academic opportunities on offer. The salient word here is 'offer'. You were 'offered' a place at Oxford. What you did with that offer, once you had accepted it, was entirely up to you. At university, particularly in those days, there was no compunction to work. Of course, you had to pass your first-year exams or else you were shown the door. And Finals would determine what degree you left with but in the meantime, it was left to you how you organised your studies. The opportunity to waste your time was therefore considerable, especially if you were not particularly academically inclined. Or if you had more interesting things to do. And George found playing games and socialising with his friends vastly more attractive than burying himself in the School of Geography for hours on end.

A typical day would go something like this. A group of them would gather in The Mitre and a beer or two would be consumed. After lunch, it would be football, or cricket in the summer. And in the evening, it would be back to The Mitre to discuss what had happened on the pitch. If the weather were inclement, as it was so often that first winter, they would go to the cinema. On one occasion, George had whiled away a lazy afternoon watching a film that he doesn't now recall. On his return home, K mentioned that there was a good film on in town that she very much wanted to see. George had no choice but to surrender to the idea, not wishing to own up to the true nature of his afternoon's recreation, and for the second time that day, he had to sit through the same film. It seems doubtful that he managed to keep his eyes open once the lights dimmed. 'Honestly,' he said, 'going into the library to get on with some work simply didn't feature in our routine.' Francis Prichard agrees. 'We weren't terribly good attendees at lectures.' He too regrets not working harder. 'I should never have got a Third [third-class honours degree]. But life was there to be enjoyed, you see.' George snorted with derision when reminded of this. 'Only a Third! Disgraceful. He was much brighter than me. As it happened, I was quite pleased with my Third.' *I have heard it said by Oxford graduates that a Third is a perfectly respectable sportsman's degree.* With a slow grin, George said that he had to agree.

I was interested in their lack of intellectual aspiration. Was it the war? The pair of them had stared down the barrel of a German gun, so to speak (Fran had served in the navy), and lived to tell the tale. Had that given them a different perspective on their lives? I was reminded of a famous riposte by Keith Miller, the famous Australian all-rounder, when he was asked about the pressure of playing in a Test match against England: 'Pressure! Pressure, mate, is when you have a Messerschmitt up your arse!' It goes without saying that Miller had served with distinction in the Royal Australian Air Force. If you've fought a war and survived when so many of your friends did not, then passing the time of day with a jar in your hand in The Mitre would seem to be an infinitely more agreeable proposition than burying your head in your books. To their credit, neither man was prepared to dart through the crack that I had just opened for them. 'No, I don't think so,' said Fran. 'There just seemed so much else to do.' George nodded. 'I was playing footie or cricket every day. I suppose I *could* have done more work. But I was having such a good time.'

And perhaps they are both being a little disingenuous here. They had to do Mods (Moderations), their first-year exams, and they passed, so clearly some studying had been going on. George particularly remembers the physical geography paper. The map was of the Isle of Wight and he felt that he had acquitted himself reasonably well in his answers. The next day, he was summoned by the head of the department and asked whether he had had any prior knowledge that the map in the exam was going to be of the Isle of Wight. George was nonplussed. Of course he didn't know what was going to be in the exam paper and he communicated that fact quite bluntly to his interlocutor. The head of department then started to laugh. 'If that is so, Mr Chesterton – and your answers in the paper undoubtedly bear this out – then you seem to be the only candidate who *didn't* know what the map was going to be!' Apparently a number of the students had clubbed together to raise the cash to bribe the map clerk for information about the map to be used. George, because he spent so little time in the department, had no idea what was afoot and therefore was the only candidate in the examination hall who was unaware what the map was going to be. 'It wasn't anything to do with principles and integrity, I can assure you,' he laughed. 'It was just luck. Anyway, they passed me, even though my answers were less than wonderful, unlike my peers!' A fearful stink did ensue, however. The map clerk was sacked and everyone, with the exception of the virtuous George, was severely rapped over the knuckles.

That summer was spent playing cricket. As if making reparation for the savage winter, the weather was hot and sunny, the sixth hottest since records began in the mid-1600s. George played for his college and joined just about every single club that he could: Incogniti, Buccaneers, Cryptics, Free Foresters, to name but a few. He was also asked to join the Arabs, E. W. Swanton's team, but he declined, not that he had anything against the great man but he simply felt that he had more than enough on his plate as it was. 'Do you know – I don't think EWS ever forgave me for that!' So he was playing almost every day, 'and bowling 30 overs every innings.' Having played for the RAF undoubtedly helped him make all the necessary contacts to be invited to join these clubs but it was not done as a means of social advancement; all he wanted to do was to play cricket. And if he didn't actually have a match, he would be down at the (University) Parks 'watching Martin Donnelly bat.' Martin Donnelly was, by general consent, one of the finest batsmen of his era, talked of in the same breath as other graceful left-handers such as Frank Woolley and Neil Harvey. Indeed, at one stage, it seemed that he was destined to become one of the all-time greats in the game and he had already made his Test debut for New Zealand in 1938 before war intervened. In 1946, he had gone up to Oxford and in this year, 1947, when he was captain of the Oxford side, he was making a stack of runs against all the counties on the sun-baked pitch in the Parks. It was the same glorious season, as if you needed reminding, that Denis Compton scored 3,000 runs. News would spread that Donnelly was at the crease and the tutorial rooms and lecture theatres would empty as people streamed down to the ground to watch him. Sadly, he retired from the game ridiculously early having played only seven Tests but for anyone privileged to watch him play that summer, it was an unforgettable experience. 'Wonderful, wonderful.' There was a wistful look in George's eye when he said this.

I wondered how close he had come to getting a Blue that year. Apparently not within a country mile. He did play one game for the university the following year, 1948, against the Free Foresters but that was it. There had been an influx of very talented cricketers just after the war, particularly from overseas, Martin Donnelly being just one, so he had to wait until his final year, 1949, to go straight into the side. It was a golden age of university cricket and the Oxford and Cambridge sides were particularly strong at that time. Football too. George is very modest about his football career, always claiming that he was a goalkeeper of limited talent. Not so, maintains a contemporary of his at Oxford, Derek Henderson: 'He was actually a much better goalie than he maintains. He kept regularly for his college and one year they won the Cuppers – the inter-college cup.' George does admit that he played one match for the full university side. It was against Tottenham Hotspur at Iffley Road, where Roger Bannister was later to run the first sub-four minute mile. The students were hammered 9–0. 'And the wretched referee played seven extra minutes because his watch had stopped. In that period they scored three goals.' K and daughter Posy came to watch. 'Mummy,' asked the five-year-old Posy, 'why is Daddy bending down all the time to pick the ball up in the net?' George didn't hear that remark. But he did hear the strident Cockney tones of a merciless barracker in the packed stands. 'Well played, mate,' he shouted at George as the disconsolate students trooped off. 'You kept like a sieve!' That was enough for George. The next day he dropped off a note to the captain asking not to be considered for the team again. So he was replaced and the chance of a double Blue had gone. 'My replacement wasn't very good, worse than me,' he said with a grin.

So how were his studies progressing as all this was unfolding? One happy offshoot of his foreshortened football career meant that the decks were cleared for the necessary cramming he needed to do for his Finals. He never, at any stage, felt intellectually stimulated but he was determined to get his degree. He was on a shortened wartime honours course, which meant that the exams were in December 1948, rather than in the summer of 1949, which left the way clear for total immersion in cricket that term. However, as he was putting in the necessary long hours of revision, a black cloud enveloped him. His mother, fell ill with a brain tumour. There is not much in the way of detail that he is prepared to divulge about this terrible time in his life. Perhaps there is no need; his feelings can be only too easily imagined. She died just after he had taken his Finals and there is little doubt that her illness took a toll on his performance in the exams. The family tried to keep the gravity of her situation from him whilst the exams were going on, but he knew. He even applied for compassionate leave from the examinations themselves, firmly believing that he had no chance of passing but that was refused. 'Quite rightly,' he admitted. 'After all, *I* wasn't ill.' When he returned from the funeral, he was required to present himself for his 'viva'. The theory amongst the students was that a longer interview than the usual ten minutes meant that you were in trouble or in line for first-class honours, and presumably we can discount that possibility in George's case. As his name was last on the list, he had no idea whether his interrogation was going to be long or short. To his relief, it lasted only ten minutes. Later, when news of his Third had leaked – which delighted him – he went along to his tutor to thank him for putting a good word in for him at the interview. 'Not at all,' said the don wryly, 'but don't cut it so fine next time!'

Ever since he had posted that 'No' letter to the RAF Commissioning Board, George had always had it in mind to become a schoolmaster. 'That was all I wanted to do. Could do, as a matter of fact.' So he enrolled for a Diploma of Education course, which would see him through until December 1950. Meantime, of course, was the pivotal season of 1949, which was going to shape his cricket career, but more of that later. What needs to be disclosed at this juncture is that he failed his Diploma of Education. I nearly fell off my chair when I heard this little piece of history – I didn't know that it was *possible* to fail one's Dip Ed. 'They kept a record of attendance,' he bemoaned, 'which I thought was a little unfair.' He was summoned to explain his absence from any of the lectures. The matter was a simple one, as far as he was concerned. He had not been able to attend lectures because he had been playing cricket. When it was pointed out to him that he would have to give up his cricket if he were going to have any chance of passing his Dip Ed, his reply was polite but firm. Nothing would stand between him and gaining a Blue. And he stuck to his guns, firmly believing that a cricket Blue would open more doors in the teaching world than a Dip Ed. Subsequent events would underline how correct he was. I was reminded of the words of his flight engineer, Jack McCready, in his Stirling crew. 'George was always so clear-headed and sensible in his decisions, which always seemed to be the right ones.'

So the runway was cleared for the pursuit of his dream – a cricket Blue. In 1948, he had been on the fringes of the team but had found his path blocked by a posse of fine bowlers. In 1949, he went straight into the side and thereafter became a permanent fixture, missing only one match (unwillingly – he was told to rest) and that was against Surrey at the Oval, which they lost. He was also asked to stand down for the Free Foresters match 'in order to let one of the other chaps have a go.' Once again, he didn't fancy the idea of idling his time for three days on the sidelines but he said nothing. His captain, Clive van Ryneveld, was like a headmaster in his lofty command and George had no intention of rocking the boat. As it happened, on the morning of the match, one of the bowlers reported in unfit. Panic stations. Van Ryneveld ordered someone to beat a hasty path to the School of Geography to haul George out to get changed and play. This caused considerable hilarity in the dressing room. 'Don't be silly,' said one, 'George doesn't know where the Geography department is. You'll find him in The Mitre!' Indeed he was. At 10.30, he was about to order his first pint. One hour later, he was measuring out his run. Not long after that, he was able to have that pint at lunch. The Foresters had been bowled out for 54 and George had taken 6 wickets for 11 runs. This was a first-class fixture, by the way, and the Foresters had put out no mean a side, including A. M. Crawley, R. H. Maudsley, E. R. T. Holmes, R. J. O. Meyer and Gubby Allen. It was just one of those days when everything clicked and he felt he could put the ball exactly where he wanted it.

By this time, of course, he was practically a seasoned pro, having played five matches and taken a stack of wickets; his confidence was sky-high. But let us retreat four weeks. The early season trial had the local Oxford correspondent purring; he reported: 'G. H. Chesterton bowled very well indeed on a soft pitch and should be a very valuable stock bowler. He relies chiefly on the in-swinger but he can also bowl the out-swinger and he varies his pace well.' *The out-swinger as well, George?* 'Hmm… The in-swinger I could bowl at will. If it ever went the other way, it was usually an accident.'

So he was in the team and first up were Gloucestershire. Tom Graveney takes up the story. His description of the individual contest between the two of them, recounted in the foreword of this book, is compelling enough without my embellishing it. Suffice it to say that the records show that Chesterton, on his first-class debut, had taken nine of the 19 wickets to fall and that Gloucestershire, the pros, were hanging on like grim death at the end to secure a draw against Oxford, the students.

Perhaps 'students' gives the wrong impression as a description of that Oxford side. This is not because they actually did very little in the way of studying. Actually, several of them were scholars of some distinction, though it must be admitted that George was perhaps not one of them. The captain, Clive van Ryneveld, for example, was highly intelligent and was destined for a glittering career at the Bar and in South African politics. No. The word 'student' hints at callowness, inexperience, naïvety, none of which this side possessed. They were older than your average undergraduates, for a start. And they had in their ranks, not only talented but untested players, such as George, but also three players who were already, or soon to become, household names. Van Ryneveld himself was already a double Blue in rugby and cricket. He was to gain four caps for England at centre in the Five

Nations Championship the following winter. He played 19 cricket Tests for South Africa and gained a reputation for himself as the outstanding fielder in international cricket. He was widely regarded as the finest all-round sportsman to have been produced by South Africa but was sadly lost early to the increased demands of his legal and political career. A. H. Kardar, a slow left-arm bowler and left-hand bat, had already played for India and after partition, he went on to represent Pakistan, captaining them to their first Test win against England on their inaugural tour in 1954. Like many of a certain age, I still have that photo in my mind's eye of Kardar shyly acknowledging the crowd from the players' balcony at the Oval on that historic day. Donald Carr, who scored 131 in that first match against Gloucestershire, became captain the next year and went on to play for Derbyshire in a long and distinguished career, which included two Tests against India. He was also a double Blue and later played on the winning side twice in the Amateur Cup Final for Pegasus at Wembley in 1951 and 1953. He became a noted figure on the administrative side of cricket as assistant secretary of the MCC and secretary of the TCCB, the forerunner of the England and Wales Cricket Board. So technically, yes, they were a bunch of students. But wet behind the ears on the cricket field, most emphatically not.

Their second match was against Worcestershire and they were beaten comfortably. As it happened, George did not have much success against his future county, taking only one wicket, but a quick glance at the scorecard underlines a salient fact. Opening the bowling for Worcestershire was the indefatigable Reg Perks and … L. Outschoorn. Now, my knowledge of the history of the game at Worcester is not encyclopaedic but I always thought that Outschoorn, Singhalese by birth, was a batsman. 'Laddy? A lovely man. I always got on very well with him. He was indeed a fine batsman. But even he would admit that he was no more than an occasional medium pacer. They had no one to help poor Reg out. That's why they signed me I suppose.' Despite a classy century from Van Ryneveld, the students were put firmly in their place.

Which made what happened next even more extraordinary. The touring side that year were the New Zealanders, regarded by many as the finest New Zealand team by some distance to tour England thus far in their history. They were captained by Walter Hadlee, father of Richard, and included in their number John Reid, Bert Sutcliff and Martin Donnelly, the same batsman who had so charmed the crowds at the Parks two years previously. They shared the four-match series with England (four draws) and of the thirty-five first-class matches they played, fourteen were won and twenty drawn. But they lost to Oxford. Even now, the shock waves reverberate. 'They behaved impeccably,' remembers George, 'congratulating us magnanimously after the game. But my God, they were upset!' To this story there is another one of those little footnotes, which George is fond of pulling out of the hat. In 1990, when George was president of Worcestershire County Cricket Club, the touring side were New Zealand and they made the customary trip to New Road for their first game. Walter Hadlee, in his capacity as president of the New Zealand Cricket Association, was George's guest. Impishly, he reminded him of events in the Parks all those years ago. Hadlee winced. He had not forgotten. Cricketers never do. 'But still the perfect gentleman,' said George, 'and we had a laugh about it.'

Oxford batted first and made 247, a respectable but unremarkable total. Then there was a sudden and violent thunderstorm. Next day, the wicket was wet, not like a pudding but moist and greasy on top of a hard surface, which made the ball fly. Oxford were fortunate to have two fast bowlers of 6 feet 4 inches in height, George being the runt of the litter at only 6 feet, and they were able to get some steepling and distinctly uncomfortable bounce. The New Zealanders were bowled out for 110. The wicket had become no less deadly when it came to Oxford's second innings and they too struggled, being dismissed for a paltry 72. 'I made a hugely important 10 not out.' I must have looked faintly amused, because he added, 'I'm serious. In such a low-scoring game, every run was vital.' The pitch had not dried out for New Zealand's second innings and they were dismissed for 126, giving Oxford a famous victory by 83 runs. With all the magnanimity that the sixty-odd intervening years can give, George is now realistic enough to admit that the tourists were unlucky to be caught on a rain-affected wicket. *But that doesn't lessen the deep satisfaction, does it?* He made no reply but the deep Chesterton chuckle said it all.

He remembers nothing about the Leicestershire match, despite a 170 from Donald Carr, but he does remember Van Ryneveld sidling up to him during the match to tip him the wink that he was a nailed down certainty for the Varsity match. It could hardly have been otherwise but George was surprised; he believed that he would have to fight tooth and claw for his place right up until the eve of the game. If the news took a weight off his mind, it certainly didn't result in any lessening of endeavour or performance. All right, he may have been demoted in the batting order to No. 10, which he made his own thereafter, in the next match against Yorkshire, bowled by Trueman for 1, but he never seriously believed that his captain wanted him in the side to play Cambridge as a batsman. In any case, he got his revenge on the Tykes by bowling them out in the second innings, to record a memorable victory against one of the country's strongest sides. Yorkshire crumbled to 141 and the match was won by 69 runs. Chesterton's analysis was 18 overs, 4 maidens, 22 runs, 5 wickets. The ball swung late and he bowled with beautiful control. 'It was one of those days when everything slotted into place perfectly and you feel that you can do what you like with the ball.' It was certainly his finest moment as an Oxford player and convinced him that he could more than hold his own in the first-class game.

The news of the humbling of the mighty Yorkshire excited the interest of the national press. The *Sunday Express* booked an interview with him but lost interest when they realised that the Terror of the Tykes was no seventeen-year-old boy fresh out of school but a married man of twenty-seven. The local press were not so finicky; the headline read: 'Father Bowls 5 for 22'. We also learned from the gushing correspondent that the tall, fair-headed Chesterton also played football: '"But I prefer to keep this dark," says the young man, "I don't play with any distinction."'

They were all brought down to earth by an innings defeat to Lancashire but George was soon in the wickets again against the Free Foresters before another astonishing result was pulled off against Sussex. I say 'pulled off' as if it had been a close-run thing but nothing could be further from the truth; Oxford cantered to victory by an innings and nine runs. Once again, Chesterton ran through the opposition in the second innings, taking 5–40. One of his victims was David Sheppard, not yet a bishop, nor even a reverend, but even then presumably having no need of divine help to know which end of a bat to hold.

The Oxford side was now on a roll, brushing aside a strong Middlesex side by 117 runs, helped by another fine century from Donald Carr. George performed his customary demolition job in the second innings, taking 4–43, including the wicket of Compton. 'Leslie, that is, not Denis,' he laughed. Perhaps not, but Leslie was still a fine county cricketer, not quite up to the standard of his brother but the equal of him as footballer for Arsenal and England.

The matches were now coming thick and fast. They lost to Warwickshire, despite Kardar's 10 wickets in the match, and also to Surrey, though clearly with the forthcoming Varsity match in mind, George had been told to put his feet up and not play. I expect it was in The Mitre that he pondered the insensitive logic of captains who were not fast bowlers. The final outing before the showdown at Lord's was against Hampshire, who folded to the students, losing by 44 runs. A look at the scorecard reveals that they were beaten practically single-handedly by Oxford's Test player, Kardar, who took 12 wickets in the match and scored 48 runs to boot. 'He was a marvellous slow left-armer,' remembers George, 'and he bowled beautifully throughout.' He was also a difficult player to manage, it was generally accepted – moody and unpredictable. 'But he was fine with me,' said George, 'and I always got on well with him.'

So, preparation for the Varsity match could not have gone better. They had played 12 first-class matches and won six of them, including the New Zealanders among their scalps. That is a fine record, by any measure, and it should not be forgotten that these were not professionals but amateurs, juggling their cricket with their studies (well, perhaps not in George's case). Cambridge, up to this point, had had a much rougher time, only managing one win. It was not as if they had a bad side. In their ranks they included John Dewes, Hubert Doggart, Doug Insole, Mike Stevenson and John Warr, future county players all. But to put it bluntly, Oxford were the overwhelming favourites.

I can think of no cricketing equivalent to the annual Oxford v Cambridge match. Everything is bent up to that one encounter. All that has happened before counts for nothing before the big game. Only the XI who play receive a Blue. If you eat a dodgy bowl of prawns the night before and you are too ill to play, you do not get your Blue. If you rick your back bending over the mirror to shave that morning and cannot play, you do not get your Blue. If you pull up lame in the nets prior to the toss and you cannot play, you do not get your Blue. It doesn't matter if you have personally put all the counties to the sword all season, if your wife says you can't play at Lord's and you are a hen-pecked husband, you do not get your Blue. Fortunately, K made no such stipulation. At the risk of labouring the point, I need to convey some sense of its immense importance to those taking part. And it is just one match. There are of course Test matches, but they are always part of a series. There are finals at Lord's, and elsewhere, but they are the culmination of knock-out competitions; you will have played, and won, games to get there. But this is, uniquely, a one-off.

That is why the disappointment to having lost to Cambridge must have been so acute. Even now, George shudders at the memory. 'We fancied our chances, certainly, but we didn't play well.' With the ball, he did not have much joy. There was not an iota of movement all day; for some reason the ball simply refused to swing. It happens. Why it does is a question that has exercised the experts and the scientists down the ages. Perhaps the conditions were not right. Perhaps the ball chosen from the box was a duff one. Perhaps they just didn't bowl as well as they could. George's figures were respectable but he felt he bowled with little penetration.

But he very nearly made a crucial contribution with the bat. On the last day, Oxford were battling to save the match but one by one their batters fell away and the tail was exposed. George was asleep in the dressing room. Cricketers often kip in the dressing room. Perhaps it is because there are inevitable *longueurs* during a game of cricket when those waiting to bat have nothing else to do but, well, wait. It's not surprising that the eyelids can get a bit heavy. So, with a rolled-up sweater acting as a pillow and a cap over your face, you stretch out on the bench and nod off. It doesn't matter if pandemonium is going on all around you, oblivion envelopes you. There can be noisy games of cards, strident debate about 12 down of the crossword, fierce games of indoor cricket, occasional bellowed appeals from outside, waves of applause from the crowd, announcements on the tannoy, loud expressions of disgust from the captain at missed singles ... but nothing disturbs you. You are adrift in another world. George was a past master at this, even then. He was awoken by one of his team-mates, Murray Hofmeyr, another South African, who spoke to him at length about concentration and the very real chance of batting through to save the match. 'And I jolly well nearly did,' said George. 'It got tenser and tenser when I was out there, batting with the No. 11, Wrigley. If we could see it through to tea, we would have stood a chance. They wouldn't have had time to knock off the runs.' As the last wicket stand went on and on, even the correspondent from *The Spectator* was moved to bring to his readers' attention 'the immaculate off-drives of Chesterton, which Hutton could not have bettered.' History records that Wrigley fell on the fourth ball of the last over before tea. George had scored 39 not out, a brave effort but one doomed to failure as Cambridge burst through the door that was now ajar and triumphed by 7 wickets.

It was a desolate Oxford dressing room. They had lost; that was the inescapable fact. But worse, they had underperformed and not done themselves justice. There was no party afterwards to drown their sorrows. They all packed their bags and went their separate ways, never to play together as a team again or even to meet up in the years to come for any sort of reunion. *What a shame. What were you like as a team then? As a group?* George pondered this for some time and his response was illuminating and intriguing.

'I wouldn't say that we were an awfully *jolly* side,' he eventually conceded. 'They were all very nice but a little ... serious.' Quite possibly the tone in the dressing room was set by the captain, Clive van Ryneveld. His talent as a cricketer was unquestioned and George respected him for his experience and knowledge of the game. But as a captain, he made a few mistakes. He picked Campbell as the wicket-keeper, whom George didn't rate. He dropped a few, including a couple off George on that frustrating first morning at Lord's, and in any case, another 'keeper, Ken Sherwood, was the better gloveman. But Campbell was a good striker of the ball and the theory was that he would contribute with a few forceful innings down the order. This never happened; the pros soon worked him out and he made very few runs. Van Ryneveld was a very proper and strait-laced South African without much of a sense of humour. 'In addition, a few of the others were Moral Re-armers.' I shook my head at this juncture; my ignorance of the term was total. 'Sort of non-conformist Bible bashers, if you know what I mean.'

Moral Re-armament was a religious, revivalist movement that was very popular at Oxford at the time, in the immediate post-war years. Its theology was very simple, based on the moral absolutes of purity, unselfishness, honesty and love. All the problems of the world, including war, were the direct consequences of personal sinfulness. The only answer was total surrender to Christ and in order to do this, you had to submit to public confession. Apparently the practice of sitting in a circle and baring your soul in front of others became the cornerstone of counselling organisations the world over, such as Alcoholics Anonymous. Its membership and popularity reached its peak in the 1940s but gradually, since the 1960s, its influence declined.

George had no problems with anyone who had strong religious beliefs. He was, after all, the son of a country vicar. He found the fervent believers delightful people but rather dreary team-mates. George was a party animal (still is, I am delighted to say) but there wasn't much fun to be had off the field with those who sedulously eschewed alcohol, sex, bars and clubs. I am not suggesting that George led a dissolute life at Oxford but he did like a pint or two at the close of play. On one occasion, he came back to his room after a night out, not very late, he assures me, to find his roommate, Brian Boobyer, on his knees at prayer. A little nonplussed but in no way wishing to offend, he got on with preparing for bed as quietly as possible, assuming that the prayers would shortly be brought to a conclusion and that normal conversation, about the day's play, could be resumed. Not a bit of it. Twenty minutes later, his roommate was still on his knees.

'They were desperately serious but I didn't mind too much. Besides, I was having the time of my life, playing cricket every day against the best in the land.'

I should say so. You took 46 wickets at an average of 21.95. That's astonishing – in only half a season! He smiled. 'It was considered to be a not inconsiderable haul.'

Now, before I comment on the 46 wickets, let me deconstruct that sentence: *It was considered to be a not inconsiderable haul.* The manipulation of language is always interesting and serves to illuminate the intentions, hidden or otherwise, of the speaker in what he is trying to convey. *It was considered...* Note the use of the passive voice. There is no subject of the verb. *Who* considered the haul? It is not made clear. This is often a deliberate ploy, used to avoid pointing the finger. *A mistake has been made. Bullets were fired. A catch was dropped.* The technical term for this is 'de-nominalisation'; it saves the writer from having to identify his subject. In this case, George probably did not want to acknowledge that there were no doubt many who considered his debut season in first-class cricket had been such an astounding success. Natural modesty forbade it. Note too the use of the double negative, *a not inconsiderable.* He didn't say *considerable*, because that too might have smacked of boastfulness. On the other hand, it was not a negligible haul – that would have been plainly incorrect. So, *a not inconsiderable haul* tells the truth but in a self-effacing manner, in keeping with George's personality. And don't you just love the use of the word *haul*, with all its undertones of a sneaky bank raid, as if he has made off with that swag of wickets, almost without anyone noticing.

People noticed all right. It could hardly have been otherwise. Let us examine the figures. The benchmark for a top-class bowler in those days was 100 wickets for the season. Nowadays, of course, the feat is rarely accomplished, as fewer games are played, sixteen, rather than twenty-six then. Chesterton took 46 wickets in 12 matches, so one assumes that the 100 wickets for the season would have been well within his grasp, had he played throughout and steered clear of injury. (Incidentally George had a very good fitness record in his first-class career.) He was 20th in the national averages that year. Just above him were Jim Laker, Les Jackson, Eric Hollies, Alec Bedser and Maurice Tremlett (grandfather of Chris, England's current giant of a fast bowler at the time of writing). Just below him were Johnny Wardle, Fred Trueman, Trevor Bailey, Eric Bedser, Tony Lock and his future team-mate at Worcester, Reg Perks. The point is that he was mixing with the very best and clearly he was more than holding his own, a bowler of considerable promise. Characteristically, he laughed off this suggestion. 'I don't know about that. But I was a vigorous polisher of the ball!' The in-swinger was natural and he could replicate it at will, because his action was natural, needed no tinkering and was mechanical and repetitive. If the ball swung late, so much the better. He reckoned he had developed this while playing for the RAF. He practised the leg-cutter in the nets and it was occasionally effective but all bowlers will tell you that if you hit the seam, which he did, the ball can jag either way – that is usually down to luck more than judgement. But his greatest virtue was his accuracy. Looking at his record shows that he was rarely collared.

Following the disappointment of the Varsity match, he went down to Cornwall to play for them in the Minor Counties. If the Oxford side was dull, the same certainly could not be said of these Cornishmen. Quite apart from the presence of the infamous Miles Gifford in the dressing room, who was later to meet his quietus at the end of a hangman's noose, there were numerous fellows who definitely were not candidates for the Moral Re-armament movement. Three or four of the team had played cricket outside Cornwall; the rest were local club players. They were an uninhibited lot, by all accounts, and quite naïve and unsophisticated. Some of them had never even seen a traffic light! When they went on tour and were exposed to the bright lights of London, all hell broke loose in the pubs and bars. 'God, they were a drunken lot,' said George admiringly. They were not the greatest team but George enjoyed playing for them, even if he found bowling 30 overs a day 'bloody tiring.' They had an extraordinary chap who kept wicket. Actually, he was good and took several sharp catches off George, standing up to the wicket. But he had an appalling stammer, quite the worst George had ever encountered. He couldn't remember the poor fellow ever completing a sentence. However, the affliction would vanish whenever he appealed, which would be instantaneous, frequent, long and loud.

Were you considering a career in county cricket? 'I can't really remember. I suppose I was. I remember a trial at Northamptonshire. God, that depressed me!' Anyone who has ever played at Wantage Road might sympathise. He got in touch with Wing Commander Shakespeare, who was an old RAF contact and who was also on the Worcestershire committee. Amazing to relate, once Shakespeare had made known to the club that George was available, they asked him to play without further ado. Without so much as a trial. 'They needed a new ball partner for poor Reg Perks who was shouldering the burden of the Worcester attack on his own.' Bowler after bowler they had signed since the war but none of them was any good. 'Had a Flavell or a Coldwell been available earlier, I wouldn't have been signed on.' George's virtues were that he was accurate and that he was willing to bowl all day. They wanted him to play full time but George didn't want that. He had his heart set on becoming a schoolmaster. They seemed to accept that he would only therefore be available in the school holidays and the secretary simply wrote to him and asked him to let him know which matches he would like to play. 'Astonishing!' I could not but agree.

It happens to each one of us all too soon – the agreeable days as an undergraduate come to an end and a lifetime of work beckons. For George, the round of interviews at schools had started. He remembers going to Portsmouth Grammar School, Monkton Combe and Wellington, all which were foolish enough to reject him. Charterhouse, where he was doing his teaching practice, did offer him a job but by then, a voice from his past had come on the intercom, as it were, and made another critical intervention in his life. Tom Gaunt, from Malvern, asked him to come back to his old school to run the cricket for a couple of years. George accepted. After all, the script had practically been written for him.

'So the lovely, lovely days at Oxford came to an end.' *Tell me, would you have got in today?* 'To Oxford? Of course I would. As a scout!' And he roared with laughter.

10

MALVERN COLLEGE – THE YOUNG MASTER 1950–61

'Your job is to provide cricket for 250 boys, five days a week.'
Tom Gaunt, Malvern headmaster 1937–53

In December 1949, George failed his Diploma of Education. In January 1950, he began teaching at Malvern College. No, we are not inhabiting some sort of parallel universe where black is white and doublethink prevails, such as in George Orwell's *Nineteen Eighty-Four*, which had, incidentally, just been published that same year. This was the time when independent school headmasters really could act independently. If the Malvern headmaster, Tom Gaunt, wanted to act on a hunch and appoint a former prefect of his to the teaching staff, he could, even if the young man had failed to obtain his teaching qualification. Of course, it couldn't happen today, but in those post-war years, when there was less emphasis on ticking boxes, Gaunt was able to back his hunch that George Chesterton would make an excellent schoolmaster.

As he walked along the corridor towards the Common Room, gently easing aside the usual knot of boys outside the door, George must have paused for a second before plunging in to pour himself a cup of coffee that first morning of term. As a boy, you are only afforded perhaps the briefest of glances over the shoulder of a master into the holy of holies. As a master, you welcome the privacy and the intimacy of the Common Room, a pleasant respite from the hurly-burly of teaching in a boarding school. And if the porter is a minute or two late with the coffee tray, there is always the glorious view out of the window over the Severn Valley to reassure you that you have made the right choice of workplace. George will not have been the only new master to be told that while the salary at Malvern might be a little below par, the view was worth at least £500 a year.

I can almost see George choking on the coffee that he had just poured himself when someone made that very point to him, as someone assuredly did. '£500!' he would have spluttered, 'Do you know what I'm on? A measly £400 per annum. My student grant last year was £450, and that was tax-free! I'm off to see the headmaster right now.' I am not sure how long it took him to pluck up courage to pop in next door to make an appointment to see the headmaster but Gaunt was good enough to put his salary up immediately to £450, rising to £500 the following September. So at least the pay cheque matched the view.

Whether he launched himself into conversation with his new colleagues or stood about nervously on the fringes, admiring the view, he must have been a teeny bit apprehensive. Half the masters he had known as a boy and no matter how well, or how badly, he had got on with them, this was a completely different kettle of fish. What to call them, for a start? Not unnaturally, he settled on 'Sir' until instructed otherwise. One or two never allowed further familiarity but Malvern College Common Room was well known on the school circuit as having a friendly atmosphere and it was not long before he was made to feel thoroughly at home. Well, it was his home, really.

As it happened, some masters did spend more time in the Common Room than at home but that would not have gone down too well with K and young Posy. Living accommodation was a problem. For a time they had to make do as paying guests in nearby Poolbrook Road but this was far from ideal. Their spirits were raised by a call from the bursar. A flat had become available in 3 The Lees, a school property. There is nothing more dispiriting than hopes dashed; the flat might have served – just about – for RAF recruits in wartime London but for a young family it was hopelessly inadequate. K was in tears afterwards; George felt not a lot better when he later learned that an assistant groundsman had earlier turned it down as uninhabitable. So it seemed that Poolbrook Road was to remain the family home for the foreseeable future. Then K got to know the wife of the bursar at Malvern Girls' College who happened to know that a property opposite the school was shortly coming on the market. She was friendly with the owners and while they were away on holiday, she gave K and George a sneaky look around the house. When the owners returned from their holiday, George paid them a visit. Colonel Davey and his wife were very warm and cordial and when George asked whether he could have first refusal on the property, Colonel Davey replied, 'Certainly, young man. Yours for £4,500.' George immediately accepted. 'Of course, I didn't have the money. Had to borrow it. K's mother was very generous.' By now she had presumably forgiven him for not informing her of the impending publication of the wedding banns. Once the money had been sorted out, the Daveys invited them round and to George's astonishment and the local solicitor's horror, the colonel there and then presented them with the keys. 'I know a gentleman when I see one,' were the uncompromising words of the colonel. What is it about George that inspires such immediate trust? There is something about him, an honest and straightforward demeanour, to which many people in his life have instinctively responded. And there they stayed until they were asked to move into a boarding house ten years later. 'I sold it for exactly the same price as I bought it. £4,500!' Astonishing. Apparently, property prices did not start to accelerate until 1963, two years later. It is somehow comforting to realise that George is not awfully good at everything.

Summer soon came around and Gaunt hauled George into his study to remind him of his principal role in the school. As if he needed a nudge. 'Your job,' he was told, 'is to provide cricket for 250 boys, five days a week.' *I see. Singlehandedly?* 'No. I was fortunate to have an excellent team at my disposal.' He had the professional, Bob Beveridge, late of Middlesex and of course George's coach ten years previously when he was a boy at the school, to beaver away in the nets. He had Tony Leng running the Second XI and Gordon Surtees in charge of the Colts and both men he trusted implicitly. In addition, all the housemasters would be out there with their boys, giving advice and encouragement that varied in their proficiency. He winces at the penetrating tones of one housemaster that he can still hear ringing around the nets: 'Keep the left leg braced, boy!'

The elephant in the room was his predecessor as master in charge of cricket, John Collinson. He had been removed from his post to make way for George. The circumstances surrounding his removal, unknown to George at the time, made for interesting unravelling, for a number of reasons. Not least, it showed Gaunt at his political and diplomatic best, a shrewd yet hard-nosed operator. It also revealed how much sway cricket, and its reputation, still had in the school. And it underlined how much influence the old boys, albeit one who was a former Test cricketer, had over staff appointments. In the immediate post-war years, Malvern cricket had been in the doldrums. So much so that a group of Old Malvernians met up at Lord's to discuss what to do about the parlous state of affairs. Their spokesman was none other than the highly respected former captain of Surrey, E. R. T. Holmes.

The story of Errol Holmes is an interesting one. Born in Calcutta, he came to Malvern where he averaged over 60 in his 1st XI career. He went up to Oxford, playing for the university for four years, during which time he made a first-class score of 236, against the Free Foresters, and in the Varsity match in his final year as captain, he supervised a thrilling fourth innings chase with a peerless century. He was also a football Blue. He played briefly for Surrey in the 1920s but then left the game to pursue his business interests. After Douglas Jardine resigned from the captaincy of Surrey in 1934, following the Bodyline series, Holmes was persuaded to return to lead the county. Seven years out of the game seemed not to have dulled his talents, for, following a successful season, he was selected to tour the West Indies with the MCC as vice-captain under R. E. S. Wyatt. (Coincidentally, Bob Wyatt was George's first captain at Worcestershire.) In all, Holmes played five Tests for England before retiring in 1938. After the war, he was prevailed upon to come out of retirement for the second time, to captain Surrey in 1947 and 1948. At his best, he was a fine attacking batsman and a bit of a tearaway fast bowler. As a captain, he was well respected as a skilful manager of men who always liked to keep the game open and entertaining. In short, his reputation was such that when he spoke, people listened. Even the headmaster of Malvern College.

On 26th November 1949, when George was wrestling unsuccessfully with his Diploma of Education exams, Holmes, encouraged by a number of worried OMs, wrote to Gaunt, expressing deep concerns about 'the low level to which the cricket at Malvern has sunk… Are we sure we have the right people looking after it? And are the cricket master and the professional the best available?' Finally, he made a *cri de coeur* that resonates down the years even to this day: 'This summer at Lord's we have been asked on several occasions by people that really matter in the cricket world, "What is the matter with Malvern cricket?"'

Gaunt's response is a masterpiece in tactful diplomacy. 'My dear Holmes,' he started, a delightful little insight into the custom and practice of addressing your peers in a bygone era. He went on to admit that he had full knowledge of the problem with the cricket but felt it only fair to put on record that he owed his hard-working staff a certain debt of loyalty. Furthermore, it needed to be pointed out that the current 1st XI had been drawn from 'a very small entry in the years 1933 to 1944.' It is somehow comforting to note that typos were also made in those days – he meant of course 1943 to 1944. As we know, Malvern at that time had been relocated to Harrow, numbers were down and the very future of the school hung in the balance. 'At the same time,' he wrote, 'I cannot be convinced that Collinson is necessarily the right man…' In the meantime, he had been scouring the country for the right man to take over from John Collinson and had indeed offered the post to Hubert Doggart, but Doggart had turned it down in favour of a post at Winchester, his old school. Coincidences abound here. Hubert Doggart and George had been rivals on the cricket pitch for years, at school and at university and this rivalry was to stretch out for many years yet, between Worcestershire and Sussex and Old Malvernians and Old Wykehamists… 'I have, however,' announced Gaunt in his letter, 'appointed G. H. Chesterton, who will come to us next term… The appointment has won considerable approval from those members of the staff who knew him and I believe he has the capability and right temperament to take Collinson's place.'

Still, Holmes was not reassured. He wrote back to Gaunt on 14th December, maintaining that the time had come to stop pulling his punches. 'We always believed that Collinson is not the right person to hold the position of cricket master.' He then went on to explain, in no uncertain terms, why: 'The tradition at Malvern has always been to "Attack!" because attack is the best method of defence… We feel very strongly,' he added trenchantly, 'that whoever takes on the cricket must believe wholeheartedly in this theory, coach on these lines and should not be one who believes primarily in defence. Further, he must be a man of character (somewhat of a tyrant) who will instil in the boys the fact that the bat is provided for the purpose of **hitting** the ball – not as a weapon of defence.' No mincing of his words there. At least it could be said that Holmes was speaking from the heart. His own career in the game had emphasised by personal example how he felt it should be played. He then took his sweater, as it were, after delivering this wicked bouncer; he made the simple but damning observation that these principles were clearly quite foreign to Collinson.

So, how was Gaunt going to play it? He was an experienced headmaster and we can imagine the political manoeuvrings that went on behind the scenes. At length, he felt able to drop Holmes a short note. 'My dear Holmes, I am writing to you to tell you that Collinson has today asked me, in view of his considerable duties as a housemaster, to relieve him of his commitments as master in charge of cricket at Malvern. I have agreed to this and have asked G. H. Chesterton to take his place.'

The die was cast. How would George respond to this difficult situation, which some patently believed was nothing short of a crisis in Malvern cricket? Would he react, as Holmes believed necessary, by operating as 'somewhat of a tyrant'? His first problem was how to deal with John Collinson. JC, as he was known, harboured some resentment at being relieved of his duties and did nothing to make George's life comfortable. To everyone's relief, JC discovered golf and thereafter spent a lot of time on the golf course instead of getting under George's feet.

The relationship with Bob Beveridge cannot have been easy either, in the initial stages anyway. Mention has already been made of the chip on his shoulder that Beveridge brought back with him from his wartime years as a PT instructor in the RAF. He baulked at having to call the boys 'Sir', though some felt that he still should, but he was expected to call the masters 'Sir', some of whom he felt hardly deserved that status. One could almost imagine him thinking, but not saying, 'Show us your medals then.' Or pips. He had, after all, gained a commission and risen to the rank of flight lieutenant. And now someone whom he used to coach as a boy had come back to the school as his boss! At first, George trod gently but soon his convivial nature began to bring the older man round. Indeed, they forged a close partnership, brought together by hours spent in the nets and strengthened by a pint or two in The Fountain at the close of play. George appreciated his qualities and Beveridge warmed to the young master. The professional's role was to provide accurate bowling in the nets so that the boys could practise their shots. This Beveridge could do for hours on end. Anyone who has ever taken a net session will know how invaluable this skill is. It would not be infrequent that a boy could bat out his ten minutes without ever managing to hit the ball, so inaccurate is the bowling. Sometimes the fellow next door would have had a better chance, though whether he would have appreciated having two or three balls coming at him at once is a moot point. That is why the invention of the bowling machine has been such a boon in the coaching of cricket, though it can be over-used. In any event, George and Beveridge worked out an amicable *modus operandi* and George was sad to see Beveridge go when it was time for him to retire. Despite George's best efforts to keep in touch, the silence from New Zealand was deafening.

As well as having to provide cricket for 250 boys five days a week, including running the 1st XI and making sure that all other teams were properly manned, George still had to do his teaching. No remission in the timetable was ever given in the summer term, and still isn't. He taught English, Geography, Divinity and History in the Lower School. In 1952, Norman Rosser was appointed to the staff as head of Geography and he proceeded to put the subject on the map, so to speak. George felt that before Rosser's arrival, Geography hadn't been taken all that seriously. Rosser was soon to change all that but before he could manage to secure George's full-time services in the department, the school had to undergo a full academic inspection. This always causes raised blood pressure amongst the staff and considerable cynical amusement amongst the pupil body. For, let's face it, the opportunities to sabotage lessons are endless and the temptation sometimes irresistible. For George, the problems came not from the boys – he could crack the whip when he needed to – but from unexpected quarters.

The teachers were told that they would only be inspected in their major subjects. George's was obviously Geography and period 1 on Monday morning was Divinity, so that lesson needed no special preparation. When he breezed into his classroom, the same one above the boiler that had so disrupted another earlier lesson observed by the headmaster, he was nonplussed to discover one of the inspectors patiently awaiting him, along with his class. He was courteous and asked George if he minded very much if he sat at the back. 'Just ignore me,' was his instruction. George took a deep breath and plunged into 'one of my usual, deeply uninspiring lessons' on the Bible. As it happened, they were reading the story of the Gadarene swine, where the possessed pigs take a tumble over the edge of the cliff into the Sea of Galilee. 'Never really did get the point of that story, but never mind. We got to the end and, without further ado, I instructed the class to turn to the next story.' The inspector coughed. 'Excuse me, Mr Chesterton, are we going to discuss this?' George wasn't very keen and made noises about being 'short of time' and having 'to get on'. But the inspector was persistent. 'Do you mind then if I came to the front of the class and asked a question or two?' According to George, he then proceeded to give one of the most interesting and inspiring lessons that George has ever heard. 'It was riveting stuff and the boys lapped it up.' At the end, the inspector warmly shook George's hand and thanked him profusely. 'I did so much enjoy that.'

The next lesson in which George found an inspector waiting for him was English. Not his major subject but it is not the job of humble teachers to question the workings of the inspectorate. The head of English, George Sayer, had been on a major drive throughout the school to improve the standard of grammar amongst the pupils. George knew a correct sentence when he saw one but he was never entirely sure of the grammatical rules. So, on his own admission, he was only one page ahead of his class in the textbook and was therefore not exactly joyous at encountering the grim spectre at the back of the class. 'Well, Mr Chesterton, what are you going to teach today?' he was asked. 'Adverbial clauses,' replied George more brightly than he felt. 'Oh my God!' exclaimed the inspector. 'How dreadfully boring!' And he turned on his heels and left.

The following lesson was history. Yet again, an inspector turned up. The lesson passed off without incident, well enough anyway for George to have no recollection of it. But there was no respite for the young master. The next lesson was Geography and he had been told that this lesson would definitely be inspected, as it was his major subject. Accordingly, he had put in many hours the night before preparing a stirring lesson on ox-bow lakes, his usual fallback topic when the going got tough. 'And do you know what? It was all for nothing. No one turned up.'

The story does not end there, even if the inspection, to everybody's relief, did. Several weeks later, the timetable for the following academic year was published. To George's horror, he saw that he was down for five periods of Divinity a week. *Five!* He went to see Gaunt. The headmaster confirmed that the timetable was correct; he was indeed down for five periods of Divinity. As best he could, George pleaded his case, respectfully suggesting that he would do more harm than good to his pupils' moral welfare if he were to be let loose on them five times a week. But headmasters have a way of politely dismissing you while giving every indication that their mind has been made up and is not for turning. Glumly, George beat a retreat. He later discovered that the inspector who had hijacked his lesson on the Gadarene swine had given George such a glowing report that the senior management team at the College firmly believed that they had an undiscovered genius in their midst. To George's immense relief, Norman Rosser galloped to his aid and made insistent overtures to the powers-that-be that the Geography department needed George as a full-time teacher. No doubt there was a bit of divine intervention too!

In any event, Divinity's relief was George's too, and Geography's gain. From his timetable were ejected all subjects save Geography and he enjoyed belonging to a single department. He believes that Norman Rosser was a superb head of department, who set about driving up standards to gain for the subject legitimacy in the school that it had not been possessed of hitherto. 'And he achieved that without ever having a departmental meeting,' said George with admiration … and immense gratitude. Rosser was a first-rate organiser, meticulous and thorough in everything that he did whilst allowing those in his team a loose rein, having the confidence in them to do what they were asked to do and only asking them to do what they could do and were good at. It's called man-management and for years the Geography department was renowned for its close and effective teamwork.

The joke for decades was that you could only get into the Geography department if you had a Blue. Denis Saunders had by now joined them. He was a football Blue and had captained the Oxford side. He had represented England as an amateur. He also captained Pegasus to Amateur Cup glory in front of 100,000 spectators at Wembley twice – in 1951 and 1953. Rosser himself was a talented games player, gaining a Half Blue in squash. He took the A-Level sets, with considerable success, and largely entrusted the lower-school teaching to Chesterton and Saunders. It worked well. George and Denis would compete with each other to see who could get the better results at O Level for their sets. To George's chagrin, it always seemed to him that Denis had the edge. Maybe he did; maybe he didn't and George is his usual modest self. But he did publicly pay homage to Saunders's teaching when he gave the address at his funeral in 2003: 'Denis was one of those truly gifted schoolmasters who had total and absolute control of every class that came before him. No one would ever think of trying to take advantage of him.'

Of his own teaching, George is typically self-deprecating but I cannot imagine that any class of his would have sought to take advantage of him. I imagine that like most teachers, he felt that he did a workmanlike job, enjoying his time in the classroom, without ever claiming to be one of those rare, truly inspirational educators. If you do not enjoy the experience of standing up in front of a class, you're in the wrong profession. 'Some days I thought I was on good form. For the most part, I thought I was competent, no more.' He does however tell a couple of amusing stories about former pupils' memories of his teaching. Not so long ago, he was at a point-to-point meeting and a bookie's runner came up to him and greeted him warmly. 'Hello, Mr Chesterton. You used to teach me Geography. And you gave me one of the best lessons of my life.' Intrigued, and not a little pleased, George demanded to be reminded of this life-affirming lesson. Apparently the boy had been inattentive whilst sitting in the front row. Annoyed, George had sent him to the back, telling him that he hated inattentiveness and that if he wanted to waste his time, he could jolly well do it at the back without disturbing anyone else. 'So I did,' said the grateful Old Malvernian. 'I read *The Racing Post* and, as you can see, I've never looked back!' On another occasion, George was watching the cricket at Worcester from his favourite vantage point, on the balcony of the Reg Perks Stand. It was a sunny day and it had been a good lunch. Slowly his eyelids drooped and he was soon doing what he has become famous for – having a nap. Later, at the close of play, he was making his way across to the car park when a Mercedes drew up alongside and down purred the window. 'Hello, Mr

Chesterton,' said the disembodied voice. 'I saw you asleep on the balcony. Reminded me of those Geography lessons you used to give us!'

As we have learnt from countless similar anecdotes that George loves to tell against himself, he is a past master at deflecting praise. He revels in the role of the bumbling amateur, making his way by virtue of a happy blend of immense good fortune and cheerful bluster. The reality is very different. He liked to give the impression that he only kept one step, or one page perhaps, ahead of his students but Norman Rosser made it clear that George knew his stuff and was an excellent communicator in the classroom. And he was far more organised than he ever let on. It would have been impossible for him to remain a teacher at Malvern College for so long, especially during a period of rising standards, if he had not been able to cut the mustard. But let me not be content with platitude; let me quote from someone who should know. By his own admission, Ian, later Lord, MacLaurin did not have a glittering academic record at Malvern. He failed most of his exams, preferring to concentrate on a successful, and more enjoyable, sporting career. Nonetheless, he is hugely grateful to the school for the 'lessons of life' which he learnt there and which prepared him for his long climb up to the top of the greasy pole in the retail business and cricket administration. Chairman of Tesco, chairman of Vodafone, chairman of the England and Wales Cricket Board … somebody must have been doing something right. If you ask him, most of the credit should be ascribed to George Chesterton (and Denis Saunders). His affection and admiration for George know no bounds. Of course they had a common interest in cricket but George happened to be his Geography teacher as well. 'He was a far better teacher than he says,' maintains MacLaurin. 'If he taught me and I managed to learn stuff then, believe me, he was a good teacher.' His point is a valid one: the trick – skill, if you like – is to engage with the less gifted pupils as well as those who are academically talented and motivated. And George apparently had that in spades.

In 1953, Tom Gaunt retired. The fact that the school was still in existence, and thriving, after the trials and tribulations of wartime and its aftermath tells you everything you need to know about the man's resilience and leadership qualities. In common with many schools of its type, Malvern had struggled with its numbers during this testing time, at one stage down to 250, and Gaunt's remit had been to restore confidence and to increase the roll. This he had achieved very successfully. The job of his successor was to build on this solid platform and to raise academic standards. If you remember, George had been critical of the quality of the teaching during his time at the school as a boy. He remembered lesson after lesson of boring note-taking and uninspiring instruction. This was all to change with the appointment of Donald Lindsay as headmaster.

If Gaunt's reputation has understandably faded over the years so that it is now no more than a distant memory, Lindsay's remains firmly fixed in people's minds, approaching what you might call legendary status. Talk to any of the masters who served under him and immediately a grin crosses the face and a story or an amusing anecdote will inevitably follow. Quite clearly, he was a charismatic figure who could carry his common room with him, however difficult or unpopular some of his decisions proved. He was a born performer and though he was short of stature, he could command the stage, whether with parents in his study or masters at a Common Room meeting or the whole school at assembly. His wit was famed. Sometimes, said George, you would come away from a meeting with him clutching your sides with laughter but not at all sure whether you yourself had not been the target of his humour. His greatest gift was an instinct for appointing the right man. Better teachers were being brought to the school. He promoted capable and accomplished lieutenants to positions of responsibility in departments and Houses. Slowly standards were driven up and Malvern started to lose its reputation of being solely a games-playing school. And this was achieved without compromising the reputation of the major games. It could not have been otherwise with men like Chesterton and Saunders in charge of the cricket and football. They would surely have bailed out if they felt that their positions were being compromised. George says that he enjoyed every minute of his time as a young master. He felt that the school was on the up and that he was part of a special time in Malvern's history. 'It was great fun,' he says simply.

As if to illustrate the point, he related a story. George had been put in charge of a coach trip of Shell (1st Year) boys to visit Westons Cider, in Herefordshire. They were greeted at the front gate by Leonard Weston, who was the firm's owner and a good friend of the College. Immediately, the boys were whisked away on a tour of the factory with George and Weston following at a more leisurely pace. All the vats, he remembers, were named after famous film stars or football clubs. When they came to the end of the tour, a table had been set out with various types of cider on offer for tasting. It soon became obvious that the boys had already been availing themselves, in copious quantities, of the samples. As quickly as he could, George ushered the boys onto the coach but he was unable to turn off the tap of Weston's hospitality because they were each presented with a commemorative bottle of the firm's finest as they filed on board. About a mile down the road and safely out of sight of the factory, George stopped the coach and confiscated all the bottles but the damage had been done; all the boys were well and truly plastered. Rumour had it that, on their return to Malvern, George was seen ushering boys up the fire escapes and through the windows of the boarding houses. This he denies. He does admit that, for some reason, No. 8 boys were in the worst state so he had to own up to the housemaster, George White, and explain the circumstances. 'He was very good about it,' said George. What happened to the confiscated bottles, history does not record.

Much fun too was to be had on the cricket field, though you might be forgiven for doubting this if you noticed the carpet of cigarette butts beneath George's feet at his favourite vantage point for 1st XI matches. His recollection is that the sides that he produced at Malvern during his time as master in charge of cricket were 'pretty average'. Many of his protégés beg to differ. Ian MacLaurin says the standard of cricket in the school was high. These things tend to go in cycles; there might be a good side for a couple of years and then a fallow period invariably follows, during which the youngsters have to be brought along. George unashamedly and enthusiastically espoused a policy of promoting younger players. Cricket lends itself to this strategy because size is not so important in such a way as it clearly is in rugby, football and the more physical games. MacLaurin himself was a beneficiary of this principle. He played for the 1st XI in his first year and he is one of the very few, if not the only one, to gain his colours for all five years he was in the school. 'I'm not sure that I deserved the honour so young,' he concedes, 'but I was jolly grateful to George for it meant that, as a Colour, I was excused fagging duties!' He reckons that Malvern, at this time, was the equal of any school in the country. Eventually, George appointed him captain and the experience stood him in very good stead for his later career as a captain of industry. 'I learnt such a lot from George,' he maintains, almost reverently. He particularly remembers, as a young lad in the side, being taken aside by his master-in-charge and asked how many he, Ian, thought was a good individual score. A little overawed, yet quite pleased with his minor contribution of 20-odd to the team's score, he answered, 'Well, Sir, I suppose about 25.' Gently but firmly, George put him right. 'No. You've got to think in terms of a hundred. Anything less you should feel is a failure.' 'And do you know what?' said Ian, 'I can think of no better metaphor for life. Never be content with 25 per cent of your potential, or even 50 per cent. Nothing less than 100 per cent should suffice.'

Another one of George's protégés has similar memories of sensible advice sensitively given. Richard Whiley, who later went off to become a headmaster in

Australia, said that playing cricket under George was always fun: 'I can think of some coaches and masters in charge of cricket whose approach was the antithesis of enjoyment.' But not George. He also owed George a debt of gratitude for re-awarding him his colours 'after an innings of 40 against the MCC which probably cost us a win!' There was another occasion when Whiley got his marching orders from the umpire and complained about it following an appeal for LBW from George who was bowling to him at the time. He was quietly informed that there had been plenty of times when George hadn't appealed, even when it was clear he was plumb! At the time, Whiley was struck how restrained George's response had been. He also made reference to the occasion in 1953 when he was having a bad time with the bat and received from George, who was playing for the Free Foresters, a gentle leg-side full toss for him to get off the mark. Somewhat ungraciously, he slogged it for four. There are times as a schoolmaster when the iron fist is called for and there are times when a little kindness is needed. George, said Whiley, seemed to know instinctively when one or the other was required.

MacLaurin has radiant memories of playing cricket on the Senior, watched (compulsorily) by the whole school. In his two years as captain, he felt the same about George as George had about John Rambridge, his master in charge of cricket – he was grateful for being treated as an adult. 'We used to discuss the game at length and he would make valued and helpful suggestions. If he ever criticised, it was always in a kind and constructive manner. He taught me how to deal with people, a lesson I tried never to forget.' He also tells an interesting anecdote about House matches. You will remember how George took almost more pleasure in School House winning the cricket cup than in any game he played, proof enough, if any were needed, of how much loyalty to their House boys feel. 'In those days, House matches were two-innings affairs, with no time limit, played over several days,' reminisced MacLaurin. 'It was George's second year in charge. No. 6 were playing No. 2 in a semi-final and were overwhelming favourites. No. 6 batted first and scored over 400 and then bowled out No. 2 for 70. Instead of enforcing the follow-on, the captain, obviously fancying a hundred (which he duly got), batted again and scored another 400-plus. The game went on for three weeks!' I checked my sources with George. Grimly, he corroborated the history. 'Completely mucked up the timetable,' he said. 'As a result, I had to change it and introduce a time limit.' Just imagine it today – an intra-school match lasting three weeks of a short, busy, exam-laden term. Different times indeed.

Not all matches were deadly serious. The Common Room had a strong side, taking on, and sometimes beating, the 1st XI. They also played in the local Barnards Green knock-out cup, a thoroughly enjoyable 20-overs thrash in the evenings after school. One day George was bowling to 'a spotty youth who fancied himself a bit.' George had him plumb LBW and appealed – just as a matter of course. The umpire demurred however and even had the gall to tell George it wasn't even worth the appeal because 'it was missing by miles.' George never lost his rag with an umpire but on this occasion he felt impelled to disagree. That was as far as it went but inside he was seething. The competitive juices suddenly started to flow. 'I lengthened my run-up and decided to bowl a leg-cutter. It was a beautiful ball I bowled, swinging in late and cutting away off the seam to hit the top of off stump – just perfect. The trouble was that was the last I saw of it, the ball was disappearing over the trees and down the M5!' The story entered Common Room folklore. I heard about it many years later. 'The young lad failed to recognise the two crowns and OUCC on George's sweater,' my informant told me.

On another occasion, they were playing against the Worcestershire Regiment at Norton Barracks, where the hospitality was second to none. A certain D. W. Richardson had been selected to open the batting for England and needed some last-minute practice. George, with his connections at Worcestershire CCC, had arranged for Dick Richardson to play for the regiment. George opened the bowling for the masters and early on in his spell had Richardson plumb LBW, or so it seemed to Pat Hooley, who was fielding at mid-off. But this time, George did not appeal and, following his lead, neither did anyone else. Richardson duly went on to score a century. Later at tea, Hooley enquired of the bowler how close he thought that ball had been to an LBW. 'Oh, that was plumb,' said George, 'but he needed the batting practice.' And, so the story goes, Dick Richardson did indeed make a score in the coming Test match.

When Bob Beveridge retired in 1957, the problem of appointing his successor was a tricky one. When professionals in the first-class game came to the end of their playing days, one of two avenues usually opened up. Either they took up umpiring or they looked for jobs coaching in the public schools. The trouble was that having an ability to play the game did not necessarily equip them to coach it – successfully coaching youngsters, many of whom do not as a matter of course possess the same level of talent, requires more than just coaching skills. The best coaches have to know their stuff, clearly, but they also have to be able to handle, and enthuse, tetchy teenagers. That is why George and his new boss, Donald Lindsay, took great care over the appointment. Of the many ex-pros to apply, one was George Tribe, the Australian slow left-arm chinaman and googly bowler and late of Northamptonshire. 'He was a wonderful cricketer,' said George, 'but Donald didn't like him. He said that chap will be running the school in three weeks, let alone the cricket!' They chose instead a fast bowler from the Lord's staff who had formerly kept goal for Watford FC, Geoff Morton. And the rest, as they say, is history. Geoff soon made a name for himself at the College, becoming part of the very fabric of the place. 'Legend' is a greatly overused term but few who knew Geoff would quibble at the description as applied to him. Many are the stories told about him, some of which will surface in this account, but there is no doubt it was an inspired appointment. 'The thing is,' says George, 'Donald Lindsay had the happy knack of picking the right man. He didn't know the first thing about cricket. But he could spot a good egg and in Geoff he saw a good character, someone who would add a lot to the school in many different ways.' In addition to his coaching duties, Geoff was put in charge of the College Store where, as the first port of call for new boys and their parents, he quickly became a resounding success.

Another example of the trust that George placed in Donald Lindsay proved a surprise. 'I was offered the captaincy at Worcestershire, you know.' I certainly had not known that, and neither had many others to whom I spoke about this. Once Bob Wyatt had finally called it a day and Ronnie Bird had given up after two years in charge, the Worcestershire Committee made overtures to George to take over. By this time he was firmly inked in for every match for which he was available, once term had ended. It was an extraordinary situation, truth be told, one that could never obtain nowadays. He would simply ring up the secretary at the beginning of the season and inform him of the games that he could play. And into the side he would immediately go, with no questions asked. No one seemed to turn a hair when he pitched up, cricket bag in the car boot, not even having had so much as a net in preparation. That, more than anything, convinces me that he had a rare talent. The professionals would not have stood for it otherwise. Which made the choice of the committee to approach George to captain the side a shrewd one. The players would have been expecting an amateur to captain them anyway; that was the way things were done. And clearly they respected George as a proper member of the team. 'Besides, I got on well with the pros,' said George, 'and I think they would have accepted me as their captain.' Of course they would, just like Jimmy Knighton, Jack McCready, Tiny Shaw and others in his crew at 190 Squadron had accepted him unequivocally as their skipper in the Stirling. But captaining Worcestershire would have been a full-time job; he would have had to get leave of absence from Malvern College for the whole summer term. His initial response was that he would like to give it a shot, for two or three years at least. On the horns of this dilemma, he approached his headmaster for advice. Lindsay did not dismiss the idea out of hand but asked for some time to consider and consult. He spoke to Lord Cobham who was on the College Council and also a member of the committee at Worcester. They both came to the conclusion that they would not stand in George's way, if that was what he truly wanted, and were prepared to give him leave of absence from school. But the inevitable consequence of this would be that he would lose his seniority in the Red Book. The Red Book is the Malvern College bible, which George many years before had resolutely refused to become acquainted with as a new boy. Now George, by this stage in his life, had set his heart on becoming a housemaster and as the Malvern way was to do these things in strict 'Red Book order', his chances would be severely diminished, if not extinguished altogether, if he lost his years of seniority. The choice was stark. The captaincy or a House.

In modern parlance, it was a no-brainer. Cricket was a hobby, albeit a passionate one; schoolmastering was his job. Although there were a few regrets at the time at having to decline the offer of captaining his county, they are not ones that he dwells on. The decision, in his mind, was clearly the right one, just as turning down a regular commission in the RAF had been too. His career at Malvern was mapped out for him. Who knows how Worcestershire would have fared under his leadership. Sport is a notoriously fickle mistress. And how could he have afforded it, playing full time as an amateur, as he was bound to do? Furthermore, he and K now had two children – their son Colin was born in 1951 – and the peripatetic life as a cricketer on the road all summer would have put a strain on family life. And afterwards, when Old Father Time had pulled stumps on his playing career, what then? What would it have been like having junior men stepping over him to become housemasters? No, he came to a practical, rational decision and cheerfully went along with it. He made just one, final observation: 'I did captain Worcester for one match, you know ... which we won *handsomely!*'

I asked him whether the family ever came to watch him play. He said that, at first, they did and K enjoyed it. But the pleasure slowly wore off. With a young family, hours on the boundary edge can begin to drag and towards the end of his career, they never came. In hindsight, he is astonished at how selfish he was and how forbearing was K. She never complained at his disappearing every summer to play cricket; indeed, she was very loyal and insisted that he go, knowing that he would be like a bear with a sore head if he didn't. The only proviso was that they should spend a fortnight by the sea in north Devon every year and this he agreed to, fitting his Worcester games around the dates. But George being George, it was impossible for him to pass even the most modest of cricket grounds without going in and asking for a game so he was allowed two days' cricket during these two weeks, and no more. The only occasion that this rule was breached was in 1953 when he was asked to play for The Gentlemen against the Australians. He tried to impress upon her that this was a great honour and an exceptional opportunity but she wasn't at all pleased. There was no suggestion, however, that he should not go. He shakes his head at the licences he took. His word to describe his decision to go on tour with the MCC to Canada a fortnight after Colin was born is 'outrageous'. K was suffering from post-natal depression and was in a nursing home while the children were being looked after by her mother and a nurse, but still he set sail with the team. To be fair to him, the commitment to tour had been made long before, but husbands have cried off for less. These days, England players abandon their team-mates to fly halfway across the world to be at home for the birth of their children, much to Geoff Boycott's disgust, but it was a little different then. Players tended not to upset the MCC if they could possibly help it. Nonetheless, there was no plea from K for George to stay and no hint of a doubt in his mind that he should go.

One other interesting reflection on his early days as a master at Malvern College concerned his relationships with his peers in the Common Room. Public schools are very conservative, traditional establishments. That is not to say that the atmosphere was stuffy or that people were stand-offish, far from it. Malvern has always been an especially friendly place – I cannot imagine anyone as gregarious as George being happy in any environment that wasn't – but there was definitely a way of doing things, an established and accepted code of behaviour. This had arisen with the dilemma over Red Book order and the captaincy at Worcester, which he fully accepted, and would recur later, with the problems arising out of his second marriage, which he found more difficult to understand. If you did something slightly unconventional, brows would be furrowed and tongues would wag.

Nearly all the teaching staff lived in College accommodation. Ordinary people had not yet started to be able to afford to buy their own houses. George and K were unusual in that they lived off-campus in their own house, albeit barely half a mile away. Nothing was ever said but George sensed from time to time a certain awkwardness whenever the subject arose, as if the Chestertons were slightly apart from everybody else – they obviously had 'private means' and were not short of a bob or two. 'Completely untrue,' he said, 'but sometimes superficial impressions are hard to break down.' Furthermore, they had friends outside the College and did not rely exclusively on the Common Room for their social life. Once again, this was not quite the form expected. Boarding schools can be very insular places and George, with his susceptible antennae, had a notion that they were perhaps a little bit on the fringes. At this point, he paused and gave the matter some thought. Then he shrugged his shoulders and moved on. Whether he was telling himself that he was being oversensitive or whether he was regretful but unapologetic, it was hard to tell.

11

WORCESTERSHIRE COUNTY
CRICKET CLUB
1950–57

*'The beauty about George was that we'd wind him up, put him
on to bowl, set him off and he'd still be bowling at ten o'clock
at night if you let him.'*

Peter Richardson, Worcestershire captain 1956, 1957

As George pushed open the door of the home dressing room at New Road, Worcester, in early August 1950, he was apprehensive and not at all sure what to expect. It was his debut for the county and one hopes that the gateman had recognised him and allowed him unhindered entrance to the ground. If the gateman had no idea who the young man was, he might have been forgiven for his ignorance. Possibly he had kept abreast of the cricket news in the daily rag which had trumpeted George's availability for Worcester with a banner headline which read: *Oxford Cricket Blue To Play For County*. But that article by the ubiquitous 'Cover Point' had been penned months ago at the start of the season, and it was now August. To be truthful, George would have been unfamiliar to the members and supporters as well as the gatemen. He wouldn't have been very well known by his new team-mates either. He was not on the staff so he would not have attended pre-season training. He had never played for the club, not even a trial match. Not even so much as a net at the ground. Nor would he have been a visitor for home matches during the season; he had been far too busy at school for that. So he was a totally unknown quantity that morning as he looked around the dressing room at a sea of unfamiliar faces.

Cricket dressing rooms are strange places to anyone unacquainted with their particular significance. They are places where you get changed, of course, but to the players they are much more than that. Cricket is a game that is played over many hours, or days in the case of the county players. They are thrust together in one room for hours at a time during the day, weeks on end, throughout the six months of a season. No wonder it is sometimes said that a professional cricketer spends more time in the company of his team-mates than he does his wife. In a sense, the dressing room becomes more like a home, with all the same potential for joy, fun, laughter and high spirits as well as introspection, stress, tension and despair. That is why players are so mistrustful of outsiders and so jealously stand guard over their privacy. Within the family of your team, you can argue and squabble and act the goat in seclusion, safe in the knowledge that the outside world is kept firmly at arm's length. Anyone who invades this space is usually given short shrift. One story illustrates the point. A committee member at Worcester in George's time clearly did not get the point. He was always wandering up the steps to speak to the players in their bolthole, as if the place belonged to him. For this he was roundly despised by the players. 'Watch out,' exclaimed Dick Howorth one afternoon, 'Here comes that ****!' The committee man was furious, telling everyone that he had heard the insult and that the perpetrator would be brought to book. Quick as a flash, Roly Jenkins, a notable wit, put the irate committee man right. 'No sir, you misheard. He called you the Count!' The name stuck. Thereafter everyone in the club knew him as the Count, and it was a sobriquet that he himself became mightily pleased with. No one, except the team of course, knew the real reason.

That is why George picked his way through the cricket bags with bats, pads, gloves, boots, clothing and all the detritus of a cricket player strewn across the floor, seeking a quiet, obscure corner to park himself. He was playing in this match against Essex for this team but he was not part of this team. How could he? The others had been together through thick and thin for the best part of four months and he was the new boy. Furthermore, he was an amateur and they were the professionals. Not so long ago, they would have been changing in different rooms. Suddenly, a voice boomed out. It belonged to Reg Perks, the side's fast bowler and senior pro. 'Come over here, George,' he instructed, 'Change next to me. I've got ten pegs and you can have as many as you like.' The ice was broken. It was a small act of kindness but George never forgot it and he gratefully took up the offer, making sure of course not to take more than three of the ten pegs on offer. And so an unlikely but enduring alliance was formed between the two opening bowlers, one an amateur and one a professional, one playing in his debut and the other who had first played for Worcester way back in 1930, when his first victim had been Jack Hobbs.

Essex won the toss and elected to bat. Undoubtedly, this was a good thing for George. He could get straight out there and bowl instead of kicking his heels for most of the day getting nervous. Perks bowled the first over, a maiden. George bowled his first over, also a maiden. With his shortish run-up and his economical action, he got through the over in one and a half minutes. As with his driving, George did not like to hang about. He took his sweater from the umpire and was about to set off for third man when he felt a tap on his shoulder. It was Reg Perks. 'George,' he said, 'you're going to have to take longer than that. I haven't got my breath back!' And so he did, for the rest of his Worcester career.

The statistics show that Chesterton bowled 25 overs that day and took 3–43, a most satisfying debut. He remembers little of the details, even though he resumed a rivalry with Trevor Bailey, his opposite number as captain in that MCC Schools match in 1941. Though their paths crossed from time to time in the game, they never became close friends. Bailey, along with others throughout the counties, played as an amateur, but these 'gentlemen players' had some sort of nebulous financial arrangements with their employers, which permitted them to play full-time and often captain the side – only amateurs could lead, you see. They were known as 'shamateurs', but never to their faces. It was widely known that no less a grand person in the cricket world than W. G. Grace earned more from the game as an amateur than any living professional. The whole ridiculous charade was swept away when the distinction between amateurs and professionals was abolished in 1962. George truly was an amateur, however. He was not paid to play and he could only turn out when his work commitments permitted. He felt that the shamateurs tended to look down their noses a little at the part-time players, such as himself, as if they were giving the game a bad name for playing only infrequently. Nothing more was offered by George on the subject but you do feel that the faint whiff of hypocrisy was not pleasing to his nostrils. In any case, he always preferred to let the ball do his talking.

He has one other memory of this day. Bob Wyatt was his captain. Wyatt was a most interesting man and had a distinguished and remarkable career. He made his debut for Warwickshire in 1923. He led England on 16 occasions in the 1930s and was widely respected for his courage as a batsman and his wholly admirable qualities as a man. Although he was an amateur, he was never well-to-do, even if he did come from a family with considerable connections: Woodrow Wyatt, the politician and broadcaster – father to Petronella Wyatt – was a cousin. After the acrimonious Bodyline tour of 1932–33, when Douglas Jardine abandoned Test cricket in the controversy of the fall-out, Wyatt was the man considered ideal to heal the wounds between the two sides and he was made captain for the visit of Australia in 1934. His Test career finished after the tour of the old enemy in 1936–37. After the war, he was prevailed upon to come out of retirement to captain Worcestershire and was well regarded and liked in the dressing room. The professionals had no problems with the amateurs provided they were good enough. And Wyatt's record spoke for itself. But by the time of this match against Essex, Wyatt was 50 years of age. And where does a 50-year-old captain field? 'George,' he commanded during play, 'come and field here with me in the slips.' George was surprised. His normal territory was somewhere in the deep. As George crouched down in his unfamiliar position, hoping against hope that a sharp chance wouldn't come his way, Wyatt engaged him in conversation. Not about the game, which, incidentally, he knew backwards, but about his new car, a Rover 90.

There was another nice touch when George was batting. He was at No. 11 and the heady days of taking a century off Cheltenham at school must have seemed a lifetime away. Nonetheless, Worcester were only a handful of runs ahead on the first innings, so any score might well have been vital. He blocked his first ball with all the insouciance that a tail-ender can muster, to show that he is in full control of his nerves and his grossly undervalued technique. As he held the lordly pose, he was horrified to see his batting partner, Roly Jenkins, almost within hand-shaking distance from him down the wicket. 'NO!' he bellowed in a tone of voice that would have had any boy in the Remove shaking in his boots. Jenkins turned tail and hared back up to the other end, only just making his ground. At the end of the over, the two batsmen sauntered up the wicket to exchange nonchalant words, the way you do when disaster has only been narrowly averted. 'What's up, George?' asked a clearly concerned Roly Jenkins, 'Don't you want to get one off the mark on your debut?' Far from trying to pinch the strike, 'the dear man', as George referred to him, had thoughts only for the debutant's one off the mark. The mid-wicket conference bore little fruit alas. Not long afterwards, George was run out for 2.

There was no time for any practice at running between the wickets for the team were soon on the road up to Old Trafford to play Lancashire. George studied the scorecard in Wisden thoughtfully, a frown furrowing his brow. 'Hmm... We were stuffed. By 9 wickets, I see. Bowled badly, as I remember. Didn't take any wickets.

Oh, yes I did. I took 6 for 61. Well I never!' He said that he could not remember a single dismissal but he must have bowled well and kept his head whilst more experienced players all around were losing theirs. This was only his second match, let us not forget. What he does remember is the 23 he made in the second innings to avoid the ignominy of an innings defeat. 'They were all going on about the promising new batsman that Worcester had just signed!' he laughed. 'Unfortunately, history was to tell a different story.'

And so down to Cheltenham to face Gloucestershire. The College ground was one that he knew well, having played there as a schoolboy. He always loved bowling on it and found the atmosphere, with the marquees surrounding the boundary and the historic school buildings as a magnificent backdrop, vibrant and intimate. He tells a story about this match that goes a long way to throwing some light on the contentious issue of amateurs and professionals. The institutionalised distinction between the two in what is a team game is a concept difficult to grasp for those brought up in more egalitarian times. But it was different then, a fact of life. That is why it is so significant that George, as an amateur, was welcomed into the Worcester dressing room. The pros, a hard-nosed lot at the best of times, must have thought he was a good enough player. And, crucially, they liked him.

Two young amateurs were down to play at this match. They were both Blues but the pros didn't want them in the side. They thought they were only in the team because of their connections with the committee. As Cheltenham was a pleasant place to play and they fancied a game, that is what they were guaranteed, it seemed. And it was wrong, the pros felt, not least because it would be at the expense of a couple of their colleagues, who were probably reliant on their match fee. Furthermore, these two Blues were considered to be poor players, not fit to wear the green of Worcestershire. Despite the misgivings in the dressing room, the team was announced and that was that. Nothing could, or would, be done. But the two young men were late and Ronnie Bird, who was captaining the side, and no doubt mindful of his team's feelings, ruled them out. When they eventually turned up and discovered that they had been dropped, they were furious and left the ground in high dudgeon, neither making much of a mark in the county game thereafter. One can scarcely imagine such a scene in a club game now, let alone a county match.

Despite taking two wickets in the first innings, but none in the second, George was worried about his bowling, not at all sure that he could cut it at this level. What occurred at Worcester in the next match against Somerset ought to have

145

banished any such thoughts from his mind for good. Before the match started, he was passing the Somerset dressing room and he happened to overhear someone speaking. The voice he recognised was that of Mickey Walford, the Somerset opener and a bit of a dour character, so George always thought. They had known each other at Oxford, and Walford was later to follow George into the teaching profession and take up a post in charge of cricket at Sherborne. 'Look, fellas,' Walford was saying, 'I know this chap Chesterton. All you've got to do is get your front foot well down the wicket and he'll never get you out LBW.' Even today, looking at the scorecard gives George immense pleasure. It reads: 'Walford lbw Chesterton 4 in the first innings and Walford lbw Chesterton 12 in the second.'

Notwithstanding settling a personal score, George could do little to stem Worcestershire's collapse in the first innings, run out (again!) for 0. Thereafter the home team were up against it. Needing a meagre total of 166 to win on the last day, Somerset had every reason to believe that a comfortable victory was on the cards. At lunch, they must have picked at their salads with little appetite. They were 128–6, still needing a tricky 45 to win. George had taken all six Somerset wickets at a personal cost of 45 runs in a magnificent display of controlled swing bowling. In the words of the local reporter, 'Chesterton had put a different complexion on the match' and he had given Worcestershire 'an unlikely, sporting chance of victory by his grand bowling.' Sadly, the unlikely victory was not to be. After lunch, Somerset pulled themselves together and eased their way past the required total without further alarms. However, as George made his way from the field of play at the conclusion of the match, he was tapped on the shoulder by his captain, Bob Wyatt, and presented there and then with his county cap. It came as a complete surprise to George but a very pleasurable one – on a par with gaining his pilot's wings, you might say. To any county cricketer, the awarding of one's cap is not dissimilar to gaining colours at school or, for someone like George, getting a Blue at university. It signals that you have arrived, official recognition of the fact that you are an integral part of the team. A county cap is not given lightly and it is a sacrilege to wear it, or the sweater, if you have no right to do so. To the professionals, of course, it meant a higher rate of pay and the chance of a lucrative benefit, awarded by the Club, in ten years' time – provided that you are still playing, or haven't lost form or favour, or been injured, or got the sack, that is. To George, of course, none of this applied, except the deep satisfaction of having made his mark and received acknowledgement of that fact amongst his peers.

So, was getting your cap the same for you as getting your pilot's wings? 'Well, it was certainly a very proud moment in my career. But a little, insistent voice in my ear kept on telling me that I should feel guilty for abandoning my family during the holidays to go off and play cricket. I could never quite shake off that little voice.' *And how were your team-mates, the pros? Were they pleased for you?* 'Oh yes, I think so. Either that or they were too polite to do anything other than congratulate me.' His team-mates were surely delighted for him but the committee were distinctly frosty about the impromptu gesture by their captain. The awarding of a cap is a very serious business and needed to be run past endless sub-committees before being ratified by the grandees of the committee room, some of whom, I have little doubt, barely knew who Chesterton was. And in one fell swoop, Wyatt had bypassed the whole procedure and they were livid. Wyatt was unrepentant however; he felt that George fully deserved the honour and besides, he was at that stage of his career when he had little need to take notice of the bruised egos in the committee room. 'There was a terrible stink about it,' admitted George, with a laugh. 'They tried to rescind it, you know. But of course it was too late. The deed had been done.' But what a shame that his red-letter day should have been spoilt by petty politics.

No time for riotous celebration. It was straight in the car for the long journey up to London to play Surrey at the Oval the following day. Strange to relate but George was still suffering from a crisis of confidence. You would have thought that getting his cap would have made him relax and start to believe in himself. But no, the doubts remained. His mood was not lightened when Worcestershire lost the toss and Laurie Fishlock, one of the most destructive batsmen of his generation, proceeded to take a wolfish fancy to the opening attack, most notably the new boy Chesterton. He hit him for 4 fours in quick succession and then for an enormous six right out of the ground. Anyone who has been to the Oval, which has the biggest playing area in the country, to say nothing of the towering stands, will know what a tremendous blow that was. 'God! That's curtains for me!' exclaimed the poor bowler. He did not just mean for his current spell. Nor for the match. He meant for his whole career. As George related the story, I scoffed – after all he had taken 20-odd wickets already in his short time in the team of only four matches. But he was insistent; he truly believed that he had at last been rumbled and that the game was up. 'And then I bowled him!' he shouted. The exclamation of delight made the gardener pruning the roses in the garden outside straighten up in alarm, the evident note of triumph in George's voice just as fervent as it must have been 60 years ago. Confidence restored, he settled down and bowled well against a strong Surrey batting line up, taking 4–106 in 34 tiring overs.

What did you think of Peter May? 'He seemed a very nice chap. I didn't know him well.' *No, I mean as a player?* Peter May was widely regarded as England's finest post-war batsman, and he was my boyhood hero. 'Well, obviously he was a good player but … well, I never saw the best of him.' *That was because you kept on getting him out, wasn't it?* He smiled bashfully, 'It is true I got him out cheaply in both innings. That's why I was selected, I think, for the MCC tour of Canada the following year. The selectors must have been watching from the president's room!' Notwithstanding George's efforts, Worcester were put to the sword by Alec Bedser in the main and suffered a heavy defeat.

The final match of the season was against Somerset again, this time at Taunton. It was a match spoiled by rain, noteworthy only for being Arthur Wellard's last appearance for the county. Wellard was a legend in the West Country, as much for his tremendous hitting (he struck over 500 sixes in his career, which accounted for about one quarter of his total runs) as his fast bowling. His final six in Somerset colours was an extraordinary shot. George remembers it well. He was fielding at long-off at the time. 'It was a curious sort of golf shot really. It was one of those low screamers. Fortunately it sailed just over my head. Any lower and I would have been forced to try and catch it. If I had, it would have taken my hand off.'

So, that was that. Shortly afterwards, he was to return to Malvern for the start of the new term. *Were you a hero back at school?* He laughed. 'Not at all. It was straight back to teaching Geography to the Remove!' As far as I know, George did not visit a gym once when he was back in harness at school. He kept his arm in, so to speak, by bowling for hours in the nets, sometimes to the boys, sometimes on his own. As for the MCC, they left it to him to prepare for the forthcoming tour of Canada in whatever way he saw fit. He did play one match for Worcestershire in 1951, the traditional early season pipe opener against the tourists. It was before the summer term started, so he was available to be selected. This year it was South Africa. One of their number, of course, he knew well, his captain at Oxford, Clive van Ryneveld. It was a pleasure to renew their friendship for they had the utmost respect for each other. So much so that each of them donated his wicket to the other, a nice touch I feel: 'G. H. Chesterton, bowled Van Ryneveld 0 and C. B. Van Ryneveld, bowled Chesterton 29'. Honours even and dignity preserved. It was highly unlikely, however, that the two old university chums hit the town that night to reminisce about the good old days of undergraduate excess. 'He was such a solemn man,' said George. *And you're not.* He smiled wryly but made no comment on that. 'But I got on well with him. After all, he gave me my Blue. So he was obviously a good chap.' In addition to his former captain, he claimed the scalps of Jack Cheetham and Russell Endean for 38 runs off 21 overs. No wonder Worcester could not wait for him to join them as soon as term ended.

You can imagine their consternation, therefore, when George informed them that he would not be available that season. In fact, they were deeply upset and for a while tried to cut up rough. But in the end, they had no real choice but to accept the inevitable. George was an amateur and bound by no contract, unlike the professionals. So, reluctantly, they gave their blessing for him to go on tour with the MCC. George had been surprised by their reaction and, on reflection, wished that he had handled the whole business with more tact. It was a rare failure of protocol for one who is well known for his good manners. 'I should have asked,' he says, regretfully, 'instead of just informing them.' Nonetheless, at the time he felt that it was an opportunity that he could not afford to miss. It was an honour to be selected for an overseas tour with the MCC and Canada was dear to his heart. He had enjoyed his time there training with the RAF and he was looking forward to catching up with old friends around the country. This was the first tour of Canada by the MCC since the war and no doubt their hosts would pull out all the stops with their renowned hospitality. All in all, he was expecting a thoroughly enjoyable few weeks. In the event, it didn't quite turn out like that. Looking back on it, he rather wished he had stayed at home and played for Worcestershire.

Not that there was any immediate indication that anything might go amiss. This time, in 1951, travel was by luxury liner, the RMS *Empress of France,* not a troop carrier slipping down the Clyde estuary by night to be escorted across the Atlantic by destroyers and an American battleship. On board was Sir Anthony Eden, the new foreign secretary of the recently elected Conservative government (later he was to succeed Churchill as prime minister), who was most hospitable and entertained them in his rooms. The MCC team were travelling second-class and Eden was naturally on the first-class deck but he kindly let them use his quarters as a conduit through to the first-class deck whenever they wished. By all accounts, his renowned charm and good looks were not exaggerated.

They docked in Montreal and had a coach to themselves, which was attached to the train carrying them around the country. In the east, the opposition were largely of West Indian extraction but when they went west, they encountered more ex-pats in the teams. They played one match at a prep school in the foothills of the

Rockies. It was a lovely ground with an idyllic backdrop but the dressing room was a little primitive. On the door was a notice: *'Beware of Rattlesnakes on the outfield'*. Quick as a flash, George volunteered for slip fielding duties. In Vancouver, they obviously wanted to see the sights so their hosts took them up the North Shore Mountains, which offered the best views of the city and the surrounding landscape. Unfortunately, fierce forest fires were raging in neighbouring Alaska and little could be seen. Indeed, all the time they were in Vancouver, they were shrouded in smoke, odourless, thank heavens, but at no time was visibility more than 100 yards. On their visit to Victoria, they caught the overnight ferry, were welcomed at the port with ceremonial speeches, treated to an official breakfast and whisked off to play the match, still in thick smoke. At the conclusion of the match, it was straight back on the ferry for the journey home. Such is the relentless schedule of touring.

As best he could, George attempted to renew old acquaintanceships from his time there during the war, but as ever with these things, especially when you are constantly on the move, it was not as easy as he had imagined. Nor was the cricket all that it had been cracked up to be. In all honesty, he said, the teams they encountered were no more than of decent club standard, if that. *And the wickets?* 'Oh, they were matting.' *Did you not like bowling on matting?* 'On the contrary, I loved bowling on matting. I enjoyed the bounce that matting gives you.' But he admitted that the matting wickets were not terribly good. In Holland, where he was to tour frequently in his latter years, the matting was excellent but in Canada, the wickets were unpredictable. *So what was the problem, George? Why the equivocation? Sounds like you could have had a whale of a time.* He sucked in through his teeth. 'We had a rebellion in the ranks, you know.'

The captain was R. W. V. Robins, who had captained England three times just before the war and had captained Middlesex to championship success in 1947, forever remembered as 'Compton's Year'. His cricket pedigree was unquestioned. He was a gutsy player, even at the fairly advanced age of 45. George remembers one occasion when they were faced by a West Indian who was genuinely quick and who had aspirations of turning out for the West Indies. Robins was determined to see off the fast bowler, so that there would be no chance of encountering him again on that tour. Instructions were issued to the team to 'hit him out of the attack.' When no one seemed able, or willing, to do that, he went in himself and destroyed the young man, thrashing him to all four corners of the ground. Needless to say, the bowler was never heard of again. 'Walter was like that,' said George, 'very courageous with a bat in his hand. But not a lovable character. He wanted to win at all costs.' While there is nothing wrong with a winning mentality – and George is of course as competitive as the best of them – you have to suit the tone of the match to the circumstances. Especially if you are the captain. The MCC were on a missionary expedition to one of the far-flung outposts of the game, where it had, and still has, a precarious hold on the national consciousness. To tour the country crucifying every team that you encounter simply isn't good form – you might just as well slog the little prep-school boys for six after six in the fathers' match – and is similarly pointless. 'But Walter wanted to win every game,' George pointed out, 'as if it was a Test match.'

Furthermore, he treated his team as if they were young professionals on the staff at Lord's, expecting them to be at his beck and call whenever he so chose and barking orders in an imperious way. Silly curfews and 'naughty boy nets' simply did not go down well with a team of amateurs. 'Of the party of seventeen, twelve of us were schoolmasters, for heaven's sake!' George exploded with a rare display of passion. Many, like George, were there in their holidays. All right, it was a reasonably serious cricket tour but a certain amount of fun could be had along the way. The team approached the manager, J. R. Thompson, to present him with an ultimatum: either Robins eased off or they went on strike. Thompson was a very talented games player himself. He had represented Warwickshire before the war and continued to do so until 1955, when his teaching commitments at Marlborough permitted. He also played Rackets to a high level, winning the Amateur Doubles at Queen's, partnered by Colin Cowdrey. So it could be said that he knew a thing or two about the amateur ethos and would have understood perfectly the grievances of the team. When Robins realised that his authority was to be challenged, he was furious and disappeared for two days. It took all of Thompson's adroitness as a diplomat to calm the troubled waters between captain and team on Robins' return but eventually some sort of truce was effected. The tour went ahead and Robins did moderate his behaviour. But George never warmed to his captain. He tells a story to illustrate his point. Some years later, he was captaining an MCC team against Ireland and Robins was in his team. Ireland were nine wickets down and battling to save the game. The last wicket pair were proving most stubborn and try as they might, MCC were unable to break through. George tried everything. He put on off-spinners, leg-spinners, donkey droppers – the lot. Still, the Irish pair could not be separated. At last he put himself on to try to break the deadlock. Robins approached him in a fury, taking umbrage at George's 'negative' tactic, accusing him of settling for a draw and threatening to report him to the match committee of the MCC. Now George is a calm and even-tempered man but only a fool would mistake an equable temperament for weakness. Robins had obviously misjudged his man. He was told, in no uncertain terms, that there was only one captain of this side and it wasn't Robins and that it might be prudent if he, Robins, returned immediately to his fielding position. *Did you encounter him again, later in your life?* George shook his head. 'I've no doubt that he did write that letter to Lord's,' he added, more in sadness than resentment. It is poignant but true that George was never again asked to captain an MCC side, despite his years of loyalty and service. Nor did he even receive a letter of thanks for his endeavours. Perhaps it was just a coincidence, as George charitably points out. But it has to be said that Robins did wield a lot of influence within the MCC. He was for several years the chairman of selectors of the England team, an MCC appointment. Typically, what bugs George to this day is not the snub by the MCC but that putting himself on to bowl to try to dislodge that stubborn last wicket stand of the Irish didn't work. The match was drawn.

But that wasn't the whole reason for George's less than warm memories of the Canada tour. He felt that he didn't bowl well. *Oh, come on George! I've heard you say you didn't bowl well and then I discover that you took 6 wickets!* But he was adamant. The problem was an injury to his back, which had first surfaced when he was at Oxford. It flared up from time to time throughout his career at Worcestershire but it never stopped him from playing. He just bowled through the pain. On reflection, he acknowledged that he did in fact miss one match, against Glamorgan, when he could barely get out of bed, but that was the one and only occasion. He struggled on throughout the tour but he was in considerable discomfort most of the time, and occasionally in agony, and was unable to do himself justice. There is nothing more miserable than being injured on tour – the choice is going home (and this was going to be the tour of a lifetime so he wasn't going to bail out if he could possibly help it – in any case, that was not the Chesterton way) or soldiering on, trying not to make a fuss but distressed that you cannot perform properly. And to have a bad back, with all that travelling in cars and trains, trying to get some sleep in a different bed every night, with a lot of hanging about, in hotel lobbies and railway stations, carting around your suitcase and cricket bag … well, it cannot have been a bundle of laughs, no matter how hard he tried to join in with the fun. Indeed, there must have been times when he wished he was back home.

Worcestershire sent him once, during a particularly bad bout of back trouble, to see the eminent orthopaedic surgeon, W. E. Tucker, the man who had removed

Denis Compton's knee cap in a medical saga that had the whole country on tenterhooks. George was ushered into his enormous consulting room, thickly carpeted, with pictures on the walls of the great man with Compton and other notable patients. George was ordered to strip off and then, summoning his assistant to observe, Tucker told him to run up and bowl an imaginary ball. He had to bowl a whole over, doubtless a maiden ... stark naked. 'No need to operate,' was the diagnosis of the surgeon. And the cure? 'Avoid eating strawberries, rhubarb and goose!' This piece of advice came at enormous cost and, needless to say, was ignored by the patient. The problem was eventually solved by an osteopath, who turned out to be an Old Malvernian whom George had no recollection of teaching. This man had hated his time at the school and had nothing but ill to say of the place. He told George that his son was once misbehaving so badly that he took him by the ear, shoved him in the car and drove him all the way to Malvern. When they arrived, he ordered his son out of the car and told him that if he did not start behaving properly, he would be sent to 'this bloody awful place'! Notwithstanding his resentment of all things Malvernian, he was a good osteopath and seemed to put George's back right. Whether he put his son right is not documented.

The season that George missed while he was in Canada – 1951 – Worcestershire finished fourth in the County Championship, a considerable achievement considering their lack of playing resources (nobody to share the new ball with Reg Perks, for a start) and budgetary restraints. It was to prove to be a brief taste of success. For the most part in the 1950s, Worcestershire were at best no more than a mid-table team, occasionally slipping down to the lower reaches. But they were not a poor side. It should be remembered that these were generally recognised as the halcyon days of county cricket, when the standard was as high as it has ever been. Just reflect for a moment on the calibre of player dotted around the counties: Peter May, Colin Cowdrey, Tom Graveney, Don Sheppard, Denis Compton, Bill Edrich, Ken Barrington, Alec Bedser, Godfrey Evans, John Murray, Jim Parks, Fred Trueman, Brian Statham, Frank Tyson, Peter Loader, Jim Laker, Tony Lock, Jim Mortimore, David Allen, Fred Titmus, Brian Close, Johnny Wardle, Ray Illingworth... One would be hard pressed to assemble a phalanx of gifted, home-grown players from the present day to match them. By comparison with the stronger counties, it is true that Worcestershire struggled from time to time but they had a well-balanced side and in Don Kenyon they possessed a batsman who scored as heavily as anyone in the country and in Reg Perks they had an opening bowler who regularly took 100 wickets and more in a season. But, try as they might, they never found anyone decent to share the new ball with Perks (that is, until Jack Flavell and Len Coldwell appeared on the scene later on in the decade, and then they were a match for anyone). No wonder the club was so unhappy at George disappearing off on a 'jolly' to Canada and no wonder they swallowed their pride to welcome him back for the 1952 season, albeit late on after term had ended. And George was only too keen to rejoin his team-mates after his disappointments abroad with the MCC.

When he did make a reappearance in the home dressing room at New Road on 2nd August, the season was well advanced and it was already clear from the championship table that Worcestershire's form the previous year had been something of a false dawn. *So, did you detect any hint of low spirits or lessening of ambition in the team when you arrived? Was morale low?* 'Good Lord, no, not at all. These were professionals. They took a pride in their job. They played to win, every game.' Apart from team members playing for their livelihoods (if you didn't perform, you didn't get a contract) and apart from bonuses for winning and prize money for finishing higher up the table, professional pride was at stake. Every run scored, every wicket taken, every catch made was important, because that is why you played the game. Complacency hardly ever crept in. If it did, your colleagues would soon put you right – eloquently. You lived or died by your performances. There was no hiding place when the national averages came out at the end of the season. It was a hard game played by hard men and only the toughest endured.

One of the toughest was Peter Richardson. On George's return, against Essex, Richardson made a typically valorous 102. In his earlier days, he had been known as an attractive stroke-maker but in a bid to make his technique more watertight, he started to eschew the flamboyant shots and concentrated more on watching the ball carefully and accumulating runs. His batting became more productive as a result and he was rewarded with 37 Test caps. He was an amateur, later taking over the reins as captain, but some of the amateur's carefree approach to the game disappeared and he became more professional in his outlook than the professionals. And this was to his credit in George's eyes. Getting the job done was what counted, always.

George certainly got the job done, in spectacular fashion, at the following match against Sussex at Eastbourne. In every sportsman's life, there is the occasional day when everything goes right and the game seems easy, though it never lasts, this flowering of form, always short-lived and elusive. 'It was one of those golden days when everything just seemed to click,' he recalled. 'It was a blazingly hot and sunny day. We lost the toss and prepared ourselves for a long day in the field, for The Saffrons was notoriously a belter of a wicket to bat on.' Which makes the Sussex score of only 179 seem well below par. Despite appearances to the contrary, there was a bit of nip and juice in the wicket and Chesterton and Perks bowled pretty much unchanged throughout, save for two overs of leg spin from Roly Jenkins. George's figures speak for themselves: 33 overs, 5 maidens, 97 runs, 6 wickets. Just consider that marathon bowling stint for a moment. George was not a gym-hardened, finely tuned athlete who had been to Dubai for pre-season conditioning or to a boot camp in Germany to toughen him up for the rigours of a hard season. He hadn't played any competitive cricket for nigh on twelve months. He had no masseur to rub him down during breaks of play. He had no team analyst on a computer telling him where to bowl. He had no 12th man (or 13th or 14th) waiting for him down at long leg to offer him a towel, an isotonic drink and an encouraging pat on the backside at the end of every over. As for plunging into an ice bath as soon as he came off the field after bowling Sussex out … well, the very idea doesn't bear thinking about. His only thought was that he could murder a pint. Accordingly, he sought out his Uncle Hugh whom he had deposited in the Members' Enclosure before the start of play. He made it a regular fixture to stay with his uncle whenever he played away against Sussex (another uncle gave him a bed and hospitality whenever he played at Lord's); the professionals had to stay in the team hotel but the amateurs could billet themselves wherever they liked. Of course he could stay with the team in the hotel if he so wished but the practice was that amateurs had single rooms whereas the professionals had to share. This meant that his single room was often in demand by a member of the team whenever a romantic liaison was in the offing but George was by nature a generous and obliging team-mate and he would rarely grumble about it, provided a pint was bought. On this occasion, given the heat of the day and the number of overs he had bowled, he was looking forward more than usual to his well-earned drink. His uncle, much loved by George, was an affable fellow who was 'a bit of a boozer.' He had been gassed in the First World War so his shortcoming can probably be forgiven. George greeted Uncle Hugh, asked him how he was and suggested that they repair to the bar for a drink. 'Jolly good idea,' agreed Uncle Hugh. 'So where's the bar?' enquired George. 'I have no idea,' responded Uncle Hugh. George made enquiries of the attendant and together he and his uncle made their way up the steps and into the bar. It was empty, save for the barmaid. 'Hello, dearie,' she breezily greeted Uncle Hugh, 'Back again?'

Worcestershire failed to press home their advantage however and the match was drawn. Not a great deal remains in George's memory of the remaining matches that summer, though he continued to take wickets regularly. I noticed that against Lancashire, a certain J. B. Statham opened the bowling. What was George's impression of him as a bowler? 'Distinctly rapid,' was his response, 'but he kept the ball pitched up, especially against the tail-enders. You see, there was none of this bouncing numbers nine, ten, jack. It was an unwritten rule in those days.' *And what about that marathon spell of 42 overs against Hampshire?* 'I just loved bowling,' he said, 'You couldn't prise the ball from my hand once I'd got it.' Just as well. Worcestershire only had three bowlers. Perks bowled 37 overs and Jenkins, a leg spinner, 32. It was hard work but George thrived on it.

One incident from that match he does recall with perfect clarity. He was wandering back from the nets at the lovely Dean Park ground in Bournemouth when he heard a voice hailing him from a distance. He looked up and saw Leo Harrison, the Hampshire wicket-keeper, rushing towards him, waving a £5 note in his hand. 'George! Here's the fiver I owe you.' Apparently, he had borrowed the money from George some half a dozen years before, when they were playing together in the same RAF side and had not met up again until that day. 'An extraordinary gesture,' said George, 'I shall never forget it.'

And so on to 1953. Two thirds of the way through the season and Worcestershire were facing a crisis. Quite simply, they had no bowlers. Or, to be more precise, no fast bowlers. Reg Perks was injured. A succession of triallists and Cambridge University amateurs ('sons of committee members,' remembers Peter Richardson, 'and all hopeless') had been drafted in, to no great effect. Without Perks, the team was toothless. So an SOS was hastily sent to Malvern College. Would the school consider releasing George Chesterton a couple of days early, before the end of term, in order that the county could take to the field against Leicestershire with at least one recognised bowler who could take the new ball? Reluctantly, and for this one occasion only, the headmaster, Donald Lindsay, gave his blessing. Accordingly, on 25th July, George reacquainted himself with old friends in the home dressing room at New Road. Rain was about and the wicket was wet, which accounted for Worcestershire's slow and painful progress with the bat. The innings was held together, as it so often was, by Don Kenyon, who top-scored with 55. At 108–8, Ronnie Bird declared, in order to allow the home side a bowl on the tricky wicket. It was Saturday evening and of course in those days, Sunday was a rest day. And who knows what the weather had in store before they all came back on Monday to resume play? One Leicester wicket did fall, Maurice Hallam, to George, in the last over of the day. Playing regulations decreed that if a wicket fell in the last over of the day, stumps would be drawn and the over would be completed the following morning, or, on this occasion, on the Monday morning. George returned home to Malvern and spent the day on Sunday as he always did during term time, starting with Sunday morning chapel. Monday dawned and it was raining, cats and dogs. George remembers it bucketing down for hours at a time. Anyone who has lived on the side of a hill, as Malvern is situated, will be familiar with torrents of water cascading downhill, bursting drains, flooding roads and pouring out of wells, springs and waterholes. There was no possibility of play that day, mused George, as he registered the fact that, sadly, he would have to attend the dreaded end-of-term Common Room meeting after all. It was a three-line whip and you missed it at your peril. Almost as an afterthought, he stopped by at the general office, dressed in his gown in readiness for the meeting, to ring up the ground at New Road to enquire when the early lunch would be taken. 'Early lunch?' said the bemused voice at the other end, 'What do you mean?' George patiently explained that the custom was to take an early lunch when rain had stopped play. 'Rain?' said the voice, 'It's not raining. We haven't had a drop here. The sun's shining.'

George gulped. He could not believe that the torrential downpour that had flooded Malvern had not similarly been visited upon nearby Worcester. As a geographer, he should, perhaps, have known that the Malvern Hills does have a strange microclimate all of its own. But now was not the time to ponder the complex details of microclimatology. He didn't even have time to think about ox-bow lakes. He was dressed in suit and gown. He was in the general office of Malvern College. It takes half an hour to drive from Malvern to Worcester. It was 11.00am. Play resumed at 11.30am. And he hadn't finished his over!

How he managed to get to New Road by 11.29am, driving at breakneck speed, changing into his whites as he sped along, one hand on the wheel, defies credulity. I cannot believe that his desperate dash in the Stirling, at treetop level out of the killing grounds at Arnhem, was any less hairy. He jumped out of the car, half dressed, and sprinted onto the field of play. The umpire, who was about to call the over null and void, remarked, 'Oh, now George is here, we might as well complete the over.' Which George duly did, a maiden, a wicket maiden therefore. And then he retired to third man, to do up his bootlaces, button his shirt, hitch up his trousers and complete the transformation into something resembling a county cricketer. And guess what? He bowled 35 overs straight off, taking 3–77. Business as usual, in other words. Well, there was no other seamer, so he had to. It still astonishes, and I fear I labour the point, that a man can come straight out of school, rather rapidly in this case, and bowl 35 overs on the spot, unchanged, with no practice or training or any sort of preparation whatsoever … in the professional game! 'The man was a marvel,' said Peter Richardson, 'We don't know what we would have done without him.' The match was lost, despite George's heroic dash along the A449 to Worcester. No rain came to their rescue and they were defeated by 9 wickets.

To illustrate his point, Richardson pointed to one match that summer, against Glamorgan, when George bowled 53 overs! I continue to marvel at his stamina and resist the temptation to add more exclamation marks after every mention of the number of overs he bowled. Such enormous spells rarely happen these days … and, let us not forget, county matches then were of three, not four, days' duration. He took 5–142, an astonishing feat of strength and sustained accuracy. By contrast, Glamorgan employed nine bowlers in their attempt to dislodge George Dews, who resisted unbeaten on 124. Dews was a good No. 5, in George's opinion, who could usually be relied upon to score a thousand runs in the season. He also played football for Middlesbrough and Plymouth Argyle. He was an outstanding outfielder in an era when perhaps not as much attention was paid to that facet of the game as nowadays. He was known up and down the land as 'Gentleman George', a sobriquet that I reckon might equally have been applied to the subject of this book but by all accounts it was an epithet richly deserved. His courteous manner and sporting demeanour made him a firm favourite wherever he went. 'Absolutely right,' our George agrees. 'A gentleman to his fingertips.'

Down to Cheltenham for the next match against Gloucestershire – a short drive but another long stint, 36 overs this time, and another five-wicket haul. Tom Graveney did not succumb to George on this occasion (bowled by Perks for 2) but among his victims were Arthur Milton and Jack Crapp. 'I often wonder why the poor man never changed his name,' George mused. 'I think I would have. Just imagine the fun the boys at school would have had with a name like Crapp.' And then he was off on one of his stories. Jack Crapp, who later became a respected umpire, was a Cornishman. As it happened, his home town was close to where Dee and the family had moved to a new parish in St Mawgan. When Crapp was playing in one of his seven Tests for England, there was understandably great excitement about the game in his native Cornwall. In fact, commentary of the game was relayed on a public address system throughout the town. George happened to be there on that day and heard it. Half an hour later, he stopped for petrol at the local garage and noticed that the commentary had been switched off. He asked a garage mechanic why and was answered with a response of just two words: 'Crapp's out.' There is another story about the redoubtable Jack Crapp. Whilst on tour with the MCC in South Africa, he returned to his hotel where he was sharing a room with Alec Bedser. Not as well known as Bedser, he was not entirely surprised, on asking for his key of the hotel receptionist, to be asked, 'Bed, sir?' 'No, Crapp,' he replied, only to be directed to the toilets along the corridor.

The game itself was another thriller. Worcester followed on after having been dismissed for 140 on a turning wicket, Chesterton run out again! They batted better second time round, Mortimore doing the damage, leaving Gloucester only 78 to win. But time wasn't on their side. Still, they went for it and then all hell broke loose. Chesterton and Perks were not the sort of bowlers that you could afford to take liberties with at the best of times and sure enough, the college ground soon echoed to the clatter of wickets. After 8 overs, the score was 44–5, Chesterton having taken 3–16, including his 'bunny', Tom Graveney. At which point, sanity prevailed, the chase was called off and the match was drawn. George had taken eight of the 14 wickets to fall in the match. Not bad for a part-timer. In fact, he was becoming indispensable.

So it must have been galling for them to see George pack his kit into his car and, with a cheery goodbye, drive off on his holidays. There were still several matches to go. But the agreement with K to spend a fortnight in Devon with the family was not to be violated. Well, not unless the MCC came calling, that is. And they did, with an invitation to play for The Gentlemen of England against the touring Australians. To any cricketer, that is an opportunity that would be lunacy to turn down. To a harassed wife, however, with two young children to look after when your husband is away gallivanting in whites, the momentousness of the occasion might very well pass you by. George employed every blandishment in the book (and his book bulges more than most) before she reluctantly gave him leave of absence from playing on the beach with the children to drive up to Lord's. Imagine preparing for the biggest day in your life as a sportsman by building sandcastles.

And imagine today, three days at Lord's being set aside for the Australians to play against The Gentlemen of England. It would seem quaint, bizarre even. But in 1953, it wasn't quaint at all. It was taken mighty seriously by both sides. Consider the talent on display. For The Gentlemen, the amateurs, in effect:

Reg Simpson, David Sheppard, Bill Edrich, Peter May, Colin Cowdrey, Charles Palmer, Trevor Bailey, Wilf Wooller, Don Brennan, Robin Marlar and George Chesterton. And the Aussies were not taking it lightly either: Arthur Morris, Colin McDonald, Keith Miller, Neil Harvey, Ian Craig, Richie Benaud, Ken Archer, Ray Lindwall, Doug Ring, Gil Langley, Ian Johnston. To all intents and purposes, it was the 6th Test match of the summer.

And at the completion of both first innings, it was nip and tuck, The Gents holding the slenderest of leads of three runs. Despite his lack of match preparation, George had bowled not at all badly, taking a couple of wickets in his 13 overs. Thereafter, the Aussies assumed full control, thanks to a hostile spell of bowling from Lindwall who took 5 wickets. But George wasn't one of them. He carried his bat proudly in both innings. Admittedly 0 not out on each occasion but what else could he do? It is the perennial grumble of the No. 11 batsman the world over – no one to stay with you! The Australians raced away to an eight-wicket victory, which might or might not have made up for losing the Ashes that summer. All George can remember is the width of Arthur Morris's bat. Nothing went past it in a chanceless innings of 126*. And that the Australians were 'a good bunch'.

There is not a wealth of memories from the 1954 season. It was one of George's least productive as far as wickets were concerned but he remained an integral part of the Worcestershire attack during the month of August. There was however a sensational spell of bowling at Hastings that he was privileged to observe at first hand, from Jack Flavell against Sussex. Flavell was red-haired and temperamental: he could bowl terrifyingly fast when he fancied it but if he wasn't in the mood he would bowl at medium pace and hang the consequences. He took a lot of handling within the team and there were times when he could be infuriatingly stubborn and wilfully uncooperative. Fast bowlers can be like that. Something needs to stir them, to fire the adrenalin, for them to gather body and soul together to strive for that absolute peak of physical explosiveness. It cannot be done every day of the week. It simply isn't a repetitive action that can be generated at will. Sometimes the muscles will rebel and refuse to respond. Sometimes the mind is not in the right place, confidence can be low or mood despondent. Or the moon might not be in the right quarter. Or the toaster might have been on the blink that morning at breakfast. Yes, fast bowlers are awkward customers and need careful managing. It takes a special type of captain to balance the demands of the team with the needs of the mercurial leader of his attack. He might be infuriatingly unreliable but you would always want him in your side. As

George was describing the hot-headed, spiky Jack Flavell, a succession of similar bowlers marched across my mind: Fred Spofforth, Harold Larwood, Roy Gilchrist, Fred Trueman, Charlie Griffiths, John Snow, Denis Lillee, Sylvester Clarke, Shoib Akhtar…

On this particular day at Hastings, the moon certainly was in the right quarter for Flavell. He took 9 of the Sussex wickets and might well have taken all 10 had not Sussex declared at tea. For once, George only bowled 12 wicketless overs. Clearly, on this occasion, it was Flavell who wouldn't give up the ball. Despite this exceptional piece of bowling, Sussex still won by 9 wickets.

The current absurd muddle that is the first-class fixture list is conveniently blamed on the computer. No such scapegoat existed in 1954 to explain away the daft fact that Worcestershire had to face Surrey twice in a fortnight in late August. At the time, Surrey were entering that sustained period of hegemony in the county game which would see them walk off with the Championship, often by hefty margins, every season from 1952 to 1958. They boasted a side almost entirely comprising Test players – with no overseas players, please note. It was unchanged for both matches and reads like a who's who of English cricket in the 1950s: Ted Clark, Mickey Stewart, Peter May, Bernie Constable, Ken Barrington, Eric Bedser, Arthur McIntyre, Stuart Surridge, Alec Bedser, Peter Loader, Tony Lock. Oh, I'm sorry – I made a mistake. In the second match, Jim Laker replaced Eric Bedser, thus weakening the side considerably! It will come as no great surprise to you to learn that Worcestershire suffered two heavy defeats. George, sensible fellow, only played in the first of these games. And then the insistent cries of his children, Posy and Colin, called him back to their north Devon beach. He must have enjoyed attempting to build more sandcastles, reflecting that Worcester's batting in the second match was constructed on similar shifting sands. They were bowled out for 25 and 40.

Before the 1955 season, Worcestershire were in a quandary. Ronnie Bird, the captain since 1952, had retired. Although a tremendously talented games player, known and respected for his courage as a batsman, George felt he had not been a very effective captain. For a start, the professionals didn't much like him; he was prone to demand respect rather than earning it and they could see through his affectations and pretensions. His requirement of a gin and tonic at the close of play was inflexible and woe betide any 12th man who forgot it. Two of the pros, Roly Jenkins and Dick Howorth, persuaded George one day to substitute the gin for plain tonic. 'Go on, George,' they said, egging him on, 'You'll get away with it. You're an amateur!' Whether or not George 'got away with it' is open to conjecture – at least he wasn't dropped for the next match – but Bird was furious. He didn't get the joke and felt his dignity had somehow been compromised. The best captains, or any leaders of men, must have a sense of humour and should be able to laugh at themselves sometimes, without worrying about losing the respect of their team; a fact which persuades me to believe that George would have made a fine captain had he been in any position to accept the club's offer of the post made that winter. But he had declined, for reasons that have already been explained, and there was no obvious alternative. Eventually, Reg Perks was appointed, the county's first professional captain. Perks was an immensely popular figure at New Road and greatly respected for his deeds as a bowler and for his vast knowledge and experience of the game. But it was a poor choice. He was revered by his team-mates but he didn't possess the leadership qualities required to lead a bunch of such disparate characters. For a start, he was a fast bowler – perhaps not so fast these days – and fast bowlers are notoriously faulty judges of when to make bowling changes. Besides, as George sagely points out, Perks's main concern was to take 100 wickets in the season, a feat he completed in his last match that year, before retiring from the game. It was the sixteenth consecutive time he had done it and no one begrudged him the achievement, for there was no more popular player on the circuit. But an inspirational figure in the dressing room he was not.

First match back that summer was against Sussex and all George can remember about it is the masterly 22 not out he scored in Worcester's first innings of 105, yet again lamenting being left high and dry at the tail of the innings. Of the 6 wickets he took when he bowled, he has no recollection. I point out to him that only three seamers, Perks, Flavell and Chesterton, bowled, sharing the immense burden of the 78 overs between them. *No spinners used, George. And Roly Jenkins was in the side. How come?* And then he laughed as it all came flooding back to him. Roly Jenkins was a marvellous bowler, a leg spinner who gave it a rip, so much so that you could sometimes hear the ball hum on its way to the batsman. He was also a very humorous man and a good friend to George. But there were times when his self-confidence would inexplicably desert him and he would wander around the dressing room muttering, 'I've lost! I've lost it! I can't bowl anymore.' And he really couldn't. In that mood, wild horses couldn't drag him to the bowling crease. And then, just as mysteriously and just as suddenly, the confidence would flood back and he could bowl again. That is what happened that day at Hove.

Another unconventional and interesting character in the Worcester dressing room was largely responsible for the team posting an unexpected victory against Essex in the following game. Laddie Outschoorn was Singhalese by birth and was an entirely self-taught cricketer. He had an unorthodox style, based entirely on his quick eye and deft wrists. He could be infuriating to bowl to because he always seemed to be on the move and hitting the ball to places where it didn't seem possible to do so. He was also a brave and proficient close to the wicket fielder; George always liked to have him lurking close in at short leg. He had suffered dreadfully as a prisoner of war at the hands of the Japanese, which possibly accounted for his assumption of airs and graces, as if he needed to assert his rank and status for the good of his own self-esteem as much as anything else. There are few more unforgiving places for an outsized ego than a cricket dressing room and the professionals, amused at his social pretensions, used to call him the Prince. Be that as it may, he played like a prince that day at Chelmsford, scoring an unbeaten 150, which set up Worcestershire's eventual comfortable victory.

That evening, the team were having a couple of drinks in a pub in town. It was unusual for such a small place in that it had two entrances, one at each end of the bar. During the evening, George noticed that at one point, without a word being said, all the locals swiftly disappeared out of the door at one end of the bar. Almost as if on cue, members of the Salvation Army appeared through the other door and set about their usual routine of shaking the collection tins. They in turn, no doubt thanking the Worcester team for their generosity and wishing them all of God's beneficence for the rest of the match against Essex, made their way out through the exit recently used by the locals. And then, as if by magic, the locals returned, just as quietly as they had left, through the first door, having completed a silent and perfectly timed circuit around the back. It was surreal and caused everyone huge mirth.

There was another entertaining incident at Swansea during the next match. Worcestershire did not play well and towards the end of the second day, they were staring down the barrel of a humiliating innings defeat. Glamorgan needed just the one wicket to wrap up the game. But time was running out. Glamorgan claimed the extra half hour to try to force a conclusion that evening. George however was at his infuriating best with the bat, determined that they shouldn't lose that evening and go home, tail between their legs. What would be the point, you might ask. The cause was hopeless. Glamorgan still had a whole day in hand and no one would want to drag the match into a third day, surely. Not the groundsmen, not the caterers, not the match officials, not the administrative staff. Not the scoreboard operators, not the gatemen, not the car park attendants. Certainly not the Glamorgan players who wanted to get away and back home that night to enjoy a rare day off. The captain, Wilf Wooller, was particularly keen to see the back of Chesterton and made that fact known to George loud and clear. But you have to get inside the mind of a cricketer to understand how and why he can be so maddeningly stubborn at such a time. For one thing, it might rain, all night and all the next day. All right, that might not be the most satisfactory way to avoid defeat but a draw is a draw. Besides, George and his partner, Hugo Yarnold, began to feel an increasing, and not wholly unreasonable, irritation with Wooller. The game would end when it ended, not at a time to suit the social plans of the Glamorgan captain. And another thing, said George with a roguish smile, 'The waitresses at Swansea had exceptionally nice legs and we all wanted to see them again the next day.' Their wish was granted. George hung on and they all had to come back again the following morning. But not for long, it has to be said.

The highlight of that season for George was, paradoxically, not a game that he particularly remembers for any personal success with the ball. Following an especially disappointing innings defeat at the hands of Northamptonshire, they travelled down to Dover to face Kent. Unpromisingly, they were bowled out for 119 on the first day. The wicket turned and bounced and Doug Wright, the England leg-spinner, ran amok, taking 8–36. At times, he seemed unplayable as he got the ball to fizz spitefully. The captain, Reg Perks, had been laid low with a bug and was unfit to play. As the only amateur in the team, George had to assume the mantle. Perhaps it occurred to him as he donned blazer for the toss and strolled down the steps of the pavilion of the attractive terraces that form the natural amphitheatre of the Crabble Ground that this is what might have been had things turned out a little differently. But it was not to be and George fully accepted the status quo, quietly enjoying the experience, if only for the once.

Mind you, with his team taking to the field in defence of a meagre 119 runs, perhaps enjoyment was not the predominant emotion. They had just been bowled out by a spinner who had found the wicket very much to his liking. But Worcestershire had three spinners in their ranks, Horton, Jenkins and Berry. Surely they would do some damage of their own. Nevertheless, George still believed that the wicket, as it had both pace and bounce, would suit the seamers. In this, he went against the opinions and advice of his team who, to a man, wanted to get the spinners on as soon as possible. George backed his hunch, which you must do as captain, and risked the wrath of his team. He was rewarded for his faith by a spell of bowling from Jack Flavell that was as destructive as anyone could remember. Bowling downhill and downwind, he was terrifyingly fast and the Kent batsmen were visibly shaken by the hostile onslaught. They crumpled to 50 all out, Flavell taking 9–30. The other wicket taker was Chesterton who toiled manfully uphill and upwind all the while. His wicket had come earlier in the innings so it was not a case, thankfully, of his denying Flavell all ten wickets at the last, as had happened at Hastings when Sussex had declared at tea to deny him the full set. George says that he has never seen anyone, before or since, bowl as fast as Flavell that day. 'And mean with it,' he added, with something like an approving shudder. You tend to do that when the nasty fast bowler is on your side.

The game wasn't yet won, however. There was still much work to be done. Worcester battled to 186 in their second innings, a healthy but by no means impregnable lead of 255. Bowling Kent out proved to be a lot harder second time round but they managed it, George taking three wickets, to win by 52 runs. It was, as George says, 'a handsome victory' and he must have basked in the glory. After all, it was his hunch about the wicket that had turned the game and, as I say, a captain needs to have the confidence to back his hunches … hoping they turn out right.

But that was it for 1955. While his team headed north to continue their lives as county cricketers, George made his way along the south coast to join his family on holiday in Devon, where, when bowling to the four-year-old Colin on the beach, he no doubt imagined he was as frighteningly quick as Jack Flavell.

The following year, the Australians were back in town. The traditional opening match of their tour was a visit to Worcester and, once again, George was able to squeeze in an appearance for the home side against the tourists before the summer term started. It is interesting to note how much the normal rhythm of school terms has changed over the years. Terms now start and finish much earlier. George would never have been able to play before the summer term now but he would have been available from the beginning of July, rather than at the end. So yet again, George, as an amateur, would not have been involved in any pre-season training and nets; he was just going to retrieve his kit bag from its winter hibernation in the loft and turn up to play. And bowl. And bowl. And bowl. Just have a look at these figures: G. H. Chesterton, 56 overs, 18 maidens, 131 runs, 4 wickets. Yes, that's right, *56 overs!* At the age of 34. Against the Australians.

Let me quote from *The Times*, whose special correspondent was casting his eye over the Australians for clues as to how the forthcoming Ashes series was likely to pan out. Worcestershire batted first and were skittled out for 90, Ray Lindwall looking particularly menacing and back to his best form. Not long into the afternoon session, Worcester took to the field and George took the new ball with Jack Flavell (no Perks – he had retired). Early on, George had Burke out, bowled. 'I remember the ball to this day,' he said with relish, 'It started off on off stump and then dipped in late. It nipped through the gate and bowled him leg stump.' Let *The Times* take up the story:

> Worcestershire dropped everything that came their way. The worst sufferer was Chesterton, who never bowled better in his Oxford days. The first Australian runs did not come until the sixth over and Burke had made only one cut to the third man boundary when he pushed forward to an in-swinger from Chesterton, which straightened and took his off stump. [Did it hit the off or the leg stump? Who to believe here, our man from *The Times* or the bowler himself?] For the next hour, the ball was as much on top of the bat as it had been when Worcestershire were batting. Chesterton shaved Mackay's off stump and then had him dropped at second slip when he was 12. In the next over, Flavell, who was hostile and erratic, had him dropped, also at second slip, and hereabout, Mackay's bat was all edge. McDonald gave two difficult leg-side stumping chances and a relatively simple chance to slip, all off Chesterton.

'Aaagh! Slasher Mackay,' recalled George with unwonted passion, 'I had him plumb LBW – twice! Not given.'

The next day, George carried on where he had left off. Eventually, he snared his prey: K. D. Mackay, caught Dews, bowled Chesterton 55. It had been an obdurate innings (all four of them, we ruefully agreed) but that was what Mackay was known for. The sobriquet 'Slasher' was bestowed entirely ironically. There is a wonderful photograph of the moment, with Mackay on the front foot, George Dews swooping at second slip, George Chesterton pulling himself upright in his follow-through, the temporary stands packed with spectators and the majestic cathedral in the background looking on approvingly. *It looks a packed house, George. How many were there?* 'It was a capacity crowd. 7,000, I think.'

The Australian innings was saved from mediocrity by a commanding 160 from Richie Benaud. *The Times* reported:

> Just as Benaud stood above the other batsmen, so did Chesterton stand alone among the bowlers. The bare facts of his feat of endurance give some idea of what he meant to Worcestershire. His only periods of rest from the start of play and the time the Australians were out at twenty five to six were

25 minutes immediately before luncheon, three minutes in the middle of the afternoon to change ends and some forty minutes after tea when rain held up play. In the remaining time, he bowled 34 overs with no luck whatever and by the end of it he was just about on his knees. Fortunately, he has an economical action but one imagines that it may be some time before he feels again the urge to go down to the nets at Malvern. [How little they knew of him!] He practised all the dictums of length and most of those on direction that he must pronounce at Malvern, generally moving the ball into the bat a shade, as well as showing a love for labour that the Australians were quick to appreciate.

Normally, your opening bowlers are given a rest before they take the new ball but Peter Richardson, the new captain, had had Chesterton and Flavell already bowling for 75 minutes when it became available. It seems he had no choice. Benaud was now on the charge and only George was able to maintain a measure of control. So on and on he toiled. Richardson laughs now when he recalls the day. 'The beauty about George was that we'd wind him up, put him on to bowl, set him off and he'd still be bowling at ten o' clock, in the dark, if you let him.' It wasn't ten o'clock when he finally took his sweater but twenty-five to six when the Australian innings came to an end, with a commanding total of 438. *You must have been knackered, George.* 'A little,' he owned. What he remembered most was the ferocity of Benaud's strokeplay. 'He hit one back at me, very hard. I suppose you can call it a technical chance. I reckoned I saved a boundary. It hit me on the hand and ricocheted out to mid-off. He ambled through for a single. Meanwhile, I was nursing my bruised hand and muttering audibly, 'Bother! Bother! *Bother!*' Richie looked at me and said, 'Is that the best you can do, mate?' They were a lovely lot, the Aussies, absolutely delightful. Especially Benaud.' *That must have been the highlight of your career, bowling so well against the Aussies?* 'I bowled *all right*. But there were times when I felt I bowled better.'

Facing such a large deficit, and with Lindwall bowling like the wind, many expected that Worcestershire would submit as meekly as they had in the first innings. Indeed, for a while, it seemed that the Australians would soon be on the road to their next match, having swiftly wrapped up proceedings but the fact that they were delayed and ultimately thwarted was owing to an extraordinary innings of 130* by Peter Richardson. He had been widely touted as England's opening batsman for the forthcoming Ashes series and this knock probably secured him the berth, but not in ways that you would have expected. 'It was the best bad hundred I've ever seen,' George deemed. That might sound like the mother of all oxymorons but anyone who has played cricket will understand immediately what George means. As a batsman, sometimes your touch and timing can desert you, your best shots go straight to fielders, you play and miss, your confidence drains away and you just do not know where your next run is going to come from. Usually, you succumb and you spend the rest of the day cursing in the pavilion. But sometimes, against all the odds, you survive. You can then try to hit your way out of trouble or you can put your head down and continue to battle for survival, utterly resistant to any temptation that you should give your wicket away. That is how Richardson played that day, never fluently but doggedly, utterly intent on denying the Australians his wicket. George remembers one over from Lindwall when Richardson played and missed at all six deliveries. And still he remained undaunted. *The Times* described it thus:

> Many would have given up the ghost after being beaten as frequently as he
> was during the first hour but instead, he grafted on so that by mid-afternoon
> he was looking much more himself. He can of course only have benefited
> from the experience yet the truth is that not until he had batted for over
> three hours did he look an England player.

But England player he became and had a reasonably successful Test career. It is not often remembered that later that summer, at Old Trafford, in what has become immortalised as Laker's Match (he took 19 of the 20 wickets), Richardson had set up England's win with a typically resourceful hundred – on the same 'unplayable' pitch.

George got on well with Peter Richardson. He was a livewire, full of energy and mischief, with an insatiable appetite for life and fun. 'Though you wouldn't believe it if you ever watched him bat' was the rather unkind observation of a contemporary reporter. George found him stimulating company and they would often share long car journeys in George's Rover, known as Sabina (opinions differ as to the origin of the name – one says that it was on account of the number plate, SAB 12A, the other remembers a photo of a 'dishy' film starlet called Sabina on the dashboard) with George at the wheel and Peter riding shotgun, tirelessly firing off quips and wisecracks. His brother, Dick, was also in the team and was another larger than life character, whose off the field activities seemed in no way to lessen his effectiveness as a batsman. In fact George believes that he was such a fine player that he was unlucky only to play the one Test, against the West Indies in 1957 (with his brother, the only occasion when two brothers have represented

England in the same match). There was a third brother, Bryan, whom George reckoned to be the most talented, but after a handful of games for Warwickshire, he concentrated on his business career, not the least acheivement of which was his chairmanship of Coventry City FC.

Looking back with a critical eye, George is unsure about the effectiveness of Peter Richardson's captaincy. He never felt that his heart was really in it, as if his enthusiastic embrace of life's pleasures was somehow compromised by the responsibility of being in charge. The professionals in the team would sometimes voice their concern that he was a little casual. Of course he had his own batting and his England career to concentrate on and none could deny his gutsiness as a player. 'But he kept me on too long,' says George, 'He would give me the ball and forget about me.' Peter disagrees. 'George gave me a measure of control that the other bowlers couldn't. Even if he wasn't taking wickets – and sometimes of course he would run through a side – but if there wasn't anything in the wicket, you could rely on George to bowl to a field and not let the opposition run away from you. Bowlers like that are gold dust to a captain.' Whatever the reason for George's frequent marathon spells, he was happy to oblige and bowl all day, if required. Bowling in the rudimentary net at the vicarage or in the more sophisticated nets at Malvern College or on a little club ground in north Devon or in front of 7,000 spectators at New Road against the Australians ... it was all the same to him; he always loved it.

He must have. There can be no other explanation for what happened at Old Trafford in mid-August 1956. George had returned to the side as usual at the end of the summer term and had already played several games with his accustomed heavy workload. Against Lancashire, it assumed heroic proportions. Peter Richardson still talks about it with respect and awe in his voice. The weather was unpleasant. Rain was about and a howling gale was blowing. Lancashire batted and eventually declared at 240–6. The Worcestershire attack was paper-thin. There were three spinners in Horton, Jenkins and Berry. George's new ball partner was Outschoorn, who bowled on the slower side of medium pace and who never managed to take more wickets in a season than the 12 he claimed in 1948. 'George bowled uphill, into the gale, for *46 overs*. All innings. Unchanged!' said Richardson, 'It was a colossal spell. I cannot praise him highly enough.' Rain ruined the rest of the match. 'I was pretty tired,' admitted George, 'So much so that on the drive home, I pulled into a lay-by to have a kip. The rest of the boys, following behind in the coach, recognised my car and woke me up as they passed with a loud blast on the horn and much derisory cheering.'

In thinking back on his 1956 season, he became a little wistful and claimed that he was beginning to feel that he should no longer be in the side. *What? Don't talk nonsense George. Just look at your performances. 5–78 against Yorkshire, whom you customarily had for breakfast. 5–81 against Notts. 6–56 against Middlesex. How can you possibly say that you were no longer worthy of your place?* 'Well, I was bowling well enough. But I was finding it more and more of a struggle in the field and I felt I was beginning to let myself down.' Perhaps there is some truth in that. He was now thirty-four, at an age when stiffness begins to take its toll, especially for fast bowlers, and it does become increasingly difficult to bend and field properly. But the team assuredly would have forgiven the odd ball going through the legs if he continued to bowl as manfully as he had been. Besides, as his former team mate, Norman Whiting said, 'George was no batsman and not much of a fielder. In those days, you see, bowlers weren't expected to bat and to throw themselves around in the field, not like nowadays. Bowler's job was to bowl. And George was a fine bowler. Would have been even better if he'd played more regularly. Looked innocuous but he bowled a heavy ball. The pros accepted him utterly, without a single moan. Just goes to show because we pros loved a good moan.'

The committee at Worcestershire clearly were of the same mind, for there was no question that George would not be welcomed back in 1957. But that was to be, as it happened, his final season. If you take a casual glance at the scorecard of his first match that year, against Yorkshire, you will perhaps understand his worry that his days were numbered. Opening the bowling for Worcestershire were Flavell and Coldwell, who would soon become the most feared opening pair in the country and who would remain as the backbone of the attack, together with Norman Gifford, for years to come, eventually culminating in the county's championship successes in 1964 and 1965. They were the future. George Chesterton, at the age of thirty-five, clearly was not. But then take a closer look at the scorecard. Chesterton, bowling at first change, returned figures that look mighty familiar: 34 overs, 4 maidens, 109 runs, 4 wickets. It seemed that there still was a vital role for him to play. George doesn't agree. The game was at Scarborough and you have to be of a very miserable disposition not to enjoy playing in that seaside resort, with the marquees flapping in the offshore breeze, the brass band playing and the Yorkshire holidaymakers enjoying the sunshine and the cricket. But George was depressed. The belief that he was redundant in the side and not worth his place any longer was hard to shake off. The despondency deepened during his next match against Leicestershire. 'And then someone missed a straight one from me, a perfectly innocuous ball, and he was bowled. I can't imagine why he missed it but he did. And, to some extent, my confidence was restored.' Indeed it was: he took 4 wickets in the first innings and 5 in the second.

That summer, Denis Compton had announced his retirement from the game and his final match was scheduled for the end of August. At Lord's, of course, and against Worcestershire, as it transpired. A large crowd was expected to turn out to bid farewell to one of England's finest batsmen and most popular heroes and sure enough, the old ground was packed. Usually, the wicket at Lord's turned (the cynics would say deliberately so, in order that Titmus could bowl sides out) and the scores accordingly were on the low side. But the groundsman's plans had been thwarted by some errant fielder in the previous match who had skidded on the wicket prepared for Worcestershire and scored a horrible gash on a length. The pitch was unusable so there was nothing left for him to do but to bring back to readiness the used Test match wicket alongside, which had of course been carefully and painstakingly prepared, much more so than any of his normal county strips. It turned out to be a belter and the Middlesex batsmen took full advantage. There can be little doubt that Compton, batting for the last time in front of his adoring public, was not too upset at the late change of wicket and sure enough, he started to make his serene way to what everybody expected to be the inevitable hundred. But even geniuses, albeit an ageing one with a dodgy knee, make mistakes. He gave a chance, a difficult one, when he was on 89, to George … and George dropped it, instantaneously becoming the most popular person in London. Compton duly completed his hundred, Flavell eventually bowling him for 143, and he departed to a rapturous and emotional standing ovation. You would have had to have a heart of stone not to begrudge the great man his final moment of glory and the Worcester players joined in enthusiastically with the applause.

George took a solitary wicket in the Middlesex innings but had bowled economically as usual. It says a lot about the easy-paced wicket that Flavell and Coldwell found the going equally tough. As did the Middlesex bowlers when it was their turn. Worcester replied to their opponents' score of 350–6 declared with 354–9 declared, the backbone of their innings being a delightful century from Dick Richardson. At stumps on the second day, with Worcester back in the field, it was felt by all that the game was interestingly poised. Middlesex could fill their boots on the last day if that was their wish but somehow George and the others didn't believe that this would be the case. Bill Edrich was captain and he hated draws. A game would be made of it for sure.

Whether this was in Bob Broadbent's mind that evening whilst he was getting drunk, no one can be sure, least of all Broadbent himself. George had always found him a most congenial team-mate and admired him for his wholehearted approach to the game and, in particular, for his sharp close to the wicket catching. He was also a bit of a disaster socially, especially where the fairer sex was concerned; if any chatting up had to be done, it were best done before Bob Broadbent hove into view. In any event, on this particular evening, he had evidently decided to give it a bit of a thrash and by the time he climbed into his car to return to the hotel, he was three sheets to the wind. This would not be as much as a rarity in the professional game as you might imagine. Not that Broadbent was any worse than anyone else, though to be as drunk as he was that night was exceptional and most would have accepted, even in those more lenient times, that it was the height of folly to drive in such a state. All teams had one or two hell-raisers in their ranks. It was always so and no doubt always will be. Compton was a renowned carouser and Edrich himself was no slouch. Colin Ingleby-Mackenzie, who was to captain Hampshire to their first championship success in 1961, was once asked about the rules he laid down to his team and the curfews he expected them to keep. He replied, 'I would like my boys to be in bed by midnight. If they're not, I expect them to come home.' He was a very amusing man and he was not intending to be taken *entirely* seriously but it is true that cricketers, by and large, know how to enjoy themselves. It is a social game that they play. Even George admits that his team-mates 'were quite a boozy lot, so unlike the Oxford side I played in.' The point was that not too many questions were asked about your nocturnal activities provided you could do the business on the field the following day. The bottom line was that if you did not perform, you wouldn't survive and your contract wouldn't be renewed at the end of the season. So, you had to know your limits.

That night, Bob Broadbent misjudged his limits. The police, inevitably, chased him down Bayswater Road, where he demolished a bollard and wrote off the car. He was duly arrested and unceremoniously bundled down to the cells, apparently fighting all the way. When he came to, on a cold, hard prison bed, it was 2.00am. He shouted for the duty sergeant and tried to convince him that it was a matter of the utmost urgency that he was brought before the magistrate first thing in the morning as he was playing at Lord's. Evidently the sergeant believed him for he so arranged it, as you sometimes could in those days. Accordingly, Broadbent appeared before the beak, was fined £100 and banned for driving for one year. But he made it back to Lord's in time and took the field, with the rest of the team, at 11.30am. The ferocity of his headache can only be imagined.

The rest of the team had no inkling of his night-time adventures as Middlesex went in search of quick runs to set up the declaration. Then Peter Richardson came up to George to ask him to take hold of the reins for an over or two while he excused himself to have a blister seen to. He never came back. While Worcestershire had been on the field, the first editions of the papers had hit the stands and there, in conspicuous headlines and lurid detail, was news of 'County Cricketer's Night of Shame'. This being the annual fixture at Lord's, the game was attended by large numbers of Worcestershire committee men who were evidently furious at what had happened and who were locked in the dressing room with their captain demanding answers to some uncomfortable questions. Presumably Broadbent guessed what was afoot, which cannot have had much of a soothing effect on his hangover.

Spice was therefore added to the game, which, in truth, had no need of it. As expected, Edrich threw down the gauntlet with a challenging declaration and Worcester were duty bound to pick it up and respond. The stage was set for one of the most exciting and nail-biting finishes to a game of cricket that George has ever been involved in. And guess who led the charge for the visitors with a brave and resourceful top score of 42 in the middle of the innings? None other than the disgraced Bob Broadbent. Wickets fell, runs came, the total inched ever closer and the tension mounted. Everyone knew it would go down to the wire. As indeed it did; 12 runs wanted off the last two overs, with George at the crease together with the wicket-keeper, Roy Booth, and only Coldwell, a rabbit if ever there was one, to come. The last over … Worcester needed 5 runs, Middlesex needed 2 wickets. At this point, Edrich gambled, true to form. He brought on Compton. Compton bowled left-arm chinamen and googlies. If that sounds double Dutch to non-cricketers, such a variety of unusual and eccentric deliveries can sometimes sow confusion in the minds of even the best of batsmen. Sometimes. They can equally easily land anywhere. Or not at all. First ball, George latched eagerly upon a long-hop and smote it for four. Then he lunged desperately at the next three balls without making contact. At which point, Booth sauntered down the wicket to engage in conversation. 'Look, George,' said Booth, 'hit it into the covers and run like hell. But not if it goes to Bennett.' Don Bennett was the team's best fielder, the Colin Bland, the Derek Randall, the Jonty Rhodes of the 1950s. 'Got that, George?' George nodded, walked back and took guard. As instructed, he hit the ball into the covers … but straight at Don Bennett. Nothing daunted, George set off on a run. Roy Booth, not anticipating this, was highly startled but had no choice but to pin back his ears and race for the far end, for the good ship Chesterton was not for turning. For once in his life, Bennett took his eye off the ball, fumbled it and Booth made his ground safely. The match had been won, by 2 wickets on the penultimate ball.

From first to last, it had been a magnificent contest, one that would stick in the memory for years to come. The Press of course labelled it 'Compton's Match' for the pure theatre of the old entertainer scoring a peerless hundred on his swansong. But it could just as easily had the headline of 'Worcestershire's Match'. After all, they had won. Or what about 'Broadbent's Match'? History does not relate what sanctions he was handed down by an irate committee but George does remember that the team, thenceforth, were not allowed to travel in their own cars but in a team coach. George, as an amateur, would not have been bound by this edict. Just as well. Can you imagine the Stirling Moss of Malvern College travelling by slowcoach?

'It was a memorable match,' he looks back now, 'for a whole host of reasons: Compton's hundred in his last game, Dick Richardson's innings, Edrich's sporting declaration, Bob Broadbent's escapades, his vital knock in the final innings, the tense final overs, that last, scrambled run… Some games you have absolutely no recollection of at all. After all, we're talking about more than fifty years ago. And some matches you can remember vividly, almost every ball.'

And what did Broadbent have to drink, to celebrate? 'No time for celebrations. We were straight in the car for the journey all the way up to Blackpool, to play Lancashire the next day.' You need stamina to play county cricket. Perhaps it might have been more fitting if the game at Lord's had been George's last match, at the home of cricket rather than at Stanley Park, an undistinguished, though perfectly pleasant, county ground. But he wasn't to know that this was going to be his farewell to the game, even if he might have had a fair idea that his career was in its twilight. After the heady delights of beating Middlesex, Worcestershire were brought swiftly back to earth by a crushing defeat, by an innings and 56 runs, at the hands of a strong Lancashire side. Brian Statham was the executioner in chief, taking nine wickets in the match. George bowled tidily, as always, taking 2–52 off 21 overs. One of his victims, his second to last, was the great Cyril Washbrook. His last wicket was a fellow named Smith. Oh, I am sure that you are agog to know how he signed off for his county with a bat in his hand. Yes, you've guessed it: G. H. Chesterton, run out 0.

Over the winter months, he was too busy teaching the formation of ox-bow lakes to consider very much his future in the game. In the end, a letter from the chairman of cricket at the club made up his mind for him. It informed him 'in plenty of time' that his services would no longer be required for the forthcoming season. Of course it was a blow; no player enjoys the brutal finality of the *coup de grâce*, no matter how inevitable its coming. The news from Worcestershire did not come as a complete surprise to George and unwelcome as it was, he had no quarrel with the decision. In fact it was met with a certain amount of relief on his part. The adventure with county cricket had been a lot of fun and had provided him with a host of happy memories and the firm friendship of so many people. 'And I didn't bowl too badly, did I?'

Indeed not. In his stop-start career for Worcestershire, he took 168 wickets at an average of 19.87. In his full first-class career, including matches for Oxford and MCC, he took 263 wickets at 22.78. These figures may not mean much to anyone who is not a cricket statistician but they do tell a remarkable story. In short, George's reputation for exceptional accuracy is borne out by these figures, which stand comparison with the best in any era. There is no doubt, given his strike rate in the handful of games that he played each year, that he would have taken 100 wickets a season – the gold standard of an outstanding bowler in those days – had he played full-time. Some of his friends and colleagues have suggested that, in that case, he might have played for England. Perhaps that is being a little fanciful. He played at a time when England was blessed with great seam bowlers – Bedser, Trueman, Statham, Tyson, Loader, Bailey, to name but a few – and, in any case, George was never 'fast'. He was a medium-pacer and their role in Test cricket has always been more peripheral.

So, what sort of bowler was he, and how good? The number of his playing contemporaries still alive is now sadly much depleted but I managed to speak with three who knew him well. Tom Graveney said that he was a 'mighty fine bowler, who could drop it on a sixpence.' This accuracy was his strength, allied to a natural in-swing, abetted by the odd leg-cutter. Graveney particularly admired the thoroughly professional way George adhered to the age-old maxims of line and length. 'You would never have known that he was a part-time amateur by the way he conducted himself on the field and in his bowling.' Enough said.

Norman Whiting, who was a team-mate of George's in the early 1950s, said that he bowled at a 'lively medium pace, inners, with the occasional one holding up. He had a 12 pace run-up and could get through a maiden over very quickly.' Some of the younger pros, especially the fast bowlers, would quietly grumble behind the scenes when George turned up during his holidays, claimed Whiting, because it meant one of them would have to make way for him. But everyone saw it as inevitable, not because nepotism had reared its ugly head again, but because it was recognised, from the top to the bottom of the club, that George was far and away the best bowler.

I had a long and interesting chat with Peter Richardson, who played with George throughout his career, captaining him in 1956 and 1957, about how best to describe George's bowling. Eventually, we agreed that Derek Shackleton of Hampshire or Tom Cartwright of Warwickshire were of a similar pace and type. 'A bit like Trevor Bailey,' he said, 'but only in Trevor's latter years. When he was younger, he could be distinctly rapid.' It is a fact, and a curious one, that no modern equivalent springs to mind. The art of medium-pace bowling seems to be in decline. Bowlers either have to swing the ball prodigious distances at a lively pace, often with minimal control, or they have to be a 6½-foot giant who bangs it in short. 'And what's all this about "reverse swing"?' Richardson declared challengingly: 'It's rubbish. It's in-swing by another name. Like George bowled. I saw Neil Harvey at a dinner not long ago and I asked him how he would have played "reverse swing". He looked at me and said, "Peter, mate, are you pulling my leg?" That was from one of the greatest left-handers who ever held a bat.' He went on, expressing his trenchant opinions. 'Medium-pace dobbers, like Collingwood, are only seen now as part-time, stop-gap fillers-in. Someone like George, who would bowl you 30 or 40 overs a day, sealing up one end ... well, you never see 'em these days.' He continued, 'George was a very good bowler.' And this was from someone who played a lot of Test cricket:

He was by far the best of the amateur bowlers. His value to Worcestershire was inestimable. About two-thirds of the way through the season, everybody, especially the bowlers, would be tired and start to moan. 'Don't worry, lads,' I would say, 'Next week George will be back!' And that cheered them all up.

According to Richardson, George was totally reliable, very accurate and bowled to his field, which it seemed some of the others could not. 'He bowled to his strengths, you see. He didn't muck around with his grip or mix it up or try to bowl fancy mystery balls. He just bowled inners at medium pace with the occasional leg-cutter. *On the spot!*' The last words could have been heard in the next county.

And what about George as a team-mate, in the dressing room, on the pitch, in the pavilion bar, in the hotel dining room, in the pub, in the car on long away trips? 'George was a thorough-going gent,' said Graveney, 'A tough competitor out there, but there was no nicer man in the game.' *And off the field…?* 'Well, there were no dull conversations with George.' Whiting told me that George got on well with everyone. The senior players accepted him in their midst without question and enjoyed his company. 'He wasn't a hell-raiser. He liked a pint and he could enjoy a party with the best of them. But you have to understand that, at that time, a lot of the senior pros were at the end of their careers, in their forties, having missed six years because of the war. So they would prefer a quiet pint at the end of the day, with plenty of reminiscing. George liked to drink with them. Unlike the young guns.' George would have been in his late twenties, early thirties himself at this time. Besides, he was probably tired after having bowled 30 overs.

But perhaps the most telling appraisal comes from Peter Richardson. 'George provided quiet leadership in the dressing room, even though he wasn't the captain. Morally, physically, mentally, he was an example to us all. Great company off the field but on the field he always gave 100 per cent. He was a part-timer yet he was fit to rank with the best. I can't praise him enough, as a player and as a man.'

Some players, when they finish their county career, dump their cricket bag and turn their back on the game. Ian Botham famously never donned his boots again after his last day on the field. Such a response to the inevitable end of an existence that has dominated your life is wholly understandable but it was never one that tempted George. He loved the game too much and he wanted to go on bowling as long as his body would allow him. In the summer of 1958, he was invited to tour Holland with the MCC. The team was managed by an Etonian housemaster, whose name escapes him, who went to great pains to reassure George that his bowling load would be light as the party was packed with bowlers. 'The "bowlers" were all ancient donkey-droppers, masquerading as off-spinners,' laughed George at the memory, 'I bowled all the time. God, I was tired at the end.' Matches were played on matting, which suited him because, with his height, he could get the ball to bounce, sometimes extravagantly.

He continued to represent the MCC on biannual tours of Ireland up until 1963, matches that still had first-class status. On the last two occasions, he was asked to captain the side. He remembers once having six former England captains in his team: Errol Holmes, Wally Hammond, George Mann, Donald Carr, Freddie Brown and Colin Cowdrey. Hammond was a particularly interesting character, if only because his physical and mental decline since those golden pre-war years when he was regarded as one of the finest players in the game was so marked and so pitiful. He was withdrawn and morose, sitting alone in the dressing room, nursing his Scotch, refusing to join the others for lunch in the pavilion dining room. 'All in all, he cut an unattractive figure,' said George, 'so unlike the handsome sportsman of his younger days.' Not long afterwards, he died of a heart attack in South Africa, a sad end for one of the most talented yet enigmatic cricketers of his generation.

On another occasion, Len Hutton was in the team. It so happened that he had never scored a hundred in Ireland, an irritating blot on his record that he was determined to erase. And he surely would have done, batting with supreme confidence and due vigilance during his innings. But this being Ireland, he was to be thwarted by an unusual agency of fate … a broken-down mower. The outfield was as a result ridiculously long and he could only manage 80. George reckons it would have been 140 if they hadn't been playing in a meadow. He may not have got his sought-after hundred but Hutton helped himself to something else. On instructions from Lord's, who obviously were of the opinion that expenses had been too liberally taken for granted, George as captain had issued a plea to his team to go easy on their wining and dining. He was not terribly impressed later on to observe Hutton, on an adjoining table at dinner, tucking into a Lobster Thermidor.

On the Sunday, a day off from the cricket, the Irish took them all to Croke Park to watch the hurling final. George remembers that the stands were awash with black and white. Neither team played in those colours – the ground was full of priests. 'It's a lethal game,' concluded George, 'but wonderful to watch.'

To round off the festivities, and the Irish were nothing if not fabulously hospitable, there was a dinner for over five hundred guests. George was informed pretty late in the day that, as captain, he would be expected to get to his feet and propose a toast to their hosts. Desperately he sought the help of his team-mates for suitable material, a joke, a funny story, anything. He was quickly coached in an amusing anecdote about a bishop. As he teetered and stumbled his way through his speech, he was aware that his team, to a man, were convulsed in helpless laughter. And then the penny dropped. He had given away the punch line in his second sentence. 'I limped on. It was an awful few minutes.' Not that the Irish seemed too disconcerted. During the response by the high commissioner, a fight broke out between some Catholics and Protestants in the audience. But that did not prevent the dance after the dinner from being boisterously enjoyed by everyone. George remembers having a whale of a time, exhausting himself with repeated jigs and reels. 'Come on then,' he exhorted his partner, who seemed strangely unwilling, 'This is a jolly tune – one more, eh?' The jolly tune was the Irish national anthem.

The last-gasp, desperate draw secured by the Irish, which prompted the unwarranted outburst from Walter Robins, and the follow-up letter to the committee at Lord's, was the last game that George captained the MCC on the biannual jaunt to Ireland. He continued to play for the MCC but his first-class career was over. League cricket never appealed to him but he regularly turned out for clubs such as The Gentlemen of Worcestershire, Cryptics, Free Foresters, not to mention playing for the Old Malvernians in the Cricketer Cup, captaining them to glory in 1968. He finally hung up his boots after an incident when he was bowling for the Cryptics on a tour of Kenya. Someone hit the ball hard back at him, slightly to his left. He dived across to try to catch it and dislocated his shoulder. He was sixty-two!

It sounds corny but I couldn't resist asking George a series of rapid-fire questions before we took our leave of his cricket career.

Your best bowling spell? 'That day at Eastbourne against Sussex, when Uncle Hugh pretended he didn't know where the bar was. It was one of those glorious periods, all too brief sadly, when everything clicked. That day I seemed able to make the ball talk. Oh, and bowling out Yorkshire for Oxford in the Parks was a good time too.'

The best bowling performance you witnessed? 'It has to be that lethal spell by Flavell against Kent at Dover when he took 9 wickets. Frightening.'

The best batsman you bowled to? And here the answer was illuminating. 'You know, the better the batsman, the better I bowled. Peter May – I knew I was going to get him out. And other Test players too. I always fancied my chances. I'm sure it was the same for you.' Well, no, George, it wasn't actually. *Nevertheless, who did impress you?* 'Neil Harvey.' Fair enough. There could be little argument with that.

The best county side? 'Oh, Surrey were supreme in the 1950s.'

Favourite ground? 'Lord's is very special, of course, but I never seemed to bowl terribly well there. My fondest memories will always be playing for Oxford in the Parks. That was a happy time.'

12

HOUSEMASTER –
NO. 5 MALVERN COLLEGE
1961–76

'The House ran like the purring of the Bentley.'

Peter Smith, former pupil, 1965–69

I f teaching Geography was his job and playing cricket was his passion, then
housemastering is what defined George as a man. It was the role that he was
destined to play and one that he was ambitious to fulfil. Many people, even
experienced schoolmasters, recoil in horror at the notion of taking control of a
house of sixty testosterone-fuelled, adolescent boys, living cheek by jowl with them
for twenty-four hours a day, and being responsible for their safety and welfare. Yet
there was no shortage of takers in a school such as Malvern College, for being
asked to become a housemaster was definitely regarded as a considerable step up
the ladder. We have already seen that George's passing up of the captaincy at
Worcestershire was prompted by his very real fear that he would lose his seniority
in the long queue for the appointment. There were then ten Houses at Malvern and
length of service was fixed at fifteen years, so vacancies did not come around very
often. And George did not want to miss the bus.

Why, might you ask, would anyone want to do the job? There wasn't any
allowance so money can't have been the attraction. It is true that there were certain
perks and benefits attached, not least living in a large, splendidly appointed,
Victorian townhouse, but could they possibly compensate for the total loss of
privacy and the round-the-clock responsibility, on top of the teaching load, that the
post entailed? It was James Ferguson, a former housemaster at the school, who
put it in a nutshell: 'It's simply the best job in the College. Why? Because you can

make a difference.' For many boys, the housemaster is the most important and most influential character of his formative years, for good or bad. An old Reptonian once told me, 'You never forget your housemaster – whether you thought the world of him or hated him. He dominated your teenage life.'

Clearly then, housemastering is no sinecure. The jobs you have to do, the roles you have to play, the responsibilities that you have to discharge are multitudinous. At various times you have to be: commander; disciplinarian; teacher; organiser; enthusiast; counsellor; cheer-leader; stand-up comic; child psychologist; motivator; recruiter; speech maker; diplomat; marriage counsellor. In case you're wondering, the last two are needed to deal with parents. And all the while, you have to teach your lessons, live a normal family life and survive on six hours' sleep a night – if you're lucky. It was once said to me that three ingredients are required to be a successful housemaster: you have to possess the constitution of an ox, the hide of a rhinoceros … and be ever so slightly mad. Leaving aside the charge of insanity, it would seem to even the most casual observer in the Malvern Common Room that George was possessed 'of the right stuff'.

Obviously, Donald Lindsay, the Malvern headmaster, agreed. Early in 1961, sometime late in the Lent term as George recalls, he was summoned to Lindsay's study and asked whether he would like to take over No. 5. George must have gulped a little at this piece of news. He had been given to understand that he was next on the list and it was No. 1, not No. 5, which was coming up as a vacancy. No, he had not misheard. It was indeed No. 5 that Lindsay wanted him to move into, and straightaway too. There was to be no waiting until the end of the school year; it was to be done that Easter. This was unusual, to say the least, and the unspoken understanding between the two men was that it was an emergency – the current housemaster of No. 5 had to go immediately.

The housemaster in question was none other than John Collinson, George's predecessor as master in charge of cricket, who had so unwillingly and ungraciously stepped aside when it was put to him that he was emotionally unsuited to the job. It seemed that the same reservations were being raised about his performance as a housemaster and the need to act swiftly and decisively would have been obvious to even the most inattentive of headmasters, and Donald Lindsay was certainly not that. It wasn't just the boys' off-drives that were being put at risk but their very welfare. At times like this, all schools tend to clam up, sharing an honourable desire not to wash dirty linen in public. And there are personal sensibilities to take into account, not least those of the person in the firing line himself. In such circumstances, the sudden and unexpected disappearance of a member of staff is officially put down to 'personal reasons' and most people are prepared to leave it at that. There may be a certain amount of private speculation and of course the inner circle of power-brokers know exactly what is going on but it is surprising how quickly the waters close overhead and how inexorably life moves on. Be that as it may, in this case, it can safely be said that the reasons for Collinson's removal really were 'personal'. Lindsay believed that he was no longer up to the task. He had already been off work for two terms and that state of affairs was clearly unsustainable. So Lindsay had to make the awkward but correct decision to remove him. The trouble was that Collinson was not for moving, at least, not willingly. In his own words, Lindsay admitted, 'It was very difficult in the end. It wasn't easy to push him out of the House. He didn't want to go.'

So much so that Lindsay had to engage the services of a psychiatrist to declare Collinson unfit for work. It so happened that not long after George and K had moved into No. 5, they invited to dinner the chairman of Elmley Castle Cricket Club, together with Donald Lindsay and his wife Gerry. George had met this gentleman who was no cricketer himself but he was a considerable worthy in the local community and he had expressed an interest in meeting the headmaster of Malvern College. When Lindsay entered the No. 5 drawing room and saw the identity of the other dinner guest, the colour drained from his face. To one side, he surreptitiously informed George that the chairman of the cricket club was none other than the psychiatrist whom he had persuaded to sign Collinson's sick note. 'My God,' he observed, out of the corner of his mouth, 'I hope JC doesn't walk in. He'll think it was a put-up job.'

It wasn't and he didn't. Despite his ruthless exterior, Lindsay was actually a caring and compassionate man and he always nursed mixed feelings over his treatment of Collinson, no matter how unavoidable had been his actions. Relations between the two of them were infrequent and frosty. 'That is, until quite near the end,' said Lindsay, 'He knew he was dying and wanted to make amends. And when I sent him off, it was as friends.' George had been equally conciliatory, when he too visited Collinson in his hospice in Eastbourne as his life was drawing to a close.

The story of the hand-over between outgoing and incoming housemasters almost beggars belief. Collinson refused to move out of No. 5 until the very last minute to which he was entitled, that is, halfway through the Easter holidays. No thought of easing the entry of a family and all their possessions into their new home by being even a little bit accommodating. He abruptly turned on his heels, took his hat from the hat stand in the hall and strode out of the door, barking over his shoulder, 'Sell all my stuff, George.' And he was gone without a backward glance. So it was left to George and K to organise for all his furniture and possessions to be moved into the dining room to be sold off at an auction. There had been little or no communication between the two men once the news of George's appointment had broken. The younger man made several efforts to engage the incumbent housemaster in conversation about the House but no tips, no advice, no guidance, no encouragement were forthcoming. 'You'll find all you need in a shoebox in my study,' George was airily informed. Later, in the box, George found nothing more than a few inconsequential letters. There were no files, no addresses, no correspondence, no personal details. Nothing. One benefit of this lack of cooperation was that George came to the job without any preconceptions or prejudices. It would be usual for a new housemaster on encountering a bit of sin from one of the boys, especially if he didn't know him well, to look up his record on file, just to check whether the wrongdoing was merely a one-off or part of an emerging pattern. George had no such documentation to delve into; he had to rely on his instincts. And learn quickly. 'Besides,' he pointed out with his usual pragmatism, 'it meant that every boy started out with a clean slate.'

In a sense, George understood Collinson's resentment because he had supplanted him in the cricket and the House, both roles which had been close to the older man's heart. But it was more than that, George felt. 'Clearly the man was ill,' he said, 'Whatever it was that had tipped him over the brink, he wasn't in full command of his actions.' This emotional and psychological meltdown that was occurring cannot have been unrecognised in those days any less than it is today, though obviously less talked about. Housemastering is a very stressful job and can take its toll. A housemaster colleague at Malvern, James Ferguson, put it more succinctly, if a little drolly: 'All housemasters go mad … eventually,' he said, 'That is if they're not mad already!' John Collinson was not a madman, nor a bad man, far from it. Nor was he an inefficient, third-rate schoolmaster. In fact, he had many apologists, who believed that he had fine qualities as a teacher, not the least of which was an overwhelming concern for his pupils. Lord MacLaurin respected him and was always grateful to him for making him head of House. Pat Hooley was his senior tutor and was quite fond of him without being blind to his faults. The trouble, Hooley believed, was that he was too intense. He desperately wanted his boys to do well and was unable to prevent himself from communicating this anxiety and tension to those in his charge. Of course, this had the opposite effect of that which he intended. The boys would sense his yearning desire for success and in their eagerness not to let him down they would get anxious and fail to do themselves justice. It goes without saying that this is in direct contrast to George's style. He felt the pangs of zeal and ambition as much as anyone but he was better at concealing them and his relaxed persona seemed to put everyone at ease and therefore better able to give of his best. But Collinson was constitutionally incapable of nonchalance. 'Everyone was on tenterhooks around him,' observed Hooley, 'It got to the stage where he couldn't even bear to watch unimportant House matches. But the boys knew he was there hiding somewhere, probably being sick behind the pavilion.' It was also known that he had financial problems. He was a mathematician and he believed he could play the stock market. He couldn't. Hooley related being surprised to see him occasionally walk out of the dining room in the middle of lunch; he would be going to phone up his broker to discuss the state of the market. All in all, the pressure must have become unbearable and he just cracked. Pat Hooley is not alone in thinking that the whole saga was a very sad story and that John Collinson was a tragic figure. He dropped out of sight when he left Malvern and it seems that he led a solitary and unfulfilled life thereafter.

Selling the furniture was only the half of it. At the beginning of the summer term, George introduced himself to the boys as their new housemaster, knowing that he was in for a rough ride. Collinson was a bachelor and had taken little interest in the day-to-day running of the House. He had a matron who dealt with domestic matters and for the management, administration and discipline he relied on his cohorts of prefects, in whom he invested a great deal of power. This was an old-fashioned way of running things, one that would not have been entirely unfamiliar to George from his own schooldays, but it was a *modus operandi* that George was uncomfortable with and one that he was determined to change. It worked well enough when you had good prefects, he argued, but too often it could lead to abuses of privilege and power. 'There was a lot of beating,' he said with some disquiet, 'and I didn't like it. I pretty quickly made sure it was discontinued.' *Did you ever beat anyone, George?* 'Yes I did,' he replied with a shudder, 'Only once. But I felt I had no choice. It happened a couple of days into the term and I knew I was being tested. Had I showed weakness, they would have had me on toast for the remainder of my time there. It was the crucial moment of scrutiny that all people in authority go through.' The boy was in the rifle club and on the way back from the shooting range in West Malvern, he had passed around a bottle of gin in the back of the minibus. He was rumbled and as custom dictated, he was reported to his housemaster. Far from being contrite, the boy was truculent when wheeled in front of George, almost as if he was daring George to do his damnedest. So George obliged. 'I didn't hold back – I really thrashed him. I absolutely hated it but I knew it had to be done.' Strange to relate but the boy gave no trouble after that. He seemed to accept the punishment and bore no grudge. He even became quite amiable and cooperative. 'But I had to win that tussle,' were George's final words on the matter.

It wasn't that the House was full of degenerate schoolboys who had descended into disorder and savagery in the absence of adult guidelines. Far from it. No. 5 was a good House with many decent individuals and had an excellent reputation in games, which suited George down to the ground. But boys are by nature a conservative lot and largely suspicious of change. Collinson had a loyal following and they resented the arrival of his successor, especially in the sad circumstances of the change. It is a common hurdle for new housemasters but it is one that just has to be cleared. The anecdote that George recounts of his first night in the House explains it all. The head of House, Robert Johnson, 'a lovely chap, now sadly dead', came through to George's office at the end of the day in his formal dress, as he usually did, to report that everyone was in and that all was well. 'Excellent,' said George, 'I think I'll accompany you on a tour of the House. Just to show my face and have a chat.' Johnson demurred. 'Oh no, Sir, I don't think that would be a good idea. Mr Collinson never did that.' 'Be that as it may,' insisted George, 'that is what I shall do.' Johnson accepted the decision with good grace and never let his boss down but it took some while for the rest of the boys to get used to the new regime. But slowly George won them round. Not before his eyes had opened wide in surprise at some of the punishment routines, however.

Early in the term, on his way up the path leading to the garden gate and his route up to school, he encountered a boy in his games kit weeding the flowerbeds. On being asked what he was doing, the boy replied that he had been given weeding the garden as a punishment by one of the prefects. George left him to it. The punishment didn't seem too draconian and it was true – there were a lot of weeds about. A couple of hours later, he retraced his steps along the garden path and was surprised to discover the same boy, this time dressed in Corps uniform, still weeding. Nonplussed, George did a bit of weeding out himself to discover the reason for this extraordinary behaviour. It transpired that the punishment comprised half an hour's weeding in his games kit, another half hour in his Corps kit, then in his school uniform, then in his Sunday suit and so on, whatever else the prefects had dreamed up. Of course George put an immediate stop to it but quietly he was amused. 'You've got to admire the originality of it, even if it was over the top,' he chuckled.

One day, the House nearly burnt down. It was Posy, their daughter, who told me the story, in that matter-of-fact manner that one tends to adopt when one lives in a boarding house. It is as if there cannot possibly be anything else that can surprise – it has all been seen before. She went into her parents' bedroom, to 'swap' a bedside light bulb that had blown in her own room. She discovered the bed ablaze. She dashed out onto the landing, leant over the banister and yelled, 'Bedroom's on fire!' George pounded up the stairs and went down the corridor in search of a fire extinguisher, completely forgetting that one was placed right outside the bedroom door. Having eventually located another one, he hurried back and, following the written instructions, dropped it on the floor to deliver the sharp shock to activate the nozzle. The fire was extinguished all right but the room soon filled up with foam and he was unable to deactivate the pressure knob. Desperately, K flung open the windows and foam burst forth all over the garden, ruining K's beloved rose bushes. They did not survive. But the House did. 'The electric blanket was to blame,' Posy said. 'My father absolutely hated fire, as you can imagine. He had seen enough of exploding aircraft in the war.'

Whether this galvanised George into having a fire drill sooner rather than later, as regulations demanded, he does not say but he was determined that he would let the House know he meant business by holding it at two in the morning. The bell rang shrilly and slowly sixty-odd boys shuffled out into the yard, bleary-eyed, half-dressed and quietly cursing their keen new housemaster. One boy, barely awake, fell through the steps of the fire escape, luckily avoiding serious injury by having his fall broken by some protective wire mesh. Four boys were missing. The prefects were all for beating the absentees before it was remembered that they were billeted in a private house over the road. Unsurprisingly, George abandoned fire practices late at night.

Just to put to bed the vexed and controversial subject of beating, which we know George hated, didn't use himself (apart from that one occasion early on), and so forthrightly discouraged so that it soon fell out of favour in his House and was discontinued, let me quote James Stredder, a boy in George's House: 'At the end of his first term in No. 5, George made his first appointments as housemaster. I was to be head of House... At the start, I announced to him that I would not beat, so breaking with a tradition founded on the belief that this "ultimate sanction" was essential for the preservation of the order prefects were charged to maintain. I don't know what he thought about this, he simply accepted my decision but from the way he exercised his own authority, I imagined he might have felt that things had changed in the world and that there was actually no need for such fearful demonstrations of discipline – which were still very much the norm throughout the school.' Stredder stuck to his guns, supported by his housemaster. He goes on to say:

> Later in the year when I became senior chapel prefect [head boy], Mr Chesterton may well have had to account for his head of House's liberalism. A school pre from No. 6, 'up town' wearing his 'basher' (straw hat), as was the rule, had had his hat knocked from his head by two boys from another House. As an 'inter-house' matter, it fell to me to call the offenders to the council room and deal with them, which I did. But not as the housemaster of No. 6 expected, which was a 'School Prefects' Beating' in the presence of the other nineteen school pre's.

So, there you have it. George Chesterton was a reformer. Although Stredder claims that he didn't know what his housemaster thought about beating, it seems almost certain that George wouldn't have appointed his first head of House without knowing of, and approving, the latter's stance on the practice. In many ways, there is much about George that does little to hint at a liberal conscience. His background, and a lot of his foreground too, would suggest a conservative disposition, from his MCC hat and tie to his old-fashioned courtesies and his uncompromisingly heavy tweed suits. But he has ever been a pragmatist and has never stood in the way of change, once he has been satisfied that it is for the best. Forget not his belief that Malvern became a better and more humane place after the evacuation to Blenheim when all the petty rules and privileges were swept away, mourned by a few but unlamented by many. And let us listen to a surprising voice, one that found George to be anything but the stuffy traditionalist he expected. I refer to the third headmaster that George served under at Malvern, Martin Rogers, who succeeded Donald Lindsay in 1971:

> Although you might have expected someone who was such a distinguished games player to be rather conservative in his approach, George was in fact forward looking and an innovator. When I arrived in Malvern, I was full of enthusiasm for the then-new idea of 'study bedrooms', which I had introduced at Westminster School where they had been very popular and had a 'civilising effect'. After a year I suggested to the housemasters that they might like to introduce them in their Houses. To my great disappointment they were not at all enthusiastic. Except George. He immediately saw their

potential and No. 5 was the first House to introduce them. They were a great success and thereafter spread around the school.

Another example of George's willingness to espouse new ideas and initiatives was his enthusiastic response to the suggestion that he introduce a cup for House art. Cups abounded for sport and academic endeavour but official rewards for music and fine art were thin on the ground. He had developed an interest in painting (though he put away his brushes for good when, following a life class, his painting of a naked woman 'made her look like a monkey!') and he thought it would be a good idea if the walls in the dining room were stripped of the traditional honours boards and replaced by displays of the boys' artwork. In fact, he later came to regret this piece of historical pillage, for the names on the boards were of great interest to old boys of the House in particular but it did show that he was unafraid to seize the bull by the horns and make changes.

I wonder, therefore, whether George had a target, a goal, a vision when he moved into No. 5. After all, he had been given a specific task by Gaunt when he had come to Malvern as a young master, 'to provide cricket for 250 boys, five days of the week'. Had he similarly been charged by Donald Lindsay to 'sort out No. 5' or some such undertaking? It seemed not. At least, not specifically. George had been at the school long enough to know the ropes. His priorities were pretty clear. First, he had to stabilise the ship, no easy exercise when there has been a change of captain, especially when it is as sudden as the departure of his predecessor had been. Then he had to do what any ship's captain has to do under similar circumstances – make sure that the ship's company is full and its chain of command and working procedures are functioning properly. In his first few weeks, I doubt that he had much time to do anything else other than to establish that he had a grip on things. It was only when he was reasonably confident that he had the ship running the way he wanted that he allowed himself a visit to the bridge, to see how she sailed before the wind and to cast his eyes sideways at the other ships of the line. How did his measure up in comparison? How was her seaworthiness? Did his ship need a lick of paint? Was she any slower or quicker at changing sail? Were his ratings as smartly dressed as the others? Were his gunnery exercises up to scratch? It is often mooted that Houses within a school are not in competition with each other and that they should aim to give parity of care and supervision throughout. Don't you believe it. What would be the point of appointing someone like George Chesterton, a competitor to his bootlaces, if that were the case? To put it bluntly, his intent was to make No. 5 the best House in the school.

To this end, he purchased a Bentley. What on earth, may you ask, does owning a Bentley have to do with being a housemaster? After all, you hardly need one, or any car, for that matter, to drive to work. The daily commute for a housemaster is a short walk down the corridor, through a door to the boys' side. Well, quite a lot, as it happens. Appearances matter to George. That is not to suggest that his conduct over the years has been a triumph of style over substance – that would be a ridiculous contention given the man's achievements – but he does like to create the right impression. He always makes sure that he wears the right tie for the occasion. He wouldn't be seen dead in casual clothes at a social event. He insisted his teams were properly attired in colours blazers for lunch. He believes in putting his best foot forward; 'suited and booted' is one of his favourite sayings. First impressions are important, he firmly believes.

When I came to Malvern College and travelled around the country with the cricket team, older gentlemen would accost me from their deckchairs and ask me how George was. No one ever added the surname; there was no need. I was from Malvern and it was taken as read that there was only one person in Worcestershire called George. When I had assured my interlocutor that George was fine, the next question would always be whether he still had 'that Bentley'. And a story would follow as a matter of course, some I would have heard, some I had not and some I could never repeat. Geoff Morton used to recount tales of journeys to Harrow, Repton, Shrewsbury, Clifton, Rugby and just about every cricket-playing school in the west of England, when they would race to see who would get there quicker. Geoff firmly believed he had the edge in map reading but he would always arrive at their destination to find George already there, leaning up insouciantly against the Bentley, lighting up the first cigarette of the day. On one occasion, he told his boss that he would take charge of a particularly troublesome boy in the team and all the way down to London (they were playing Harrow) he lectured the boy on the importance of civility and good manners whilst representing the school. For once, Geoff's self-proclaimed prowess at map-reading deserted him in Harrow-on-the-Hill, which is surprising given that was where he was brought up, so he instructed the boy to wind down the window and enquire of a passer-by directions to the school. 'Oi!' shouted the boy, 'Where's Harrow?' Geoff was outraged at the boy's tone of voice. 'What 'ave I bin tellin' you these past two hours about manners, eh?' The boy was crestfallen. 'Oh, sorry, Geoff,' he said, 'I didn't know we'd started.'

I digress. The Bentley, whatever you thought about it, was a car that you could not disregard. It was there and defined a certain panache that George was trying to engender in Malvern cricket that had been languishing in the doldrums in the immediate post-war years. And of course it made its mark within the school itself, which was very much the effect that George wanted it to have. Quite simply, the statement he was making was that the best House should have the best car. He would drive down to the pitches for House matches and emerge from the Bentley, dressed in a huge coat, known popularly as the 'horse blanket', exuding style and self-assurance, confident that his team would be winning. And if they weren't, then the arrival of their leader in his chariot would soon put the score right. And amazingly, according to Alan Carter, a tutor in No. 5, it worked. George would scoff at this but you can never underestimate the importance of presentation. Alexander the Great unfailingly rode his favourite horse, Bucephelas, into battle. Nelson always wore his medals. Churchill was never without his cigar. George had his Bentley. And, as we now know, Bentleys are much sought after because of their well-marketed reliability: they regularly produce goals. Or points. Or wickets. That there has always been something of the showman in George is undeniable. He doubtlessly inherited it from his father. Like all great commanders in history, he was very much aware of the usefulness of image.

Apart from its sleek lines, the Bentley was *fast*. George did his best to conceal this fact from his wife but, as with any thoroughbred, the car had to be put through its paces from time to time. Colin, his son, remembers many a time on jaunts and excursions when K wasn't a passenger, urging his father to put his foot down and let the old girl fly. Apparently George required little encouragement. Frequently, he was requested to reprise his historic race to Worcester to finish his over and George duly obliged, the speedometer flickering on the 90mph mark. 'Go on, dad, see if you can do the ton!' roared his son as he appropriated the middle lane of the A449. That middle lane no longer exists. It has been replaced by double white lines. A source within the Highways Agency informed me that a certain black Bentley was responsible, but it was always going too fast for them to identify the number plate... There were other racetracks in Worcestershire however. Peter Smith was a boy in No. 5 under George. He is the son of Lister Smith, who was a contemporary of George's as housemaster of No. 7 and as two boys of the same age whose fathers were fellow housemasters, he and Colin were thrown together a lot and became firm friends. He remembers those outings in the Bentley with a frisson of excitement, even now: 'Colin and I shared a common aim, to annoy our elder sisters. As this fast developed into a finely honed skill, George was frequently drafted in to take us out of harm's way. We would climb into his stunning black Bentley and set off into the Worcestershire countryside. Each of these trips was an adventure. Although I don't remember the Bentley actually taking off, the wartime pilot was not averse to putting it through its paces. To the loud encouragement of his passengers, the speedo would hover at 90 … and sometimes creep upwards.'

One day, the car developed a leak in its radiator. George took it to a garage in Worcester and the mechanic assured him that there was no problem about getting it fixed: the cost would be £600. George baulked at this. £600 was a lot of money in those days so he and Colin decided to replace the radiator themselves. The total expenditure was £6. 'But do you know what?' hooted George with laughter, 'We were left with a bag full of screws we didn't know what to do with!' 'That's right,' agreed Colin, 'but the car still went like a bomb.' Another piece of Heath Robinson home mechanics occurred when the exhaust needed replacing. Once again George jibbed at the quoted price of £60 (this was at a time when a brand-new Mini cost only £400) so he and 17-year-old Colin got the old girl up on some bricks in the yard on No. 5 and had a look underneath. The exhaust pipe was shot. Nothing daunted, they sawed off a piece of pipe, which seemed to be more or less of the same diameter, from the antediluvian central-heating system in the House and banged it into the Bentley, securing it with tape and gum. 'Amazingly, it worked,' said Colin. 'Dad sold the car not long afterwards and someone was driving around in it with a bit of No. 5 in it. Seemed fitting really.' Perhaps 'fitting' is used loosely here but the old central heating system appeared not to notice that a piece of its pipework was missing; it clanked and hissed for a good few years afterwards.

Colin also remembers a slightly dodgy game that his father indulged in when he used to pick him up from his prep school. The Elms is situated on the other side of the Malvern Hills and when they reached the Wyche Cutting at the top of the hill, George would put the car into neutral and see if he could free-wheel downhill, all the way through town back to their home. The hill is very steep, needless to say. It just so happens that, many years later, my two sons attended the same prep school. I used to try to perform the same operation, to the great glee of the boys, but the other way, from the Wyche Cutting down to the Elms School. In my defence, I will say that travelling through Colwall at an uncontrolled speed was less dangerous than doing the same through Malvern, which is a much busier town. I never quite succeeded in the attempt. Naturally, George did.

The Bentley's usefulness was not limited to just its image and speed. Colin developed a fascination with history and George would take him, accompanied by

Peter Smith, to such places of interest as Hartlebury and Berkeley castles. These outings, says Peter, were not only highly educational but also entertaining. Once George spotted a man arranging lawnmowers in front of his gardening shop. George screeched to a halt, wound his window down and enquired of the man why he needed to mow a pavement. Such shameless waggishness would be manna from heaven to boys of that age. But never mind what age the boys were, this story of Peter's would entertain any age group. One day, George was trying to take a photo of the Severn bore, a natural phenomenon when, at certain times of the year, the tide rolls up-river like a mini tsunami. The Geography teacher needed more material than ox-bow lakes for his lessons. But the camera was an old one and the viewfinder made everything seem a lot further away than it actually was. The Severn bore rolled right over him. Peter fondly recalls those days: 'Travelling like royalty, Colin and I would fall about in laughter in the back of the Bentley at these endless quips and anecdotes.'

It is no great surprise that Peter went into George's House after Common Entrance. Colin, by contrast, went to Harrow. (Housemasters' children were not allowed to go into their father's House – a sensible rule, thought George, and probably even better if they didn't go to the same school, hence the choice of Harrow.) Peter had spent long enough in the Chesterton household to know it suited him. His views on his old housemaster make interesting reading: 'In my first week in No. 5, there was a pillow fight after "lights out". Under normal circumstances, such activity would have been tolerated; no self-respecting boarding school is pillow-fight free. However, we were oblivious to the fact that the dormitory was immediately above George and K's bedroom. Suddenly, the landing light, shining beneath the door on the shiny linoleum, darkened. Someone shouted, "George!" but too late. The door was flung open. We all froze. A dozen statuesque pillow fighters were caught red-handed in the bright dormitory light.' He was unable to recall any subsequent pillow fights. George's brand of discipline was not recriminatory, maintained Peter, like some regimes they had encountered at their prep schools. 'He didn't lecture us or needlessly hunt down culprits. Rapid action and a few well chosen words were usually enough.' Quentin Hayes, another boy who was in No. 5, says that he has no memory of George ever losing his temper. 'In all my time in No. 5, I only heard him get cross once. The offender was Simon Smith and all George did was growl that he was a worm! Retribution just didn't seem to be in his repertoire. He saw the bigger picture and we all respected him for it.'

Gentlemen of England v Australia at Lord's, 1953. Standing left to right: Colin Cowdrey; Peter May; David Sheppard; George; Don Brennan; Robin Marlar. Sitting left to right: Charles Palmer; Bill Edrich; Trevor Bailey (captain); Wilf Wooller; Reg Simpson. Practically a full England side! David Sheppard later became bishop of Liverpool.

Worcestershire v Middlesex at Lord's, 1957. 'Compton's Match', said the press, because the old entertainer had scored a hundred in his farewell game. 'Worcestershire's Match,' said George, 'After all, we won!' Or was it Broadbent's Match for his off the field antics? In any event, 'it was the finest match I have ever played in,' George reckoned. Worcestershire won on the penultimate ball with 8 wickets down. Standing left to right: George Dews; Dick Richardson; Bob Broadbent; Roy Booth; Jack Flavell; Len Coldwell; Martin Horton. Sitting left to right: Don Kenyon; George; Peter Richardson (captain); Roly Jenkins; Laddie Outschoorn.

Above: Worcestershire v Yorkshire at Scarborough, 1957. Worcestershire line up in front of the pavilion. Left to right; Dick Richardson; Bob Broadbent; Len Coldwell; George; Martin Horton; Roy Booth; Jack Flavell; Peter Richardson (captain); Don Kenyon; George Dews; Laddie Outschoorn. With Flavell and Coldwell forming a formidable new ball partnership, George knew his days as a county cricketer were probably numbered. This proved to be his final season. 'But I didn't bowl too badly, did I?' he said, with typical understatement.

Left: MCC in Ireland. George is standing in the middle, at the back. Just look at the front row: Billy Griffiths; Bob Wyatt; George Mann; Freddie Brown; Robin Marlar. Three England captains – Wyatt, Mann, Brown.

George in his natural habitat, bowling in the nets at Malvern College. This photo, taken in 1965, is a perfect shot of his distinctive action. 'I had a good action,' he said, 'It was entirely natural and had the beauty of never breaking down.'

Job well done. George contemplates a pint after his stint with the ball. 'In The Cricketer Cup,' he told me, 'I had to bowl my 12 overs straight off. Otherwise I would have seized up.'

Old Malvernians win The Cricketer Cup, 1968. George strides forward, having donned his MCC blazer, to receive the winner's pennant from Gubby Allen, chairman of MCC. The smile says it all. (Photo reproduced by kind permission of Patrick Eagar)

Three generations of cricket masters at Malvern. Left to right: Alan Duff; George; John Collinson. Taken at Lancing College. Behind them can be seen the famous school chapel, at 50 metres high the largest in the world. Alan Duff was a great friend and George mourned his premature passing. John Collinson looks a bit grim but he was ill and soon after died of cancer. By then, George insists, all bitterness had dissipated.

George giving away his daughter, Posy, at her wedding in the chapel at Malvern College in October 1965. The car that carried them all of a couple of hundred yards from No. 5 was none other than the famous black Bentley. When George opened the door to help Posy in, he was horrified to see his cricket gear spread all over the back seat.

George and Vanessa on their wedding day, August 1981. Here they are pictured together with the bishop of Bath and Wells. Before he agreed to the marriage, the good bishop had George on his knees for half-an-hour, testing the groom's moral and spiritual fortitude. The only other time he was on his knees like that was after bowling 56 overs at the Aussies.

*Acting Headmaster,
Malvern College, 1982.
'The headmaster would like
to see you in his study.'
The words every boy dreads
to hear. But he doesn't look
so fierce, does he?*

*Presenting a silver salver to the captain, Phil Neale, on the steps of the pavilion at New Road while the president
of Worcestershire CCC. 'I thoroughly enjoyed my time as president. Wherever I went, it would be, 'Good morning,
Mr President' and 'What can I get you to drink, Mr President?' Great for one's morale!'*

An unusual picture of George and Vanessa at yet another function, if only for the fact that George's glass is empty.

George and Vanessa on holiday in Madeira, a frequent destination.

Off to the Palace. George was invited, together with Vanessa, to take tea with the Queen in 2010. 'Not just us,' he hastened to add, 'There were one or two other people there as well!' The honour was in recognition of his work as president of the Malvern Civic Society. He is wearing his RAF tie.

President of the Malvern Civic Society. Here George and his Rastafarian friend are unveiling a plaque outside the Abbey Hotel in Malvern. 'He was a lovely chap,' he said of his guest, 'We got on famously.'

*Official opening of Chesterton Nets at Malvern College in 2003. George, Tom Graveney and Will Gifford,
XI captain. What on earth is Tom Graveney doing behind the stumps? He never kept wicket in his life.
Poignantly, this was the last time George ever turned his arm over and the last time Tom picked up a bat.*

George with Roger Tolchard. Malvern College 2011. 'My glass is empty, Roger. Would you be a dear and get me another.' 'Sorry, George. My pockets are empty, as you can see.' George believed that Tolchard, who played for Leicestershire and England, was the 'most charismatic cricketer' that ever passed through his hands. (Daniel Eglin, Malvern College)

Daughter Posy, son Colin, Vanessa, George, 2011.

George delivering the exhortation at the Menin Gate, Ypres, Belgium in 2011. The Menin Gate is a memorial to British and Commonwealth soldiers killed in the Ypres Salient in the First World War. Every evening at 20.00 hours, buglers from the local fire brigade sound the Last Post and the exhortation is delivered.

> *'They shall not grow old, as we that are left grow old:*
> *Age shall not weary them, nor the years condemn.*
> *At the going down of the sun and in the morning,*
> *We will remember them.'*

*The wrought-iron
Chesterton Gate, inscribed
with his initials – GHC –
is situated on the balcony
of the cricket pavilion at
Malvern College.*

*George addresses the
unseen audience from the
steps of the cricket pavilion
at Malvern College at
the official opening of the
Chesterton Gate. On his
left is Lord MacLaurin.*

George on the golf course, 2011. He and Vanessa share a passion for golf. He is still proud of the fact that he can manage a round or two in his ninetieth year.

George at his favourite pastime – watching the cricket, Malvern College 2011. (Daniel Eglin, Malvern College)

So, this would be a timely moment to ask the critical question: what calibre of housemaster was George Chesterton? If a housemaster can have a pivotal role to play in a boy's schooling then it is not unreasonable to examine his legacy in the job by asking how George has been remembered by those with whom he came into contact. He left No. 5 in 1976. His pupils are now well advanced into middle age, and it is to be expected that over the years memories have dimmed and details blurred. But it appears not; those to whom I have spoken recall incidents and conversations as vividly as if they happened yesterday. George, in point of fact, has a very good memory, remarkable really for his age, but when I prompted him about some of these events, he was forced to give an apologetic shrug and say, 'Well, if that was so then it must have happened but honestly, I have no recollection of it.' To be fair, this is not really surprising. George had something like one hundred and fifty boys who came under his care during his time in No. 5, but, all of those boys had only one housemaster.

The advice that I was given by other housemasters before going into a House myself was that you have to be yourself, for boys can smell a fraud a mile off and, in any case, you cannot keep the mask firmly on twenty-four hours a day, seven days a week, without it slipping from time to time. I think it safe to say that we can guess what sort of housemaster George was if he remained true to his nature. Pat Hooley remembers arriving at the school as a young master and finding his colleagues a quite terrifying bunch. Some softened over time but others remained haughty and aloof. 'But not George,' he laughed, 'He was like an amiable teddy bear!' He described George's style of leadership as 'relaxed but disciplined'. He also went on to underline the faith that he put in his lieutenants, a theme that is taken up by Alan Carter, who succeeded Hooley as House tutor. 'He got me doing all manner of different jobs,' remarked Cater admiringly, 'tutor, cricket captain, Father Christmas, proof-reader, bingo caller… And why was I fool enough to do them all? Because George asked me and you just cannot say no to the man.' George was particularly grateful to Carter for one, all-important task. This was the vetting of the House skits, which traditionally take place after Christmas Supper. The opportunity for umbrage and disaster are limitless. Let us just say that the boys relish the opportunity for a bit of quid pro quo and the housemaster dreads not so much being held up to ridicule, which goes with the territory, but needless offence being given to someone who doesn't have such a thick skin. A female guest at one of these performances once fled in tears when some rather savage lampooning took place. There was never any such trouble when Carter was on the case, remembers George; the boys wouldn't have dared.

Carter also remembers the enormous trouble that George went to in organising games and competitions for the new boys, almost as if he wanted to make them understand that they were entering what was essentially a 'family'. For that was what it was; No. 5 was an extension of his own family. The door, for example, between the boys' side and the private side was always open and anyone could pad across the carpet, day or night, if the need or inclination was there. Because of this, one episode deeply upset George and left something of a scar for many years. He had been contacted by the head of a local prep school, Seaford Court (subsequently it went out of business and is now the site of the new Malvern Hospital), asking him whether he was interested in a talented young boy who was a particularly good off-spin bowler. Of course George signed him up on the spot. Unfortunately, The King's School in Worcester thought that they had first claim on the boy and were pretty cheesed off with George for 'poaching' him. Now George was never averse to a bit of poaching, especially if a good cricketer were involved, but on this occasion he felt that he was guiltless; it was the prep school that had contacted him, not the other way round. In any event, the affair burst into flames and spread quickly, like a forest fire, with the headmasters of Malvern and King's getting involved. Donald Lindsay, Malvern's headmaster, acted as he customarily did: he supported his man to the hilt in public but in private he gave George a dressing down for behaving without due professionalism. George was a little peeved, not believing that he had done anything wrong, but the happy upshot was that he had secured a fine off-spinner.

In fact the young lad offered much more than accurate off-spin. Anyone could see that he was destined for any number of the glittering prizes on offer. Then he fell into bad company and foolishly got involved with minor drug-taking on the Hills. Martin Rogers, who had by this time succeeded Lindsay as headmaster, was all for sacking the boy without further ado. But George managed to change his mind. He believed that the boy had only been involved on the fringes, that he had enormous potential and that he deserved a second chance. Accordingly, he was rusticated, probably for two weeks; George has forgotten the exact length of the suspension. When the boy returned after his punishment, George hauled him into his study to read him his fortune. He made it crystal clear that the young lad was a very lucky boy to be given a second chance and under no circumstances was he to let anyone down by squandering it. He was very much on probation and the best thing he could do to rehabilitate himself would be to go away, keep his head down and his nose clean. Et cetera…

Lo and behold, five minutes later there was a knock on the door and the sorrowful head of House informed George that the aforesaid probationer had just been caught in the yard smoking. The boy had to go – for good. His father, a colonel in the army, came the next day to take him away but not before bringing his son to George's study to apologise. And then he was gone. Any housemaster goes through unpleasant emotions of sadness and regret when one of his own is expelled. No matter the circumstances, you cannot help but feel deep disappointment and responsibility. After all, you are *in loco parentis* and it is one of your boys who has let the side, and you, down. And, as far as George was concerned, he was part of the family of No. 5. That was why he took it so badly and so personally.

The story doesn't end there. The boy grew up and, as predicted, made a name for himself in the world. Ten years later, George was visited by a distinguished-looking chap in a bowler hat. He was from MI5 and he wanted to know whether this boy, now being rapidly promoted up the ranks in the army, had had any problems whilst he was at school. It was likely that he was soon going to be involved in highly sensitive operations and the Secret Service wanted to do a thorough sweep through his personal record. Regretfully, George had to explain that he been expelled. 'Oh, we know about that,' the functionary airily informed George, 'but is there any reason that you might doubt his trustworthiness and loyalty to the Crown?' George assured him that he did not.

Years passed. Then George was rung, out of the blue, by none other than the very person who had prompted the visit from MI5. He explained that he was now a lieutenant-colonel in the army, married with two boys and at the stage of considering what school to send them to. He had visited establishments the length and breadth of the country and in his opinion none of them could hold a candle to Malvern. In view of his own chequered career at Malvern, did George see any insuperable reasons why his sons should not be allowed to sign up and come? George could not. Though now retired, he sought the headmaster's blessing and in due course, the two boys arrived. They made a great impact in their time at school, gaining colours in all the three major sports, including cricket (of course) and one of them was appointed senior chapel prefect. Needless to say, George kept an eagle eye on their progress and took great pleasure in their successes.

The role of *paterfamilias* that George assumed in the formative years of his boys' education is made mention of by many people who have spoken to me. David Bailey, who experienced life in No. 5 before and after George's arrival, touches upon the contrast between John Collinson and George as housemasters. 'One almost felt the aura of calm and contentedness which prevailed over all matters – so different from before.' He became George's head of House: 'My instructions from George were to get on with it and if there were any challenges to bring them forward. That we had the odd challenge was inevitable but he dealt with them in his own way and normality returned very quickly.' He also refers to George's proclivity for a nap at whatever time of the day. As previously noted, all cricketers are consummate snoozers; it is a talent that does not fade with age. 'Many a time,' reports his former head of House, 'I would "cross the hall carpet" to his study for a quiet word only to find him in the midst of forty winks. A quick and discreet exit and never a mention followed.' Tim Forrester was another, later head of House. 'It was a very happy period of my life. I felt completely trusted, valued and empowered. George seldom instructed me but was always readily available when I wanted advice… The thing was, he created an appropriate environment. He was an easy communicator and always very approachable. I don't think anyone feared him but everybody respected him. He was genial, interested, supportive and had a ready smile. If I was playing sport as he walked by, I would try twice as hard. He never made a fuss but his opinion mattered.' James Stredder, George's first head of House, explains further his housemaster's style. 'George made me feel that the next phase for No. 5 was to be a joint exercise. I would visit his study, notebook in hand, and we would discuss all the day-to-day running of the House. My memory is that these were easy and pleasurable occasions. George organised things with a complete lack of agitation or tension – and, inevitably, with good humour… I never felt any sense of restriction or interference in the way I carried out the responsibilities delegated to me.'

Of course it was not all plain sailing. Obstacles have to be circumvented and occasionally disaster or tragedy strikes. One such hidden iceberg was the death of a boy, David Beckenn. James Stredder remembers the harrowing occasion very well: 'It was the worst thing and I sensed it distressed George deeply. David was a delightful member of the House and he tragically died after an accident, just a few weeks short of his sixteenth birthday.' The 'accident' was caused by a pillow fight in one of the dormitories. During the cheerful high spirits, the boy tripped and hit his head on one of the iron bedsteads. The next morning, he reported to Matron, complaining of a headache. He was sent to the doctor who found nothing untoward. As it was the end of term, school broke up and everyone went home. During the holidays, a blood clot developed in his brain and he died. The post mortem revealed that he had a very thin skull and an accident like that could have happened at any time. The school, and the housemaster, were absolved of any culpability at the inquest. Nonetheless, George took it badly and even today, he grimaces at the memory. On occasions like that, feelings of guilt and responsibility are hard to shake off. The parents of the boy, to their credit, never sought to lay the blame for their son's death at George's door but they never spoke to him, at the funeral or at any time subsequently. 'I can understand that,' says George, 'It was a terrible thing to happen.'

These setbacks aside, it seemed that the Chestertons led something of a charmed life, in many people's eyes, a golden couple. Accurate or not, this popular perception of them cannot have been diminished by their success in a national competition. George was bedridden with the flu sometime in 1965. To alleviate the boredom, he was reading the current issue of *The Cricketer* (well, it wasn't going to be *Geographers Weekly*, was it?). He turned to the competition page and his eye was immediately caught by one of the questions: 'Which international cricketer never watched a game of his 1st XI when he was at school?' George happened to know the answer to this – D. J. Knight. He was a Malvernian. The story was part of Malvern sporting folklore. Knight, who played for Surrey while still at school, opening the batting with Jack Hobbs and later playing for England, never actually *watched* a match on the Senior because he was always picked to play, even as a first-year boy. That was the trick of the question. Then George spotted another question he could easily answer: 'Which two brothers played together for England in the same Test match?' Once again, there was a Malvern connection. The answer was of course Peter and Dick Richardson, former team-mates of George's at Worcestershire and older brothers to Bryan, who was in the XI when George was master-in-charge. With mounting excitement, he sent K hotfoot up to the Long Room in the cricket pavilion to fetch some past copies of Wisden. The other answers were unearthed and the form sent off to *The Cricketer*. Later he heard that he had won! Many people apparently had got all the questions right except one – only George had correctly identified the Old Malvernian, D. J. Knight, as never having watched his school XI play. Most had assumed it was Colin Cowdrey. But in fact Cowdrey had been selected as a young boy at Tonbridge for the *second* match of the season, so he had in fact watched one match from the boundary. George's delight knew no bounds. The prize was a holiday for two in Corfu. They had a marvellous time, no doubt made the sweeter as it was at the expense of his old chum, Ben Brocklehurst, the editor of the magazine.

George is the first to admit that his wife was a reassuring and inspirational figure at his side, and not only for running his errands up to the Long Room. Indeed, when anyone, colleague or boy, talks about George as a housemaster, K's name is always mentioned, almost in the same breath. They were a team. 'Of course we were,' he exclaims, 'I couldn't have managed it without her.' George and K. The partnership rolled off the tongue as easily as ... well, how about Hobbs and Sutcliffe? Am I being a little fanciful here, or even a touch flippant? But hold on a minute – they had a pair of dashing dachshunds known by those very names, fondly remembered by generations of young boys who used to take them for endless walks, to the point, says David Bailey, that 'there was some concern that their legs were long enough to put up with it all.' But when new school caterers were appointed, who happened to go under the trade name of 'Sutcliffe's', George knew that in order to head off any potential embarrassment, Sutcliffe's name would have to be changed. And you can guess the new name – of course you will – Trumper! Sadly, Hobbs and Trumper did not survive as a partnership. They didn't get on and Hobbs had to go, taken on by an adoring cook. But the other partnership, the one that had first taken seed all those years ago only a short walk up from No. 5 to the Senior, had flourished and was now in full bloom.

The role of a housemaster's wife in a boys' boarding house can mean different things to different people. For generations, when a housemaster was appointed at Malvern, his wife very much came into the reckoning. Though no official guidelines were set down and none followed, it was accepted that the 'suitability' of the wife was taken into consideration. Although this did not preclude the appointment of bachelor housemasters (John Collinson, for example, was not married), in effect, it rarely happened and was not generally considered a great success when it did. Thus the merit and importance of the wife's role were fully understood. The trouble was that the job came with no remuneration, and therefore with no official recognition. As one housemaster's wife said to me, 'Our job is undefined, unprized and unpaid.' So why on earth would anyone want to do it? Well first, there is the not unreasonable desire to support your husband in his career. Second, a wish to get more involved in the school that takes up so much of your husband's time and energy. Third, you may like the contact with the boys and want to care for them and help them in their social development. And of course there is always the seductive fancy of residing in a large house with a nice garden, free of charge! Whatever the motives, it is, or was, of the utmost importance that the husband and wife see the job as a partnership and that both throw themselves into the fray with equal gusto. Anything less, any wariness or reservation felt by either party, will not do. If either betrays the merest hint of half-heartedness, it will quickly be detected by the boys, and probably by their parents as well, and trust will break down. After all, a couple cannot act *in loco parentis* if one of the surrogate parents cannot be bothered. Crucially, both husband and wife must want to do the job and be determined to enjoy it.

It very soon became clear that K would make a success of the role; indeed, she seemed to thrive in it. David Bailey, who had spent three years under the previous regime of John Collinson and actually respected him as a housemaster so he had no axe to grind, certainly noticed the difference: 'Then along came George and K, two children and two darling dachshunds. What a contrast!' Very soon, K came to be known popularly as 'Lady C'. It was the time of the great controversy over the publication of *that* book but there was never any hint that the title bestowed on K had anything to do with the sad life of D. H. Lawrence's eponymous heroine. It was just that it tripped off the tongue; there was no irony intended. She was immensely popular, with boys and staff alike. James Stredder, another boy who was with Collinson beforehand, said that she was an instant hit. 'We were under her roof and we sensed that she liked us and cared for us.' Quentin Hayes remembers her kindness when he was a young boy, a very young boy, before he had even arrived at Malvern. His parents had driven him over for interview from his prep school in Leicestershire and, not unusually, he was feeling sick from the car journey. 'K calmly grabbed me by the hand and ushered me speedily into the toilet before I could damage the carpet. Both George and K seemed unflappable.'

Ian MacLaurin told me that K was a lovely, beautiful woman and was the perfect foil for George as a housemaster's wife, with all the imprecise functions that that role implies. For a start, she transformed the No. 5 garden from its previous jungle-like state to one of colour and pleasing proportion. Although its grandeur is now a little faded as a result of neglect or amateurish care, it is still the finest garden in the College, a place of beauty, elegance and peace. 'She loved that garden,' said MacLaurin, a little wistfully, a keen horticulturalist himself. The image of two bottoms, one belonging to K, the other to their houseman, William, bent over a bed of flowers, as George made his way down the garden path on his way up to his classroom haunts George's memory to this day.

It was not only in the garden that her impeccable taste in décor was felt. The House was beautifully decorated and furnished. 'Style all the way,' commented

Alan Carter approvingly. 'K's influence could be seen everywhere,' noted David Bailey, 'from the colour schemes to the entertaining. There would be dinner parties in their own dining room, followed by coffee or iced tea with party games in the drawing room afterwards. All part of our extended education.' He believed that she was a wonderful woman, 'very pretty, with all the time in the world for the boys.' Alan Carter agrees. 'She got involved, becoming interested in the boys and concerned for their welfare.' Her generous hospitality was legendary. Martin Rogers remembers when he arrived as the new head, he and his wife were invited round for dinner first by the Chestertons. Alan Carter was also grateful for the meals that she laid on for bachelor masters like himself. When George was ill or laid up, Carter would take over running the House but after lock-up, he would be unable to get home as he did not drive, so K would give him a lift. At this point, lest anyone should think that sainthood is being bestowed posthumously upon her, it might be as well to comment here upon her driving. 'She learnt to drive late,' admitted her son Colin, 'and she was always a nervous driver.' Her husband drove the Bentley, pretty fast. K drove a Morris 1000, pretty slowly. She just about got to grips with the gyratory system in Worcester but then they changed it, and she never went back. I am reminded that George's mother was very nervous of the internal combustion engine, a trait obviously shared by K. 'She was never the most confident of drivers,' George confirmed.

Confident or not behind the wheel, she was poised and self-assured at the helm of No. 5. 'She set the tone,' said Pat Hooley, 'and the boys were very fond of her. Some of the Houses at Malvern were … *nondescript*. Ha! Not No. 5!' He added that his wife's brother had also been in No. 5 with the Chestertons and he had adored K. She would go into lunch every day and sit next to different boys and engage them in conversation about their day, all in the most relaxed and easy fashion. This may seem undemanding, making small talk and bothering to take an interest. And probably it is, on the odd occasion. But lunch takes place every day and there are undoubtedly occasions when school food and adolescent chat begin to pall and a wife would no doubt rather go up town and share a coffee with friends. As a housemaster, such temptations simply do not arise; it is your job and no matter your state of mind, you put on your smile and plunge into the lion's den. Your wife, however, might be forgiven for occasionally throwing over the traces and fleeing. Not K. She had an immutable sense of duty and she would never have deserted her husband. Besides, she had that natural grace and charm that would have put the boys at ease immediately, whatever her mood.

Her son Colin shares a flavour of the way that she ran No. 5: 'She was very organised and ran the House like clockwork. Punctuality was very important to her. Lunch would be at 1.00pm. By 1.10pm, it would be finished. And by 1.15pm, the washing up would be done.' George laughed at the description and took issue with the timings. 'Not that rigid. My son does exaggerate a little.' But he agreed that she liked to get a move on. 'And no tomato ketchup on the table,' Posy told me, 'That was one of her pet hates. She thought it was a bit, well, *common*.' Colin remembers the long dining table in their dining room. Breakfast, lunch, tea and supper would be laid up early every day and as the day progressed, the family would work their way down the table, clearing away each sector at the completion of each meal. 'Well, it made sense,' he said with affection.

The relentless pace of life in a boarding house, together with the accompanying stresses and strains of communal living, did however begin to take its toll. 'She started to run out of steam towards the end of term,' remembers Pat Hooley, 'and one or two crises seemed to take it out of her.' George agrees. 'She got very tired towards the end and certainly the energy seemed to drain out of her.' Whether this was the first sign of the illness that would eventually kill her, it is impossible to say. George is convinced that it was, and it has to be said that he has forever afterwards been consumed with guilt at her death and wonders whether the pressure of life in No. 5 in any way contributed. That is natural and wholly understandable, given the circumstances, but before we move onto that sad stage in his life, let us remember the happy times. For happy times they were, for them, and for the countless boys who passed through their hands at No. 5. 'I believe that George, with K's help, knew how to create a sense of well-being around the House,' wrote James Stredder, 'I felt that all you had to do to be accepted by George was to be yourself, though somehow he made you feel it was quite possible, likely even, that you would be much better than that. Such was his gentle nature. And such was the nature of the example he set.' And Tim Forrester: 'No. 5 was the happiest time of my life. I consider myself terribly lucky to have spent five key years of my life under his guidance. I think he was a truly great schoolmaster.' Quentin Hayes: 'No. 5, with K and George, was a very happy place to be.' And Peter Smith, who knew them both as house parents and family friends: 'I owe an important part of my education to their masterful acts… George's wit and extraordinary equanimity made life as a boarder in No. 5 run like the purring of the Bentley.'

13
CHESTERTON TALES
Miss Prior and sundry other comic characters

George Chesterton is a consummate storyteller. One friend of his once told me that, as a storyteller, George was fit to rank with his namesake, the great G. K. Chesterton, 'not that they're related of course.' As it happens, they are from the same family. 'GK was my father's first cousin,' confirms George, 'He and Dee got on very well and he was an occasional visitor to our house.' Needless to say, this piece of information went hand in hand with a story or two. GK was a large man, some 6 feet 4 inches in height with a considerable girth. He was persuaded on one occasion by Dee to give away the prizes and make the keynote speech at Founders' Day at Lawnside School in Malvern, now no longer in existence, where George's sister was a pupil. GK magnanimously agreed. It goes without saying that he had a reputation as a very fine speaker. Welcomed by the headmistress, he was asked if he minded planting a rose bush in the school grounds, as tradition dictated. He genially assented to this too. 'By the way,' he was asked, 'what is the subject of your speech?' He replied that he was going to speak on the joy of youth, which he thought would be appropriate. The headmistress was horrified. She believed that such a topic would be *wholly* inappropriate for her gals and she couldn't possibly countenance such unorthodoxy in her school. Unperturbed, he said, 'Right. Then I shall talk on the League of Nations.' No doubt it was a learned discourse but what the girls thought of it is not recorded. And he refused to plant the rose bush. Dee had to step in with the spade instead. On another occasion, he stayed at the vicarage with his wife on the way to lecture somewhere, George forgets where. His wife remained at home with George's parents while GK caught the train to Birmingham. When he arrived at New Street

Station, he rang up the vicarage and asked his wife, 'Where and at what time am I expected to be?' Apparently this was not an uncommon occurrence. When he visited for the last time not long before he died in 1936, George, as 'a little boy' (he was 14!), was instructed by Dee to keep out of the way because 'uncle was very tired'. Later, of course, George discovered that, on account of his worsening medical condition, he had been put off the booze and 'was very grumpy'. So, GH and GK are cut from the same cloth – not I hasten to add on account of any grumpiness – but because they both can spin a yarn.

Sit around any dinner table, prop up any bar, sip cocktails at any party and if there is a housemaster in your midst, almost certainly he will soon take centre stage and entertain everyone with tales of teenage boys. Living cheek by jowl with sixty of them for ten years (fifteen in George's day) can be many things … but it is never dull. The experience may sabotage your sleeping patterns, take a toll on your emotions, ruin your health, wreck your marriage, or drive you insane but it will provide an inexhaustible supply of humorous anecdotes until the day you die. George is still recounting his – some of the stories I have heard, some have entered Malvern folklore, some are new to me but they are all told with the born raconteur's sense of timing, with the wide grin splitting the face and the famous low Chesterton chuckle accompanying the punch line or denouement.

Remember the words of George's boyhood friend, Francis Prichard, describing the scene as he entered the vicarage for the first time all those years ago and seeing Dee on the top landing attempting to pour some syrup onto a tray on the hall floor. Skip forward a generation and it seems that the atmosphere in No. 5 was very similar. James Stredder writes, 'I remember a great deal of laughter.' David Bailey: 'The laughter that George produced was all spur of the moment stuff.' Tim Forrester: 'I remember George roaring with laughter at our failed attempts at conquest at a school dance. He had such a wonderful sense of humour.' Peter Smith: 'His speeches at House Suppers were eagerly anticipated and he always came up trumps. Using a clever formula of nicknames linked to the term's events, he would make us all roar with laughter and surprise us at how well he knew our foibles.' Well, it is scarcely necessary to draw your attention to the common theme here. No doubt many fine things were achieved in No. 5 – after all, George was fond of referring to the rows of cups adorning the trophy cabinet as 'the family silver' – but clearly much fun was had along the way.

He tackled me not long into the process of writing this book, asking whether I was going to give Miss Prior a chapter of her own. Ah yes, the redoubtable Miss

Prior. While she has not been given a whole chapter, she does loom large in this one. And I use the term 'large' advisedly. She was, not to put too fine a point on it, an enormous woman. Miss Prior was the matron in No. 5 throughout the time that George and K were there and she seems to have been a figure fit to rank with all the great comic female characters in literature, from Chaucer's Wife of Bath to the nurse in Shakespeare's *Romeo and Juliet* to Austen's Mrs Bennet in *Pride and Prejudice*. Even now, some forty years on, George cannot help himself giggling whenever her name crops up. Not the least of her strange personal traits was that she was incorrigibly untidy and everything about her was chaotic. Somehow you expect matrons to be spruce and organised, a beacon of efficiency in the cluttered world of a boarding house. Not Miss Prior – she was a shambles. When George and K moved into No. 5, she took it upon herself to escort them around the premises. The priority was to find the most suitable rooms for the two children, Posy and Colin. George pushed open a door. 'Clearly this is a junk room,' he announced, 'Colin can have this.' He felt Miss Prior stiffen, but she said nothing. To his chagrin, George later discovered that the 'junk room' was none other than her bedroom.

A day or two later, she knocked on the study door. 'Housemaster,' she announced, 'I never stay anywhere for more than three years. Well, my three years are up and I want you to know that I am giving you my notice.' 'And she stayed for the full fifteen years!' roared George, with a mixture of mirth and amazement. In some ways, he wished that she had gone early for, to be truthful, she wasn't much use as a matron, though she did have one or two saving graces. But she remained loyally at her post and unwittingly provided George with a fund of amusing dinner stories.

It wasn't long after George and K arrived at No. 5 that they began to smell a rat with regard to the laundry arrangements. The monthly accounts were published by the bursar with a breakdown of each House's expenditure on domestic matters itemised and it was immediately clear to even someone with no accounting skills whatsoever that in the column for laundry, No. 5 was remarkably low. Down at the bottom, in fact. Almost falling off the page, it seemed. A little bit of digging threw up the unwelcome fact that the boys' bed sheets were only changed once a month. This was clearly a dreadful state of affairs and K at once insisted that they be changed more frequently. She also discovered that Miss Prior had been taking the shirts to be ironed by a woman in town who charged peanuts, so she was able to make a tidy little sum on the side. This too K stopped. Miss

Prior was not best pleased but she accepted the changes without demur. 'She was very loyal,' George admitted, 'and she never gossiped. Whatever happened in our House and in our family, she never passed on any of the tittle-tattle. But she was pretty useless!'

Whether she was just lazy or whether her enormous girth did make just getting around the place a struggle, George never really knew. But he remembers that she used to slide along the linoleum in the dormitories between the cubicles on her huge bottom, dragging a laundry basket with her, chucking the clean sheets onto the beds for the boys to change. The dirty ones she did not collect herself. That was too tiring. The boys were expected to bring them to her. They were mainly indifferent about her, it has to be said. One or two quite liked her but her lack of personal warmth meant that she had very little social contact with them. It was K who provided the feminine touch around the place. Somehow, femininity and Miss Prior did not sit together well.

Because of her size, any expedition up town was a major undertaking for her. Malvern is situated on the side of a hill and some of the streets are quite steep. Church Street, where the shops are, was a huge stumbling block to her progress. She could only negotiate the journey uphill if she walked backwards. *Don't be so ridiculous, George. You're pulling my leg.* 'No,' he cried, the tears rolling down his cheeks, 'It's true. She was so large, that was the only way she could manage it.' And if I still doubted the authenticity of the story, Pat Hooley confirmed it. He too was laughing as he remembered it. On one occasion, she had finally made it to the top of Church Street and paused to get her breath back, as if she had just conquered Everest. A kindly, junior member of the Common Room spotted her and recognised her. Because she was still facing downhill, he assumed that she was on her way back to school. He gave her a lift back down to No. 5 and she was too embarrassed to put him right. As she painfully eased her way out of the car, she had no option but to resume her trek up town again. Backwards.

In 1965, the centenary year of the college, Posy was getting married. What better place to hold the reception than in No. 5? True, it was in October, during term time, and the row of roses in the garden, K's pride and joy, had gone over. This minor inconvenience was resolved by K buying fresh roses and artfully entwining them onto the stems of the bare bushes. With the marquee erected, the whole scene was utterly charming. The prefects had been invited, as had Miss Prior, and were making small talk with the guests. The Champagne was flowing and everybody was in a good mood. What could possibly go wrong? Well, put adolescent boys anywhere near alcohol and the outcome is usually predictable. Accounts vary as to who was mostly to blame. George blames his tutors for not keeping a weather eye on how regularly the boys' glasses were being topped up. Alan Carter, George's faithful sidekick, blames Miss Prior. The boys just helped themselves. Two of them were violently ill and had to be carried physically from the fray. Miss Prior ordered that they be put in the sick room, aptly named, it transpired. And then she began to worry. Panic even. Not having had children of her own, drunken teenagers were completely outside her range of experience. They were unconscious. Perhaps they were dying. Hastily, she consulted all the textbooks in her possession, such as *The Book of Home Nursing* and *Medicine Made Easy* and *A Guide to Family Health*. Desperately she scanned the chapters on 'Alcoholics' and 'Drunkenness' but could find no suitable advice. The two boys' state had not seemingly improved the next morning. In some alarm, she approached George who was having his breakfast. She explained that the boys were still unconscious, they had 'very shallow pulses' and she feared for their lives. Colin's godmother and a very good friend of K's was staying with the family and was present at the breakfast table while Miss Prior unburdened herself of her fears. 'Angela was a doctor, as it happened,' recounted George, 'and she gave Miss Prior some very simple advice. She told her to get a jug of cold water, pour it over the boys and send them to class.' Miss Prior always did as she was told, whatever her private misgivings; the water cure was administered and worked a treat and the boys were none the worse for it. 'Poor dear,' said George kindly, 'She was so naïve.'

The story has a postscript. Stories usually do with George. One of the miscreants went into the army and had a very successful career. (It is extraordinary how often this happens.) One day, many years later, George was reading the paper and noticed an article reporting on this man's retirement from active service, with the rank of major general. George, as is his wont, wrote a letter to him, congratulating him on his career and retirement. 'I had a very nice letter back,' he reported, 'He told me that the rank he attained was not major general but lieutenant general, one step up. And also he had just been knighted.' The letter went on to tell George that his former pupil had rummaged around in his personal files and found George's final report on him at school. 'And do you know what I had written?' reported George, chortling, 'This boy betrays few signs of leadership qualities!' The laughter at his own expense was long and loud.

Once, a good-looking woman came to the front door of No. 5 to complain that a boy had just flashed at her from one of the windows. George was appalled and felt that he had no option but to contact the police. The initial stratagem of detection was to get the lady to cast her eyes over the boys as they came past the dining room hatch at supper. She seemed unwilling, which was perhaps understandable, so the next idea was to present her with a House photo, to see if she could identify anyone. Immediately she picked out a boy but George was unconvinced. Her finger was jabbing at the most unlikely flasher in the history of exhibitionism. But she was insistent and three times she identified him so some sort of process clearly had to be set in train. At that moment, the phone went. George answered it and for the next ten minutes he was distracted by a conversation with a parent. When he returned, he was horrified to discover that the suspect had been hauled in and charged with the offence by a policeman. As a minor, the boy should of course have had his housemaster, in *loco parentis*, in attendance, at the very least. George was sure that this boy was not guilty and what's more, he had a shrewd idea who was. In the meantime, the policeman's prime suspect had rung home and spoken, in some distress, to his father. He was, as it happened, a chief constable. At which point, Detective Inspector Chesterton swung immediately into action. As a housemaster, you soon learn all the tricks of the interviewing technique and it was not long before the real culprit's resistance had been broken and he confessed. The upshot of the episode was that the police agreed not to charge the offender provided he underwent a course of treatment with a psychiatrist. The therapy apparently worked. The boy grew out of his exhibitionist tendencies and went on to lead a blameless life. The chief constable, however, was not best pleased at the treatment his wholly innocent son had been subjected to and took a lot of placating. Wryly, George pondered on the fate of the young constable. He reckoned that his decision that day to charge the chief constable's son had not been a particularly shrewd career move. And Miss Prior's contribution to the whole episode? When the name of the real culprit had been established, she entered the sitting room where all the adults involved were gathered and announced gravely, 'The offending article has been identified. And it is nothing to write home about.'

During Wimbledon fortnight, she became transfixed by the tennis. She had an old, tiny, black and white television and she would sit in front of it for hours. In order to create a more realistic atmosphere, she would place the TV set on a small table draped with a green baize cloth, the better to imagine the green grass of SW19.

One day, she appeared at the door of George's study. She had a strange habit, when she was agitated, of lapsing into a kind of pidgin French, though there was no hint, as far as George knew, of any French ancestry in her family. 'Monsieur Housemaster, Monsieur Housemaster,' she wailed, and George knew he was in trouble, 'Monsieur Housemaster, I will not have it! I will not have it!' What 'it' was and why she would not have it took some patient unravelling. The school medical officer, Dr Payler, had bought a plot of land opposite No. 1 and a stone's throw from the front gate of No. 5. He intended to build a house there and had been granted planning permission. So far, so good. It seemed an eminently sensible idea for everybody concerned to have the school doctor almost on site as it were. He had started casting around in his mind, helped by family and friends, for a suitable name for his new house. It was situated right at the bottom of Priory Road, which led directly from Malvern Priory. The road is as old as the priory and probably dates back to mediaeval times. Eventually, the good doctor hit upon the name 'Priors Bottom'. To him, it came across as totally appropriate, being geographically accurate and historically apt. To Miss Prior however, when she got wind of the proposal, it felt all too apposite; she was beside herself with distress at the perceived slight. 'I will not have it!' she persisted. Though quietly amused by the whole thing, George had to admit that she had a point so he assured her he would do what he could. He went to see Dr Payler to discuss it and was relieved to hear that a change of heart was already in the offing. No one liked the name 'Priors Bottom' and further thought was going to be given to the matter. The new house was later named – and remains so to this day – 'Priors End'.

The boys were not terribly fond of her, George acknowledged, a fact borne out by several old boys to whom I have spoken. K got on with her ('perhaps a case of the devil you know', said George) and she was utterly loyal to the pair of them during their fifteen years working together. However, one employee who lasted but a fraction of that time, much to the boys' disappointment, was their cook. This had absolutely nothing to do with her culinary skills; in fact neither George nor anyone else could fault her professionalism, her punctuality or her puddings. The trouble was that she was a stunner. David Bailey wrote, 'Of particular success under the new Chesterton regime was the introduction of a very pretty young cook. Volunteers for help in the house kitchen got completely out of hand and space in the ground-floor TV room was hard to find when she was off duty.' 'Ah, Gail,' said George wistfully, 'You might find this hard to believe. She was a discus thrower – a very good one apparently. She had the most fabulous figure and she used to put on her games kit – which didn't amount to very much – and go outside onto the grass to practise. The effect on the boys can be imagined.' And not only the boys, it seemed. One after another, young masters would take her out and she wouldn't get back to No. 5 until well into the early hours. 'But she was never late on parade the next morning,' he said admiringly, 'and she was always looking spruce and presentable, whatever she had been up to the night before.' As you might expect, K disapproved of her and wanted to get rid of her, not because she was jealous or anything but, with a woman's awareness and intuition, she could see that Gail was becoming a distraction in the House. George felt that he was between a rock and a hard place. He could understand his wife's disquiet but he had no grounds to dismiss her. What can I do, he fretted, sack her because she's too good looking? In the event, circumstances came to his aid. One evening he was doing his round of the dormitories. All seemed quiet and unremarkable. But then a housemaster's sixth sense made him double check on the still and recumbent form of one boy. Sure enough, his suspicions were confirmed. The figure in the bed was artfully formed by pillows – the boy was missing. Hmm, thought George, I wonder… He crept up towards Gail's quarters, even removing his shoes the better to deaden his footfalls, he later shamefacedly admitted. The bedroom door was open and the bed, he was relieved to note, was unoccupied. But the TV was on in the sitting room. George took a deep breath and walked in. 'Yes, Mr Chesterton, what can I do for you?' said Gail, as coolly as you like. George gambled: 'Gail, I know he's here. Come out, young man!' And out crept the boy from behind the sofa. Of course, she had to go. But not for three days. She went down the next morning with a temperature of 103 and K had to nurse her. 'Strange,' mused George later, 'The boy in question was rather nondescript, the least likely Romeo I could think of.' And by all accounts, interest in discus throwing among the boys immediately tailed off.

The luscious Gail may have gone but boys are, on the whole, a resourceful bunch and further ways of admiring the fairer sex could be devised. Peter Smith recalls one particularly cunning ruse to extend their limited opportunity for contact. 'One of our study windows faced due west, with a clear view of one of Malvern Girls' College's boarding houses. Roger Hargreaves, one of the occupants of this study, spotted a business opportunity. Having smuggled an enormous, brass, Navy surplus telescope into school, he trained it on the boarding house and began charging people for a "look". I remember a long queue leading down the corridor to his door. As he was not a prefect, it quickly became obvious that this was not a queue of boys for fagging. GHC acted swiftly. I don't know what happened to the telescope.'

The odd boy, it has to be assumed, got within more than telescope distance of girls at MGC as it was just down the road. One boy certainly did, though he was not from No. 5, George assures me. One day, he was contacted on the phone by the formidable Miss Owen, the headmistress at Malvern Girls' College. 'Your boy Dodd was in one of our dormitories at 2.00am this morning,' she announced uncompromisingly. George gulped. That was indeed a serious scenario, one step higher than being caught in the cook's apartment on home territory. But yet again his knowledge of his own boys led him to be sceptical of the intruder's identity. Dodd was just not the type. He plucked up the courage to demur with Miss Owen, but she was not for turning. Dodd it was and Dodd it would remain. And what was his housemaster going to do about it? It seemed that nothing much less than a public whipping for the interloper would placate her. Perhaps, George pluckily suggested, she had mistaken him for Dodds in No. 3? For the first time, a crack appeared in the indomitable lady's façade and slowly she backed off, conceding that that was possible… In fact, George was right. The boy was from No. 3 and no doubt his housemaster came in for a fair bit of flak from his colleague in No. 5 when their paths next crossed in the Common Room.

On a similar topic, George received yet another phone call, one of those unmistakeable, insistent ringing tones which herald trouble. Sure enough, it was the school doctor on the line. Would George come across to the surgery; the matter was too delicate to discuss on the phone. 'Delicate?' George told me, 'I should say so!' He was ushered inside and quietly informed that one of his boys had just been diagnosed with a sexually transmitted disease, or VD, as we used to call it. On this occasion, there was no possibility of mistaken identity, no chance of fobbing off the problem on to No. 3. What to do? It is on occasions like this that George's coolness under fire quickly rises to the surface. The poor boy obviously needed treatment and that could not be done at school. Could his enforced absence, up to six weeks, be laid at the door of some other ailment? This could only be engineered if total secrecy were preserved. Did any of the boys know? As it happened, the boy had confided in his study mate. It all hinged on this friend's total discretion. In the end, the secret never did get out. The boy returned to school after a period of convalescence from 'smallpox' and none of the pupil body, save one, was any the wiser. I loved the delicious irony of the utilisation of smallpox as a red herring for another kind of pox. Always best to keep your little white lies as close as possible to the truth. The infection, by the way, was contracted in Paris. Not on a school trip, you will be pleased to hear.

There are different, though no less startling, ways of leaving your mark on College life. It was around the time of decimalisation in 1971. Martin Rogers was the new headmaster and in a housemasters' meeting, he delivered the shocking news that wholesale forgery was rife in the school. Well, in the tuck shop anyway. The chocolate bar machine had been converted to accept the new 10p coin, and it had emerged that the machine was being milked with counterfeit coins. Rogers thundered on about 'gross dishonesty' and instructed his lieutenants to investigate the felony robustly. On his walk back to No. 5, George allowed himself the smug but misguided sentiment that he was glad that no such villain ever drew breath in his House. By chance, he made a detour via the new workshop that he had fitted out in the old coke store, a room that had become redundant when oil central heating was installed. He had wanted to encourage handiwork skills, in the same way that he had tried to champion artistic endeavour. He came across a single figure hunched over a Bunsen burner, a pile of the new 2p coins at his elbow on the bench. The significance of the scene did not take long to sink in. What the boy was doing was soldering on a tiny amount of copper to make the coins the same size as a 10p coin. The boy was David Pegley. George knew the family well. Pegley's father, John, was 'the best straight driver of a cricket ball I've ever seen.' Martin Rogers, understandably, was furious and wanted to give Pegley his marching orders forthwith. But not for the first time, George made a convincing case for clemency. The boy was not a bad 'un, and, to be fair, his misdemeanour, though reprehensible, had shown a certain amount of ... shall we say *enterprise*. Rogers, an essentially charitable man, allowed himself to be persuaded. George got on the phone to Pegley senior, who had by now forsaken his superb straight driving for the rather less straight dealings of the Turf. There was a big race meeting on at the time and Mr Pegley was unwilling to forego a profitable day in the bookie's office. George tried to impress upon him the seriousness of his son's offence and the gravity of the punishment – not expulsion, he'd be relieved to hear, but rustication, ignominious enough. Mr Pegley reluctantly came to take his son away for his enforced furlough but George doubted that much in the way of disapproval was voiced in the Pegley household.

And what of David Pegley? Did he return to school and sink into unremarkable anonymity? Hardly. A year later, he made such an indelible mark on the folklore of Malvern College that old masters still talk about him with a mixture of awe and laughter. The story is known simply as The Great Potato Saga. George was in bed with a temperature when he was visited by a colleague. Far from enquiring after George's health, he informed him that one of his boys had been making illegal use of the school printing press, apparently for the purpose of advertising door-to-door selling of potatoes. The boy was David Pegley. Now, a housemaster learns to be prepared for most surprises but this was a new one on George. Rising heroically from his sickbed, he collared Pegley, who immediately owned up. George gave him the usual housemaster's flea in the ear and gated him for the rest of term. And then returned to bed.

One hour later, a senior housemaster happened upon the said Pegley in a room in the Pavilion Block, almost hidden by mounds of King Edward potatoes, busily weighing and bagging them. 'Oh, hello David,' said the housemaster, renowned for his trusting nature and gentle demeanour, 'What on earth are you doing?' The reply was commendably instantaneous. 'Geography project, Sir.' 'How very interesting,' commented the housemaster, and went serenely on his way.

The following afternoon, Pegley was nowhere to be found, and George suspected that he had disregarded his gating punishment and broken bounds. In the meantime, his head of House had informed him that he had evidence that Pegley had a car, which was against school rules, and that he was using it to deliver potatoes, together with a friend, to customers in Worcester. It went without saying that the boys had to be caught red-handed and the most obvious time to nab them would be when they returned to the car park in Malvern just before suppertime. But George was *hors de combat*, still in bed. It was left to K to accompany another housemaster to the stake-out in the dark and deserted car park and she only agreed to go because she had to pick up a prescription for the stricken George from the chemist. Sure enough, a car pulled up at the expected time and out leapt two boys. But not Pegley. Nor was it Pegley's car. Undeterred, the housemaster chanced his arm and challenged them. Somewhat taken aback by the ambush, the boys admitted that yes, indeed they had been selling potatoes in Worcester; but confused as to how the housemaster had known.

That evening, several interrogations by the relevant housemasters took place simultaneously in different locations. Yet again, George rose from his sickbed in order to confront Pegley. The exchange went something like this:

George: You don't deny that you have been carrying on an illicit potato business?

Pegley (indignant): Not illicit, Sir. My customers had good value for money.

George: And you were selling them in Worcester today?

Pegley (piously): Oh no, Sir. I am gated.

George: I know you were there, David.

Pegley (virtuously): Well, I had to go, Sir, with some assistants to show them around myself. I can't let my customers down while I am gated.

George: Hum. You will be rusticated and you will drive that car of yours home. Make sure you are out of Malvern by 9.00am tomorrow.

Pegley (politely as always): Thank you, Sir.

'And do you know what?' said George with tears of laughter rolling down his cheeks, 'There was a thick blanket of snow the next morning and he never did go home!' After leaving school, David Pegley made a great success of contracting out heavy farming machinery. 'He is an absolute dear,' were the final words George had to say on the business, 'but a rogue!'

Another business, of an altogether less agreeable nature, was brought to his attention by a slightly embarrassed head of House. 'You'd better come and see, Sir,' he told George. There, in the passage, was a pile of recently deposited human faeces, with – comically, providing you weren't the poor unfortunate who had to clear it up – a plastic flag planted upon the summit. For the next few days, piles were discovered in different places in the House, each with a different flag raised in its honour. 'They were those flags you put in sandcastles on the beach,' said George, 'One day it would be the Union Jack, the next day the Saltire of Scotland, the Welsh Dragon, the Stars and Stripes...' Soon the joke began to wear thin. The hunt for the PC (the Phantom Crapper, as he was labelled) was really on. Then the PC altered his tactics and struck in the Music School, which helped to narrow down the field of suspects. George and K hid themselves in one of the classrooms over there and lay in wait. But their vigil was in vain. Their prey eluded them. Eventually, the headmaster, Donald Lindsay, suggested that George approach a child psychologist for advice. The expert was inclined to laugh it off. He reassured everyone that it was the sort of adolescent behaviour that wasn't sinister or pernicious, it wasn't uncommon and it would soon cease. He was right. It did stop. And the culprit was never uncovered. 'But I had a shrewd idea who it was,' George indicated to me, with a little grim nod of the head.

During the war, when the school had been requisitioned by the Ministry of Works, No. 5 was used to billet numbers of the Free French cadets. One night General de Gaulle was a guest and it is said that he danced the night away. When the buildings were handed back to the school at the completion of hostilities, the connection with the Free French and No. 5 was continued, and still is today. Quentin Hayes recollects one such visit by the French: 'In 1972, before the cubicles were demolished to make way for study bedrooms, No. 5 played host to some of the Free French who had been there in the war years. One of them, on being shown around the cubicles, asked for a leg-up into the roof. He reappeared with a tin from which he proudly produced a packet of Gauloises cigarettes he had hidden there thirty years earlier!'

Although it wasn't quite in the same category of irregular activity as David Pegley's potato merchandising, Hayes remembers a spoof film they made in No. 5, what he called 'our own surreal cinematic take on school life.' 'This included an edition of Colditz (No. 5), minor sporting feats such as caber tossing on the Junior (tartan rugs and CCF berets made ideal costume) and driving golf balls off the Worcestershire Beacon which then supposedly knocked people out down below in Barnards Green.' He also had a hand in releasing the hand brake from the car of one of the masters during lunch and shifting it a couple of hundred yards down the road. 'His bemusement and subsequent horror were recorded on the House film.' Hayes's report of George's reaction to their Monty Python-esque home movie is interesting and tells its own story. 'Rather than seeing it as subversive, GHC seemed quite proud when the finished product was shown at Christmas Supper.' In fact, he goes on to say, 'Although No. 5 was a house of sporting excellence, as you would expect, GHC benignly facilitated some great artistic and musical happenings… For those who were no good at football, there was the infamous motley collection of Middle Leagues. No. 5 very proudly won the Middle League Cup and had a celebratory photo taken with a miniscule cup that was about 3 inches tall. The rest of the school thought we were bonkers to take it seriously but I think GHC was quietly amused. Maybe even proud.'

Quentin Hayes does not however count House prayers as one of the 'great artistic and musical happenings' in No. 5. George winces at the memory: 'The trouble was that, for a short period, we had no one who could play the piano,' he explains, 'The hymn singing was excruciating.' In fact the whole House could only manage one discordant hymn. Everyone knew what he meant when he announced, 'Let us now turn to Hymn No. 5.' It's funny how boys can sing lustily in a football coach but come over all demure and timorous in a building.

Occasionally George himself took centre stage in the high jinks. Though, to be fair to him, this episode, which Alan Carter described with such relish, occurred out of town. On the other side of the country in fact. The two of them were invited to a Cambridge college, where there was a dinner for Old Malvernians. Carter cannot remember the name of the college nor the date but they thoroughly enjoyed the hospitality at dinner in hall. The port flowed after dinner as easily as the conversation. To their consternation, when they eventually took the trouble to look at their watches it was past midnight and the college doors were locked. They were blithely assured by their hosts that they would be 'easily able' to climb out. It had been successfully accomplished many times before. Not entirely serene about this state of affairs, the two of them allowed themselves to be escorted onto the roof. It was a dark, murky night in November, the street lights swirling in a thick, malevolent mist such as you can only get in the Fens. They had to clamber over the rooftop, a little the worse for wear, scared witless that each step would be their last. The final obstacle was the wall. 'If you climb over and hang on by your fingernails,' they had been told, 'you will find that the drop will only be a foot or so. You'll be fine!' George went first. He hung on grimly. The drop zone was pitch black and he felt he was suspended over a cliff. He took a deep breath and let go. But his advisors had failed to notice that George was a big man. The drop was at most a couple of inches.

One richly colourful character in the bulging *dramatis personae* of this story has hitherto kept largely in the wings. Step forward the Shoulder. You would expect a quick bowler to have trouble with his shoulder, especially later on in life, but the troubles that George has had with his do not stem from countless spells of bowling into the wind but from football. Specifically, keeping goal. George was a far better goalkeeper than the nine goals conceded against Spurs hint at. Several of his former colleagues and adversaries have scoffed at George's own modest assessment of his skills. So he was always going to be a shoo-in between the sticks whenever the Common Room football team was announced. You always wanted your best players in their best positions when it came to the Match of the Season, the hotly contested derby against Shrewsbury Common Room. At the time, both teams boasted an England amateur international, Denis Saunders for Malvern, and Robin Trimby for Shrewsbury, as well as a number of talented footballers, so the standard was pretty high. What was never in doubt was the intensity of the rivalry. The matches were no strolls in the park, no gentle kickabouts on the common.

So you can imagine the tension in the air and the pressure on the Malvern goalkeeper as he stood tall in his goal, his eyes narrowed in concentration as he observed the Shrewsbury master lining up to take the last-minute penalty that would win the game for his side. George doesn't do icy stares. Not very well, anyway. His displeasure conveys itself in more subtle ways. No less effective for all that, but at that moment, he was probably deciding which way to dive rather than engaging in any psychological eye contact with his adversary. He might even have permitted himself a quiet little chuckle; he relished these sporting confrontations.

In any event, he guessed right and made a fine, sprawling save. At the same time, he felt a searing pain in his right shoulder and a glance down at the limp, useless arm confirmed his worst fears – it was dislocated. Roger Gillard, a former colleague of his, takes up the story: 'As he lay prone in the Shrewsbury mud, unable to move having dislocated his shoulder, he was surrounded by his adoring team-mates, one of whom was heard to remark, "Never mind, George, it was worth it!" George's reply was unprintable!' 'Well, I don't know about that,' demurs George, 'but I do remember shouting out "Don't touch me!" And I remember their bursar driving his car onto the pitch to take me to hospital.' Gillard again: 'The tradition was that we would meet up in the pub afterwards for a meal. Suddenly there appeared the hero of the hour, his arm in a sling.' Nothing daunted, the Bert Trautmann of the Malvern Masters joined in the game of darts and played left-handed. 'A nice radiographer put it back,' he explained, accepting a pint. They were late back home. George's 'adoring team-mates', having liberally supplied him with liquid painkiller, were fully aware that K would be unimpressed with his heroics and even less impressed with the lateness of the hour, so they made a lot of noise outside No. 5 as they helped the stricken goalkeeper out of the car, loudly congratulating him on his gallantry and praising his spirit and bravery. It made not a jot of difference. She was cross at his foolhardiness: football was a young man's game.

Martin Knott, another colleague, drove him down next morning at 8.00am to pick up Colin from Harrow at the end of term. For the return journey, George insisted on driving himself. He jammed the car into gear and effectively drove one-handed. 'It wasn't that he disapproved of my driving skills, I think,' explained Knott, 'but George is a stubborn fellow. He wasn't going to let a minor problem such as a dislocated shoulder inconvenience him any more than it had to.' Nonetheless, the 'inconvenient' shoulder was to trouble him for the rest of his life.

The next time he did it, he was playing squash. 'Against a peer of the realm, Lord Anderson, as it happens.' Pat Hooley was there and drove him up town from the squash club in search of a doctor. One was found, who immediately gave the stricken patient a shot in the arm of 'something pretty strong'. The last thing he could remember was his friend Hooley 'floating on the ceiling' before the offending joint was put back into place. Hooley was there again the next time: 'For some reason, George and I arranged to play golf during our holidays in Cornwall. We both must have been staying nearby. Anyway, we arrived at the first tee. George struck his first drive and staggered away clutching his shoulder – which had let him down again. I am afraid that was the end of the contest as he was unable to continue. So I won!'

Darts was to feature in the next episode, a classic of the Chesterton Tales. One perk of his long service in the Air Section of the school CCF was a trip to Malta to spend two nights in the mess at the RAF station. Bruce Burnett was the RAF liaison officer at the time and it was his job to organise the trip, from the flight out from Brize Norton, to the two days and nights of 'conferences' (well, let's not beat about the bush here, he meant two days and nights of partying) to the flight back home. Burnett remembers the trip vividly. 'It was a sort of reward for the work done for the RAF in schools by these schoolmasters. We tried to look after them well.' 'We were treated very well,' agrees George, 'I parked the Bentley in the car park at Brize Norton, introduced myself to the other officers, clambered aboard and settled down for a pleasant couple of days.' At dinner, on the second night, the wine flowed even more copiously than on the first. George admits that he 'had a few'. A game of darts was suggested. George is as incapable of a friendly game of anything as much as his father was incapable of paying a bill. It got a little serious. He needed a double top of some number or other to win the game but missed the board completely with his first throw. He put a little more power into his second dart and then staggered away with the old shoulder *hors de combat*. He explained through gritted teeth that it was very painful and he would need anaesthetic for it to be put back. An ambulance was called and he was taken to the Naval hospital on the island.

The matron was a dragon. Most are, perhaps especially in Naval hospitals. Even Nelson didn't have the highest regard for the behaviour of his sailors. This matron certainly didn't. She reminded him of that crone at his prep school, Wells House. Immediately, she detected alcohol on George's breath ('She could hardly have missed it!') and what little sympathy she harboured in her stony heart disappeared out of the window and over the Mediterranean Sea. He was unceremoniously bundled into a ward full of old salts, despite his protestations that he was an officer and could he, *please*, be seen to as swiftly as possible because he had a flight to catch the next morning. But his entreaties fell on deaf ears and that was that for the night. His shoulder was put back the next morning by the duty surgeon. Expecting to be discharged, George was confounded when he was wheeled back to the ward. It was now ten in the morning. The flight back to England was scheduled to leave at eleven. He was in a hospital on the other side of the island, in a surgical gown, and his clothes had disappeared. 'I was a little strapped for time,' he reflected, with masterly understatement. The amused sailors in the ward told him where the ghastly matron had hidden his clothes so, gratefully, he got dressed and made the dash for the air base. He arrived just as the aircraft was taking off. Disconsolately, he shambled into the mess. The first person he saw was Bruce Burnett. 'Oh, my God, George!' he said, 'You're meant to be on that flight!' George was careful not to shrug his shoulders but could think of nothing to say that could alter that undeniable fact. 'I shall never forget that look on Bruce's face,' said George, 'He had obviously waved me off and the bedraggled figure standing in front of him must have been his worst nightmare.' 'How could George possibly be anyone's nightmare?' protested Burnett chivalrously 'But it was a bit of a shock.'

Somehow – he still shakes his head at the improbability of it all – George managed to wangle a lift home on another flight. But only to Southampton. And the Bentley was at back at Brize Norton. It was now well advanced in the day and unsurprisingly K was getting anxious at his non-appearance back in Malvern. Eventually, she asked her friend, Eileen Saunders, to ring up the aerodrome. Oh yes, he was definitely on the flight, she was assured, his name was on the manifest. So where is he, she persisted, adding pointedly that Mr Chesterton had been in the 'real RAF, young man.' The duty officer was unabashed but helpful nonetheless and told her he would attempt to find the missing hero. Eventually, the Bentley was located in the car park (you could hardly miss it) so he hadn't had an accident driving home, which she feared and which would not have been unheard of. When he was eventually able to ring her to assure her he was safe and well, darkness was well advanced and her relief can only be imagined. 'All right, I was a bloody fool,' George admitted, 'but it was hardly the RAF's second finest hour. There must have been an almighty hoo-ha when the inevitable questions were asked.' *Did no one notice that you weren't on the plane when they took off?* 'No. They must all have had the most terrible hangovers!' And then the familiar low rumble expanded onto a full-throated laugh.

The Cryptics Cricket Club were embarking on a tour of Kenya in 1984 and, as their president, George felt duty bound to accompany them. He also packed his cricket boots. He was 62 at the time but still felt that he had an over or two left in him. They were playing at the beautiful Nairobi Club and George was bowling. Of course he was bowling. What else would you expect him to be doing on a cricket tour – discussing politics with some local worthies over a gin and tonic on the veranda of the clubhouse? The batsman facing him was not a bad player. He had just hit George back over his head for six. No bowler likes being hit back over his head. It is a personal affront and unless you are a master of the wily arts of slow bowling – although George's pace was now much reduced at this stage in his career, he still had the instincts of a fast bowler – such an indignity demands an immediate response. He strode back a few more paces than normal and let slip a delivery appreciably quicker. The batsman, little daunted, tried to do the same again. He middled it and it flew 5 yards wide of George. At a catchable height. Or so it seemed to George who launched himself sideways, arm outstretched. As he hit the unforgiving baked turf of Kenya, the familiar shuddering pain immediately suggested to him that perhaps a diving caught and bowled was not such a good idea after all. Of course he had to go straight to hospital. A German doctor attended to him, assuring him that he could fix the shoulder but first he needed to find an anaesthetist. That was easier said than done. The first one, a Swedish woman, refused point blank to administer any anaesthetic because the patient had not starved himself for the requisite period of time (George had tucked into a very pleasant tea in the interval between the innings). 'Neffer mind,' announced the resourceful doctor, 'We shall find someone else.' And he did. The anaesthetic was given and the shoulder replaced in its joint. 'That was, incidentally,' said George sadly, 'the last game I ever played.' Regretfully, and not a little unwillingly, he was forced to join the gin and tonic brigade on the veranda for the rest of the tour, and the rest of his cricketing life. And as cricket *is* his life, that means until he draws his last breath.

Some characters never seem to know when it is time to shuffle off-stage, their business finished. George knew that his playing days had come to an end but the Shoulder continued to make unwelcome appearances. I remember seeing George at a social function, his arm in a sling. 'Yes, I know,' he sighed, 'You're going to ask me how I did it this time. I might as well tell you and get it out of the way. I did it in bed!' His wife, Vanessa, obviously saw me turn towards her because she immediately disappeared into the throng before I could offer comment. It is a never-ending saga. That was why I was so concerned when he turned his arm over for the cameras to bowl to Tom Graveney at the opening of the new nets at Malvern. Thankfully, the Shoulder decided not to spoil the day. But he is still there, lurking in the wings.

14

SECOND MASTER
1973–82

'George Chesterton is a very remarkable man.'
Martin Rogers, Malvern headmaster 1971–82

I
n 1979, when I came for my interview at Malvern, to teach English and run the cricket, it was not at all what I expected. To be truthful, I didn't know what to expect but to be invited to lunch at the delightful cottage of the head of English was a clear surprise. To be introduced to a line of Malvern grandees – and their wives – was positively daunting. Together we sat down to our meal, created and furnished forth with great panache by my future boss, and I tried, whilst carefully minding my table manners, to put names to faces and personalities to names. At the head of the table was the unmistakeable *eminence grise* of the gathering. He had been introduced to me as the second master. Second master? It didn't seem to amount to much. I knew that teachers were called masters and I very much hoped that I would soon join their number. But second master? After all, second lieutenant, second fiddle, second division were all states of existence that you would want to move up from, as rapidly as possible. In fact it sounded, well, second rate. Vice-captain, vice-president, viceroy ... now, they bestowed authority and status, don't you think? As I say, I was a raw interviewee.

Second master, vice principal, deputy head, whatever Malvern chose to call its right-hand man, George Chesterton was seated at the far end of the table from me that lunchtime. My memory was that K was not present. Although I would not have been aware of it, that was not surprising; she was very ill. There was a lull in the proceedings, which had seemed to me up to that point to be mainly concerned with the fortunes of my team, Hampshire, in the County Championship, during which everybody tried to coax Alan Carter's little daughter,

Sarah, to eat her food. She was a Buddha-like figure in her high chair, imperturbable and deaf to all the entreaties and strategies of the grown ups. Slowly, deliberately, she then upturned the contents of her bowl over the top of her head and stared back at us expressionless as the food dripped down her face. At which point, a slow rumble emanated from the far end of the table. It was my first experience of the Chesterton chuckle.

Very soon everybody was laughing. Napkins, cloths, towels were hastily produced, the mess was soon cleared up and the jolly conversation resumed. The Buddha was unmoved, however, and continued to observe us with magnificent detachment throughout the rest of lunch. I had been greatly reassured by that chuckle, however. Of all the members of the interviewing panel, for that is what it was in essence, George Chesterton was the one I couldn't get a handle on. Obviously older, obviously senior, obviously of a different generation altogether, he could have been a slightly serious and remote lord lieutenant of the county at a cricket club dinner. Later, I was to discover that, in company, he wasn't like that at all but his rather distracted air could have been explained by the fact that his wife was desperately ill. Still, if he could laugh at a moment of low comedy at a lunch table, then surely he could look on my long hair without too much exception.

So it seemed, for it was not many months later that he was welcoming me with urbane charm to the inner sanctum of the Common Room. I say 'inner sanctum' but it was several years before I would be able to join the senior men on the carpet in front of the fire and a full term before I realised they were pulling my leg. Even to a new boy like me, it was clear that the role of second master fitted George like a glove. One just couldn't imagine a common room run with such good-humoured authority by anybody else. In fact, he had neither sought nor expected the job. That he was offered it had come as a complete shock to him.

It was 1973, and the headmaster Martin Rogers assured George that no, he was not joking and yes, that was right, he had heard correctly, he did indeed want George to take on the role in succession to Malcolm Staniforth, even though he still had two years left as housemaster of No. 5. 'But what do you want me to do?' blurted out George. Rogers simply told him that he wanted George to support him in the Common Room and to take over the discipline of the school, whilst still remaining in his post as a housemaster.

So that is what he did. 'I felt a bit of a fraud, really. I tried to do what Martin wanted. I made sure that the machinery of discipline, already well-oiled, ran smoothly and of course I was loyal to him and did my best to explain his decisions and initiatives to the rest of the school.' Only once did he jib at his boss's wishes. A pottery teacher had taken to wearing an earring. Questionable nowadays perhaps but positively controversial then. George was deputed to tell the man to remove it, in school at any rate. George wasn't too happy about it; he felt it was the headmaster's job, not his. The pottery teacher exploded in indignation. George put his foot down. He told him that he would not be allowed to attend Commemoration (Speech Day) if it was not removed. The thought did occur to me that this would be an ideal and welcome excuse to get out of Speeches but the pottery teacher's dignity was clearly put out of joint and an ugly scene started to brew. In the end, a sensible compromise was agreed; he could attend if only the stud were visible. 'Other than that,' George mused, '…well, I can't think of much else I did.' Nonsense, of course, so I sought the views of others who gave a fuller picture of his work and his impact.

Martin Knott, a colleague of George's, felt that the appointment was an inspired choice. If Rogers had wanted someone in the Common Room to keep everyone on board when unpopular decisions had to be made, 'then George was the obvious, the only, candidate.' For there were unpopular decisions aplenty to be made. Rogers had the unenviable task of following a charismatic and greatly loved figure as headmaster, Donald Lindsay. Rogers was no fool and recognised this, just as much as he recognised that changes had to be made if the school was not to stagnate. And he was not afraid to make them. Inevitably, he ran into a wall of resistance from some of the senior masters who were perfectly happy with the way things were and couldn't see any reason for change. The stand-off between the old guard and the new boss was a difficult situation, and one as old as the hills. Who better suited than George, thought Knott, to effect suitable rapprochement? For example, he went on to explain, the appointment of housemasters had hitherto been done strictly according to 'Red Book order', that is, by seniority. Not unnaturally, Rogers wanted his own men in these key positions and felt that waiting for dead men's shoes was stultifying and not conducive to the changes he wanted to put into operation. So he broke with tradition and started to appoint housemasters on merit, not on years of service. You can imagine what a storm this was likely to unleash in such a comfortable and deeply conservative institution as Malvern College. 'George was crucial here,' said Knott, 'He was superb at pouring oil on troubled waters, taking the trouble to explain the headmaster's position, at once tactful and sympathetic to the feelings of his colleagues without being disloyal to his boss.' Pat Hooley, a good friend and ally of George's in the Common Room, agreed. 'George was a very good second master. He ran meetings with an assured and light touch. He would let everyone have his say and then bring it all together with the result that he wanted in the first place. And no one's nose was put out of joint.' It was a continual exercise in careful man management. 'He was a natural leader of men,' was Knott's verdict.

Martin Rogers was grateful for his support on more than one occasion, when the heavy flak opened up. 'He proved to be an outstanding second master, extremely effective in guiding the staff through potentially divisive decisions. When he saw difficulties, he would go round talking to those most concerned and, somehow, the problems would evaporate.' And how about this as an example of the legendary Chesterton charm: 'I remember him coming to talk to me,' said Rogers, 'usually about some contentious issue of the day. He would start with the words "I am sure that you will agree, Martin…" and I found that I had agreed with him before I knew what he was going to suggest!' As many of us have discovered, it is simply impossible to say no to the man. To do so, even if he gives you ample and generous opportunity to decline, would simply be a gross dereliction of good form.

Mind you, he could be a wily old devil and resolute about getting his own way, without ever appearing to be ruthless. One of the roles of second master was to take the chair as president of the Common Room whenever meetings were held. He valued the title, saw it as no sinecure and prided himself in the helping hand he could provide to colleagues, much of it done behind the scenes. If there was one institution at Malvern that came anywhere near as close to his heart as the cricket, then it was the Common Room. On one occasion, he faced down a potential *coup d'état*. At the AGM of the Common Room Club, a motion was tabled to separate the two positions, second master and president of Common Room. George was horrified. He took both roles very seriously and believed strongly that they were part of the same remit and therefore indivisible. Of course, nothing so squalid as electioneering and canvassing would take place but it was clear that the motion would have to be put to the vote. 'Don't worry,' his friend Pat Hooley whispered in his ear, 'I'm in charge of the count and they won't get rid of you.' And so it turned out, though there is no record of the actual size of the majority.

He was still a teacher of Geography and a housemaster of course and continued to take an active role in extra-curricular activities. He had given up running the cricket in 1965, which had seemed an apt moment for two reasons: his lieutenant, Alan Duff, was straining at the leash and was a more than competent successor; and 1965 was the College centenary and George, with his usual sense of theatre, was keen to bow out on an appropriate note of celebration. Accordingly, he pulled a few strings at his old club and arranged for the county side to come and play the XI on the Senior. However, this was to be no exhibition match, with the pros easing off and giving the boys a gentle run around. Ever the competitor, he devised a format, a sort of handicap, if you like, which demanded that the game be played full tilt. It was simple really. The boys were given 150 runs start. He reckoned that would more or less provide the incentive for the pros to take it seriously. And he was right. Worcestershire won but only just. 'They were good enough to bring a decent side,' said George, 'Most of their first team were playing, including the captain, Don Kenyon, and of course my old friend, Tom Graveney.' The cricket was hard fought, the weather was kind, the Senior was at its picturesque best and everybody had a good time. 'It was just a perfect day,' George called to mind. I doubt a single person begrudged him his day in the sun.

So, looking back, who was the best player to pass through your hands? He gave this some thought. 'The bowling was usually adequate, without any real stars. The batting…? Hmm. Ian MacLaurin was one of the best.' I reminded him that Lord MacLaurin had told me the story about George laying stress on the importance of setting one's sights high and never settling for second best, batting for hundreds, not pretty 20s and 30s. And this lesson, MacLaurin asserted, was a lesson for life. 'Lesson for life!' chortled George, 'Nonsense! It was a lesson for the next match! I knew he was a good player, capable of getting big scores. I wouldn't have said it had he been a run-of-the-mill player.' *Any others?* 'Bryan Richardson – fine, fine player. I always thought he was the most talented of the three brothers but the world of wheeling and dealing proved more attractive.' Praise indeed given the cricketing pedigree of Peter and Dick. 'But the best cricketer I ever had was, without doubt, Roger Tolchard. Not necessarily the best batsman – I thought his brother Jeff was perhaps technically more proficient with the bat, though he was unlucky with his career at Leicestershire – but Roger was the most *charismatic* player I have ever seen.' I played against Roger in my time at Hampshire and his brilliance, behind the stumps and as a match-winning middle-order bat, stood out even in a very strong Leicestershire side. Had he played in any era other than the one overlapping with the peerless Alan Knott, he would surely have played more than four times for his country.

George saw no reason, during this period of time, to relinquish his close association with the Air Section in the school's Combined Cadet Corps. For a start, the pay was a welcome addition to the meagre salary of a schoolmaster, especially so for one who had school fees to pay for his two children. 'And it was enormous fun,' he conceded with a wide grin, particularly when his old friend and colleague, Denis Saunders, was part of the same section. 'Fun? I should say so!' observed Pat Hooley, 'Ask him about the glider. And the comical order to the cadets, "Adopt the gliding attitude!" when the Heath Robinson contraption never got off the ground!' George felt this was a little unfair. 'It *did* get off the ground,' he demurred, 'sometimes 5 feet, up to 20 on occasions, I remember.' To get the truth, I enlisted the testimony of one who was actually there – Quentin Hayes was in No. 5 and in the RAF cadre, so he could describe what happened precisely: 'To launch the glider, it was attached to the middle of a 100-metre-long bungee rope. Five or six cadets would then march off at 45 degrees to the glider, holding the rope. This acted as a massive catapult and on release of the ground pin, the glider would shoot forward and rise about 20 feet in the air!' In this century risk assessment would not have allowed the glider to be even wheeled out of the garage.

'There you are!' George laughed. But he had to admit that often the launching process was a bit of a shambles. 'It was more of a team-building exercise,' he contended, not entirely with conviction. Mind you, there was one horrible accident and he winced at the memory. It was during the annual general inspection, when the service bigwigs visit the College to see for themselves the marvellous work being carried out by the cadets. Needless to say, everyone is in his best bib and tucker and the visiting senior officers are always greatly impressed. Just in case they're not, a lavish lunch is laid on. The launch of the glider had gone well. So well that Denis Saunders, who was in charge of the gliding team, was persuaded by one excited boy to do it 'one more time, Sir!' The elastic rope was pulled back to full stretch, the pin was removed and the glider shot up to 60 feet, when it stalled and plummeted to earth, disintegrating like matchwood. The boy was badly hurt but thankfully made a full recovery. And luckily, the inspection party had already moved on.

It is interesting to note, asserted Hayes, when recounting his memories of George, the respect Squadron Leader Chesterton was paid everywhere he went, at stations up and down the country, such as RAF Wattisham, RAF Brawdey, RAF Shawbury, RAF Defford and others. George, of course, had been 'in the real RAF', as Denis Saunders' wife once asserted, not 'playing at soldiers', as some colleagues used to remark disparagingly of the CCF. This respect, even awe, accorded to true veterans, even by the professional servicemen, was something that many of George's friends and pupils always noticed. Major Nigel Stewart remembers one occasion in particular when George's experience as a wartime pilot came in useful. It was 1969; Nigel Stewart was a teacher of English at Malvern, but also commanding officer of the school CCF. Thanks to George and his myriad contacts in the RAF, a joint service camp had been organised for the cadets at RAF Luqa in Malta. George had arranged for the contingent to be picked up by plane at the old RAF aerodrome in Defford, Worcestershire. It was noticeable, said Stewart, that the most important officer wherever they went, no matter what rank greeted them, was Squadron Leader Chesterton. Now, as we know, George and Malta went back a long way and it was unlikely to be an uneventful trip. And so it proved, though not in quite the same comic fashion as before. Nigel Stewart's account: 'As we were walking away from the aircraft at Luqa, we saw an RAF aircraft falling out of the sky and crashing just below us. The crew ejected but were too close to the ground and were killed outright.' George remembered it all too well, that telltale plume of black smoke. 'It was a Canberra. It was too steep on the turn and I could see what was going to happen. Pilot error, without a doubt.' The accident marred the trip from the outset and the boys and adults were visibly shocked. This was an occasion when George was seen at his best as Stewart describes: 'He had lived through such events in wartime, as we all knew, and he was so calm and a pillar of strength throughout that our cadets escaped any mass hysteria.'

That wasn't the end of it. Their quarters were in the barracks that overlooked the drill square. They were awoken the next morning by a detail of airmen practising the slow march for the funeral of their fellow servicemen. 'Horrible,' said George. Not surprisingly, the Malvern officers, once their cadets had been safely handed over to their training staff, sought some solace in a snifter or two. According to Stewart, George's favoured tipple was a horse's neck. Not being entirely familiar with the exact specifications of fancy cocktails, I sought elucidation. Cognac and ginger ale, I was told. The party moved on to the residence of the British high commissioner, Sir George Tory, whose son was in No. 5. On arrival, Sir George asked George what he would like to drink. 'Oh, a horse's neck would go down very well,' said George. 'Oh dear, I'm so sorry,' said the crestfallen high commissioner, 'I only have VSOP Cognac.' 'That'll do nicely,' responded George, with commendable alacrity. 'I've always admired George for many reasons, and that's just one of them!' was the final comment of his commanding officer, Major Stewart.

During the Easter term of 1976, the school was visited by a virulent outbreak of 'flu. It soon took hold and spread like the plague through the student body. The school sanatorium was unable to cope, so the burden of looking after the sick fell upon the individual Houses and their staff. As this involved constant running up and down stairs to dormitories and bed-studies to minister to the stricken, fit muscles were called for. Now, whatever qualities the matron in No. 5 – the corpulent Miss Prior – brought to the job, and they were few, as we know, bustling up and down stairs wasn't one of them. In fact, at this time of crisis she was almost totally useless. Voluntary help from among the College community alleviated the strain to some extent but the bulk of the burden fell upon K. At one stage, there were forty boys bed-ridden and it seemed that she was looking after them night and day single-handedly. 'It nearly killed her,' said George. And he wasn't joking. At the end of term, she suffered what can only be described as a total mental and physical collapse. So alarmed was George that he was forced to take an immediate and serious reassessment of his position. His fifteen years as a housemaster were up at the end of the next term. He was still second master, but by mutual agreement with the headmaster, Martin Rogers, the plan was that he would leave No. 5 in July and hand over to his named successor, John Blackshaw. The problem was that he did not believe he could wait until July. His wife's total prostration indicated quite clearly to him, if not to everybody else, that he should leave with immediate effect. Rogers was sympathetic and Blackshaw generously agreed to take over early, so it was done, and with little fanfare, George and K quitted No. 5. The circumstances bore uncanny resemblances to those surrounding their arrival, when John Collinson left prematurely, though George's was not nearly so melodramatic. In fact there was a neat mathematical parity to his departure. He had taken over at Easter and now he was leaving at Easter, after the full fifteen years *in situ* – forty-five terms in total. The exactitude of the timing appealed to George's sense of order.

The decision was undoubtedly the right one but it did not seem to solve the problem. 'She never really recovered,' admitted George sadly. 'Whether the strain of that last term hastened the onset of her illness…' It was pointless trying to steer him away from this line of introspection for he had obviously been mulling it over for years, decades even. His voice tailed off and I attempted to change the subject. He would come to the painful bit when he was ready. They had bought a charming house that backed onto school grounds, overlooking the tennis courts. Away from the responsibility of running a boarding house, she could indulge in her passion for gardening, the fruits of which are still in existence, for George remains in residence in Orchard House to this day, and he could concentrate on his teaching (he was now back to a full timetable, which must have been a shock) and keeping the school and Common Room functioning properly in his role as second master.

There was plenty going on. There was The Fire, for example. George was in the nets at the time. 'Sir, Sir,' cried the batsman to whom George was bowling, 'there's a fire in No. 5!' 'Nonsense, boy!' said George in his follow-through. 'Do you think I'd fall for that one?' 'Honestly, Sir, there's a fire!' Picking up his ball, George turned on his heels to return to his mark and was horrified to see that indeed No. 5 was ablaze. The back of the house was engulfed in flames and swirling black smoke and you would be hard-pressed to believe that the building would not have been completely destroyed. In fact, the blaze was brought under control and miraculously No. 5 did not suffer a great deal of structural damage. 'A boy had lit some joss sticks. He heard footsteps in the passage and fearing it was his housemaster, had hidden them in a drawer. And forgotten about them.' Every housemaster's nightmare. But George was no longer in No. 5. It was his successor who had to deal with the aftermath.

In the Geography department, a young student teacher arrived to do his teaching practice and to learn the ropes. His name was Nigel Starmer-Smith. George was assigned to keep an eye on him and to monitor his progress. If you were looking for a punctilious and hands-on sort of mentor, then probably the choice of George Chesterton was not the most inspired. George was firmly of the belief that the young man would flourish without having some crusty old beak continually looking over his shoulder, so he left Starmer-Smith to his own devices. The day came when the supervisor arrived to sit in on one of the student teacher's lessons. George thought that it would be a good idea if he cleared his desk so that Starmer-Smith could conduct the lesson unencumbered with the usual detritus that covers any teacher's working space. Dutifully, he removed notes, essays, books, maps and any other flotsam and jetsam that had accumulated during the term. Unfortunately, he also cleared away Starmer-Smith's lesson plan. And when the time came to deliver the carefully prepared lesson in front of the boys under the pitiless gaze of the supervisor, the student teacher was totally confounded. Apparently, he dried up and the lesson was a disaster. 'Ah well. Geography's loss was television's gain,' was George's verdict. That is quite true, for the former rugby union international went on to have a respected career in journalism and television presenting.

George and K enjoyed their time in their new house. The pace of life was less stressful, away from the relentless labour and responsibility of running a boys' boarding house. It is not until housemasters, and their wives, come out of the House that the physical and emotional toll can be gauged. Few regret having done the job but most are happy to claim back their lives. There were several agreeable holidays that they had together; one, in particular, stands out in George's memory. It was to Lake Como in Italy. There were little ferries that plied their trade around the shores of the lake. Every couple of stops, they would get off to have coffee, or a drink, or a light lunch. 'She enjoyed it,' said George, 'because it was peaceful, relaxing and above all undemanding. You see, she always seemed so tired.' At first he put this lassitude down to a natural reaction following the dreadful last term in No. 5 and the inevitable aftermath when her body and mind seemed to shut down. But worryingly, her strength and her spirit refused to revive. Her energy was slowly draining from her and the old zest had gone. Then she developed problems with her throat, which proved to be stubbornly difficult to shift. At length, they sought medical advice and she was sent to see a specialist. The consultant was sufficiently alarmed to arrange for her to have an exhaustive and exhausting round of tests. She was quickly taken into hospital for an operation during which it was discovered that she was riddled with cancer. There was nothing the surgeon could do. The news was immediately broken to George. His feelings at that moment can only be imagined. He was unimpressed by the insensitive way that he was told and still feels angry at the memory. The message was blunt enough as it was. K returned home to die. She and George had barely six months left together.

It was now at the turn of a new decade, 1980. No more than a few days into my first term at Malvern that January, I pushed open the heavy oak doors of the Main Building and made my way along the corridor, my footsteps echoing on the large, square, grey flagstones. It was early in the morning (well, I was new to the job and keen) and no one was about. I entered the Common Room and George was straightening up, having just pinned a notice to the notice board. He hesitated as if to say something, then obviously thought twice about it and hurried on his way.

Curiosity took hold and I approached the board to read his note. The headline was a single capital letter 'K'. Who or what was K? It took a second or two for the penny to drop. K was his wife. Of course she was. I knew that. But I had assumed that her name was spelt 'Kay'. I had no idea that it was an abbreviation. The message was terse. K had undergone an operation from which she was recovering as well as could be expected. But the news was not good. Much that was nasty had been uncovered. The last sentence of the bulletin shall remain etched on my mind for evermore, stark in its simplicity: 'The outlook is bleak.'

The room soon filled with masters busily emptying their pigeonholes and casting their eyes over the notice board. Inevitably, a knot quickly gathered around the note from the second master, many fumbling for glasses and peering short-sightedly. Individually and collectively, George's colleagues would back away, muttering and shaking their heads while others craned to look. Some reeled in shock. If there was any ignorance in my mind of the regard in which the Chestertons were held, then the distress that was almost tangible informed me.

As winter rolled around to spring, it must have been a desolate time in the Chesterton household. There were some poignant moments. On one occasion, K got up and looked at herself in the mirror. 'Oh good!' she said, 'I've got my figure back.' Another time, she roused herself to do two hours of gardening but that exhausted her and she had to return to bed. For the rest, it was a steady and rapid decline. No doubt, much was said. And, probably much was left unsaid. Probably there was little need. Their love for each other, fostered initially on the Senior Bank, a short stroll down the hill from where they were living, had survived a world war, and countless games of cricket. One doesn't like to pry too deeply at a time of personal sadness and intense emotion. Instinctively, one feels that it is best to shut the door quietly and allow the family some peace. She died in July 1980.

The funeral took place in the College chapel. It was filled to bursting with friends and old boys, many who had been with them in No. 5. George did not give the eulogy. He couldn't. It occurs to me that this must have been just about the only memorial service that he has attended in the chapel when he has *not* spoken. He remains to this day the 'Emeritus Professor of College Eulogies'. He is the one whom everybody instinctively turns to for an address in memory of friends and colleagues, a sure measure of the man. But not on this occasion – it was simply beyond him.

I didn't attend the service. I was in Barbados with the school cricket team at the time. One morning, Alan Duff, who was in charge of the tour, told me that K's funeral would be taking place back in England on that day and asked me whether I would accompany him to the local church to pay his respects. Of course I agreed. Leaving the fielding practice in the hands of Geoff Morton, our coach, we made our way up a dusty track to where the church was situated on the rise of a gentle hill.

I say a church but in truth it was no more than a little wooden barn with a door hanging perilously from a rusty hinge. Inside, however, was cool and peaceful with a few chairs arranged neatly in front of a makeshift altar, bare except for a heavy brass cross. It was also spotlessly clean.

Together we sat in silence, lost in our own thoughts. Doubtless the official service back in Malvern was impressive but I like to think that our two-man effort was touching too, in its own way. At length, Alan stood up and suggested it was time to go. We stepped out into the bright sunlight, the heat and the dust catching at our throats, the cheerful shouts of the team at practice floating on the breeze up the hill. Slowly we returned to the quick and the young.

Beside the field where noisy catching practice was taking place stood a man, leaning against the gate, his powerful black limousine parked on the verge. He was observing with some interest Malvern's finest throwing themselves around loudly as balls were fired at them. He was tall, if a little stooped but that might have been his posture with his elbows on the iron bars. He was dressed in a crisp, white, short-sleeved shirt and dark trousers and his hair was short, crinkly and snowy white. In the bewitching, rumbling tones of the native Bajan, he bade us good morning and noted our emergence from the local chapel. There were no services that day, he told us, it not being a Sunday. Alan explained to him the nature of our pilgrimage up the hill. He sucked in his cheeks and said that the lady was at peace now and with God. It might have sounded corny but somehow it didn't, coming from him. He also offered us the sincere hope that our team didn't drop as many catches in the match on the following day, 'or else your boys are goin' to get a whippin'.' With that, he climbed into his car and drove off, the dust from his tyres making us choke.

'Do you know who that was?' asked Alan.

'No.'

'Wes Hall.'

'Not … not *the* Wes Hall! The great fast bowler who broke Colin Cowdrey's arm at Lord's?'

'The very same. He's a big cheese on the island, you know. A senator now. And a very religious man, by all accounts.'

In my mind, I tried to square how an avowed man of God would want to try to knock a batsman's head off but the metaphysical tussle was too much for me, especially in that heat. It did occur to me, however, that George would have appreciated the kind words about K, coming as they did from a fellow fast bowler. And, for the record, Wes Hall was right. We did drop a lot of catches the next day and, sure enough, we got a whippin'.

In the words of his own son, Colin, George made 'a hopeless, grim widower.' It was the long summer holiday, so at least he was able to get away from Malvern to try to come to terms with life without K. Colin is sure that he wouldn't have made it on his own. So too were some of his colleagues. 'That man,' said one of them to me, indicating George on the other side of the Common Room, 'is not long destined to be amongst us.' 'What!' cried I in disbelief, 'Do you mean George has got a new job?' 'No, you imbecile! I mean on this earth.' I cast my eye across at George and thought that was a bit harsh. True, he looked rough but any man whose wife has just died has every right to look rough. Besides, his back was playing up again and he was in a lot of pain. It was a wonder he was at school at all. As soon as it was practicable, Colin took him away to Kilmington in Devon, put him in whites, wound him up and got him to bowl for the local cricket team. 'His nickname was Metronome, so he soon hit a length,' said Colin, who kept wicket. 'Dad cannot bowl without the competitive juices flowing and it did occur to me as he was running in, s**t, if I drop a catch now, that's me out of the will!'

George was still on this earth thankfully when I bumped into him in the queue for the post office in Malvern, not long before the start of the new school year that September. 'Oh hello, Andy. How good to see you. Tell me, how did the tour to Barbados go?' Typical. It should have been me enquiring after him and how he was coping but all possible embarrassment on my part was instantly dislodged by his civility. As I was recounting our adventures, we were interrupted by a shriek. 'George! What are you doing here? How *are* you? And how's K, dare I ask?'

Enter, into our story, stage right, Vanessa. *Alarums and excursions.*

There was a pause of only a second.

'I'm afraid she died. July.'

Vanessa's face fell, mortification writ large. But George is not one to allow another's discomfiture to endure.

'I think we could do with a drink,' he announced and off they went to the Foley Arms. I shuffled along the queue and got my book of stamps.

Looking back on that extraordinary chance meeting, I count myself privileged to have been present at the birth of something momentous. For, gentle readers, yes, they married. 'Vanessa – my second wife and glorious salvation' is how George ardently puts it. However, there is no glossing over the fact that for some, his family included, the relationship between him and Vanessa, in the early days anyway, was controversial and caused much pain.

Vanessa had been married to Johnny Clegg, the headmaster of a prep school in Lancashire, who was also a talented sportsman. He knew George because he used to send some of his boys to Malvern and as George was well known as a cricketer, it was unsurprising that the keen games players ended up with him in No. 5. They had played golf together, Johnny trusted that George would look after his boys and the two of them got on well. It so happened that Johnny and Vanessa were looking for a suitable school for their daughter and had come to Malvern Girls' College to be interviewed by the formidable headmistress, Miss Owen, who has already featured in these pages. The interview proved daunting, not so much for their daughter but for Johnny, who was so stressed as they emerged from Miss Owen's study that he demanded they go forthwith to No. 5, a short walk away, to have a drink with George to recover his composure. As you would expect, George ministered to the distraught couple with open arms and open drinks cabinet. It was the first time he and Vanessa had met.

Following her divorce from Johnny, Vanessa found employment at The Downs, a prep school just over the hill from Malvern, and was working there in 1980. 'Quite by chance, we met outside Malvern's post office not long after K died,' Vanessa told me. I gently reminded her that I had been present, 'Of course you were! Well, anyway, as you know, we went off to the Foley for a drink. And we never looked back!'

The romance was a whirlwind one. 'Well, it had to be,' she asserted in her typical no-nonsense fashion, 'George said to me, "I'm 59. No time to waste. We'd better get a move on!"' With due regard to the sensibilities of others, at first it was conducted in secret. As well as generating a little *frisson* to their meetings, this also provided ample scope for hilarious ruses and stratagems to avoid detection. They were like a couple of naughty sixth-formers trying to outwit their housemaster and housemistress. It must have been comical realising that the boot was now on the other foot. One is reminded of George's antics all those years ago at Blenheim when he broke curfew to go and feed the rabbits with the duke's daughter. Vanessa would come to dinner at George's house but he always bundled her into the car and off home by 10.30. Old habits die hard. 10.30 was the time for lock-up in the boarding houses and besides, he didn't want tongues wagging any more than they already were. Vanessa was quietly amused by the charade but in deference to his feelings, she went along with it. There was one occasion when they went to watch a golf tournament at St Pierre in Chepstow. The television cameras were there and George was terrified that someone watching the box back home might recognise his face in the crowd. They bumped into a friend of Vanessa's. Without so much as a second's pause, George introduced himself as Henry Watson. He felt he was on reasonably secure ground here. Henry Watson was no fictitious name; he existed all right. At least he had existed but he had been killed fighting with the 8th Army in the desert in the war. He had been head of House at Sherborne and had been a rival for K's affections. 'But I managed to see him off,' said George with a grin.

It soon dawned on both George and Vanessa that their relationship was more than a fleeting distraction and that they might as well come clean about it with their family, their friends and the wider community in the College. Why prevaricate? Why dissemble? All this ducking and diving was becoming tedious and unseemly. They were hardly a pair of teenagers with stars in their eyes. They were both middle-aged with families, and knew the score. Clearly, it wasn't going to sit comfortably with everyone but waiting for an appropriate length of time wasn't going to change anything. And how long was 'an appropriate length of time' anyway? No handbook on the correct etiquette had been written for them to consult. So they decided to get married. They went to Cheltenham to buy a ring. 'Good morning, Mr Chesterton,' welcomed the jeweller, 'And how is Mrs Chesterton? I hear she hasn't been at all well.'

I guess they would have told each other – once they had recovered their composure – that such awkwardness would probably be the first of many, so they might as well prepare themselves for it and get on with it. After all, there was no doubt in their own minds that what they were doing was the best thing for them. And the rest could go hang if they didn't approve. Except the family, of course. That was going to be a tricky one to negotiate but they would cross that bridge when they came to it.

George's leg, not his back on this occasion, was playing up so he was forced to spend a few days in the school medical centre. A colleague, Robert Stobbs, who taught Spanish and was known affectionately by one and all as 'El Stobbo', stopped by for a friendly chat. Out of the blue, George announced that he had just got engaged. El Stobbo, one of the most affable and kindly men you could ever wish to meet, graciously congratulated him but once he got home to break the news to his wife, the telephone wires around the school were soon red hot. Ruth Stobbs, it has to be said, was the first to extend an invitation to the newly engaged couple; she was, she later admitted, desperate to meet George's new lady. Vanessa now stepped into the limelight. She may not have relished it but she could no more have avoided it than Camilla Parker-Bowles.

Vanessa's three children were young, teenagers in fact, and could see no problem in their mother remarrying. George was on tenterhooks before he met them. Running in to bowl against the Australians wasn't nearly as daunting as having his prospective step-children come to tea. In preparation, he made a cake in the shape of Orchard House. Bashful introductions were made and, to put them at their ease, George immediately instructed them to call him by his first name, George. This caused them much amusement. 'What do you expect them to call you, Georgie – *Sir?*' cried Vanessa. George moved onto the cake. 'Now children, what does this cake remind you of?' he asked. Bemused silence. 'What does it look like?' Eventually one of them tentatively offered the thought that it might be 'the ayatollah's hat'. Whether it crossed George's mind at that point that his artistic endeavours had once made a drawing of a naked girl 'look like a monkey', I cannot say, but it certainly crossed mine. He had more important matters to worry about.

'Now look, darlings,' said Vanessa, trying to introduce a note of seriousness into the proceedings, 'George and I are going to get married.'

'Of course you are, Mummy,' they choroused, 'We know that.'

And everyone tucked heartily into the ayatollah's hat. 'From that moment onwards,' said George, 'we got on famously. Still do. I have made it clear that Vanessa's children – and now grandchildren of course – are very much mine too. It's as it should be.'

Tamsin, the second eldest of Vanessa's children, is in no doubt that the marriage was the best thing that could have happened to both of them. Not all second marriages are a great success and no doubt all of us can bring to mind associations formed on the rebound, as it were, of friends and acquaintances that have been, at best, ill-advised. She speaks for herself and her siblings when she says that they were delighted for them. And subsequent events have borne out their confidence and optimism. 'What better stepfather could we possibly have had than George?' she said, 'The kindness, generosity and steadfastness that he has shown us, all of us, grandchildren too, has been just...' She tailed off, quite overcome. It helped of course, certainly early on, that George and Johnny Clegg, Vanessa's first husband, got on so well together. Tamsin remembers her own wedding day in 1998. Everyone had left for the church. The only ones left in the house with her were her father and stepfather. 'And do you know what? They were talking about cricket! "Sorry to interrupt," I said, "but don't you think we ought to be making a move? Everyone's waiting for us."' She is full of admiration for her mother and how she dealt with any possible embarrassment about K's memory. The garden had become overgrown after K had died, which was wholly excusable, but it did need cutting back and weeding. Vanessa took the bull by the horns and enlisted the help of her children. 'Come along, darlings. Wellies on and let's get on with it!' Tamsin described, 'My mother's like that. She is a tower of strength and just gets on with things, no matter what problems present themselves.'

She and her brother and sister would spend many a happy day in the summer holidays following the fortunes of the Old Malvernians in the Cricketer Cup and on tour at Eastbourne, noting the miles eaten up by her stepfather as he used to pace nervously around the boundary's edge. 'George opened his house to us and has made my mother very happy. As she has him. It's wonderful to see them together. "The light of my life" he calls her. No,' Tamsin finally declared, 'In their case, second marriage is *definitely* not second best!'

Philip, her brother, is in complete agreement. He senses that his mother is happy and that is all that matters to him. 'It just felt right,' he said, 'I was only eight when my parents got divorced. As you can imagine, that was a stressful time for everybody. And then, six years later, George appeared on the scene and almost immediately everything seemed to calm down.' The expansion of the family, now that grandchildren have arrived, far from presenting problems, has in fact added immeasurably to their lives. 'As soon as the kids burst through the door, George's face gets a lift and his whole demeanour is energised. He is a wonderful grandfather figure.' Philip cites one of many examples. George suggested that the children might like him to read *Winnie the Pooh* to them. Perhaps the choice of book was less than exceptional, as they knew the story backwards but when Philip later eavesdropped on the reading, he saw that both children were rapt. Mind you, he admitted that they have 'on occasions observed, with all the candour of youth, that George sleeps a lot!'

As if to sum up George's influence on him, Philip made this telling comment. 'If ever I wonder what is the best course of action to take at any given moment, I ask myself, what would George do? And I wouldn't go far wrong.'

Nonetheless, they all understand the sensibilities of the other side of the family and have always tried to tread carefully. George's son, Colin, has by all accounts, despite his original unease, been very friendly and welcoming, 'as you would expect,' says Tamsin, 'of someone who is so open-hearted.' Besides, as Philip points out, Colin sees that his father is happy and well cared for. Posy's misgivings they fully acknowledge and understand. 'K was her mother,' said Tamsin, 'and she died in extremely distressing circumstances, just when Posy herself was going through a dreadful time. It must have been awful. But I think, I hope, we all appreciate that George's health and well-being are crucial here, especially as he is not as young as he once was and he hasn't been all that well recently. It puts things into perspective. My mother battles on, cheerfully and staunchly, looking after him, as she has always done. And I think Posy now recognises that.'

Posy does. Though it has not always been so. She was good enough to open her heart to me, in the interests of historical accuracy, about a time in her life that still distresses her. She took great pains to ensure that I did not misunderstand or misrepresent her feelings and I tried to reassure her, as best I could, that I would set down what she said fairly and accurately. However, you would have to possess a heart of stone not to be affected by her story. She adored her mother and her death affected her badly. In addition, she was pregnant, with triplets. George still flinches at the memory of the physical discomfort and mental stress she was suffering at that time. She was able to tell K before the end that she was expecting. 'Good,' said K, 'I hope it's a girl.' She died before they realised it would be a multiple birth. In fact, scans had suggested twins; the other foetus was hidden behind them. The babies were born ten weeks early and the first two were conjoined, hopelessly so, from the abdomen up, sharing the same heart. They were not 'viable' and died five hours later. Freyja, the third, survived but weighed only three pounds; it was touch and go. On countless occasions, hope was all but abandoned yet somehow she pulled through. She suffered no end of scares and complications and was not discharged from hospital for another five weeks. Not to put too fine a point on it, that period was 'absolutely dreadful'. It was Christmas too. Posy's husband, Rory, is full of admiration for George at that time for the way he rallied round and did his best to keep everyone's spirits up.

But Posy's spirits were not for raising, not for a long time. And then came the body blow that her father was going to remarry. 'I know, I know,' she acknowledged tearfully, 'perhaps it wasn't very rational of me to take against Vanessa but you have to try to understand how I felt. There was another woman in my father's life and ... well, even Orchard House was no longer my home.' For a time, she fell silent. I said nothing. There was nothing to say.

There is no doubt, a fact confirmed by both, that relations between Posy and Vanessa were strained for many years. The *froideur* was probably exacerbated by the fact that Vanessa is a mere seven years older than Posy, more of an age that 'you would expect of an older stepsister than stepmother,' Posy said. But time has been a great healer. The two of them have become, if not close, then certainly more amicable. 'We've both mellowed,' said Posy, 'It was difficult, early on, but all has been forgiven and we get on much better now. I've seen how well she has looked after my father, especially latterly, when he hasn't been at all well, and I'm grateful.' Rory offered an interesting take on George's remarriage: 'In a way, it was a tribute to your mother,' he told Posy, as she was speaking to me, 'It was such a happy union that he couldn't possibly live alone. And Vanessa came to his rescue.' 'Anyway,' said Posy finally, 'We all had a lovely family party a few months ago and everyone was on good form. It's all fine now and my father is happy. And that is what really matters, isn't it?'

Many of George's friends, especially the close ones, were delighted with the marriage. Two staunch allies were Alan Duff and John Blackshaw, the former George's successor as master in charge of cricket and the latter George's successor in No. 5. Both men sadly died prematurely and George still mourns their passing. 'They were dear, dear friends and I miss them.' But it has to be conceded that there were those in the Common Room who were unhappy about it. They thought it was all too soon. 'You have to understand,' Martin Knott told me, 'that a lot of them knew K well and were very fond of her. She was a very special person.' Indeed she was. There has never been the slightest suggestion, not the merest hint, in all the long hours of conversation that I have had with George that he has ever thought otherwise of his beloved K. To this day, he remains racked with guilt about the onset of the cancer that was to kill her and how much that punishing last term in No. 5 was a contributing factor. Pictures of her still have pride of place in his sitting room and I firmly believe that her memory and her legacy occupy an impregnable fortress in his heart. 'But there was no way George could have coped on his own,' Knott went on to say with a knowing smile, 'Men are hopeless widowers. Most marry again. And Vanessa was marvellous. She rejuvenated him.' He continued to explain that at the time of K's death, George was in great pain with his back (when she had her operation, he was laid up in bed) and the stress of nursing a dying wife had taken its toll. And throughout, he still had to teach his lessons and carry out his duties as second master. 'The strain must have been intolerable,' Knott concluded, 'Who could deny him some time in the sun?'

The sun that is Vanessa has now shone on George for 30 years, giving the lie to any suggestion that the relationship would be a flash in the pan. He was married to K for 37 years, 'So that means, in total, I've been under the whip for 67 years,' he grinned. George and Vanessa were married in Wells in Somerset. The bishop of Bath and Wells was an old friend of Vanessa's and agreed to take the service for them. But before the ceremony, the good bishop took George for a walk around the castle walls, just for 'a little chat', to determine the probity of the groom's character and the worthiness of his intentions. Vanessa of course was a divorced woman and, though this no longer barred her from remarrying in the church, quite clearly this minister wasn't going to serve up a succession of half volleys for George to nonchalantly put away. 'He took me to the chapel and had me on my knees for half an hour,' said George grimly, rubbing them both gingerly. But the wedding on the next day in the beautiful private chapel in the bishop's palace was a lovely occasion. Both Colin and Posy were there, as well as Vanessa's children, 'though Posy spent most of the day in tears, poor thing.' Then it was off to Greece for their honeymoon. It was a year and a bit since K had died. George was insistent that at least a year should elapse before remarrying. He felt that was a decent period of time, even if others, a few only, were still uneasy. For George, there were no mental obstacles. 'I have been twice blessed,' he said simply.

I only met K once. I remember little of the encounter, other than recognising, just as I had been told, that she was desperately ill. I have seen photos of her, naturally, but I only have the words of other people who knew her well, her family and friends, to paint the picture of a woman who featured so large in the earlier part of George's life. Vanessa I do know well and that picture is much easier to paint. Tom Graveney remarked to me in passing that there could never be a dull conversation with George around. Let me turn that observation around a trifle. There can never be a dull moment with Vanessa around either. To put it simply, I think she and George were made for each other at this stage of their respective lives and that chance meeting outside Malvern Post Office was a serendipitous turn of fate. George is in no doubt of the influence that Vanessa has had on his life. 'Good God! I wouldn't have survived without her.' I'm inclined to agree. There have been times, particularly later on in his life, when his health has faltered, at times alarmingly so, and Vanessa, with her happy mixture of cheerful optimism and solicitous nursing, has eased him back into good shape. He once said something to me that I found very surprising. 'You know, she gave me *confidence*. All that I have done since I married her would not have been possible without her encouragement and support.' The surprise was not that Vanessa was such a caring partner but that he suffered from any crisis of confidence. But I understand what he means about Vanessa. She is like a force of nature, blowing away the dusty cobwebs of any room she enters. Her exuberance and her vitality are irrepressible. Any crusty, doubting member of the Common Room would have been swept along by the sheer force of her personality. Well, if he didn't, I imagine he would have had to cling on to his gown and his prejudices pretty grimly. It is no wonder that George was smitten. He reckons she was brought on to bowl in the nick of time.

And looking at the scorecard of the last 30 years, there is little doubt that he is right. Plainly, they adore each other and both feel blessed to have found happiness in their second innings, if you will pardon the extended metaphor.

In the meantime, life at Malvern College carried on much as usual. The mysteries of the ox-bow lake were laid bare to young geographers, the secrets of the in-swinger were demonstrated to young bowlers in the nets, weekly meetings with Martin Rogers, the headmaster, still took place, at which the smooth management of the school was discussed, and the Common Room remained a generally happy and cohesive group under George's avuncular leadership. A £10 take in Premium Bonds realised a prize of £1,000 for the Common Room on one occasion and there was much discussion on how best to spend it. George, as their president, insisted on a party. They hired a boat on the River Severn and though it was no floating gin palace, a good time was had by all and no one was lost overboard. The remainder of the money was entrusted to Michael Harvey to buy some pictures of artistic merit. George did not think a great deal at the time of the prints chosen but bit his tongue and bowed to his colleague's judgement. 'They're now worth thousands!' he guffawed.

And what of Vanessa? She could have lived in K's shadow but chose not to. 'You see,' she said, 'no one in their right mind could really have seen me as a rival! We were so totally different. K was so amazingly efficient. I'm untidy, chaotic.' If Posy has found it difficult to come to terms with another woman in her father's life, Colin seems to have come to an equable acceptance of it. 'Oh, we're fine,' he adds breezily, 'I told Vanessa early on that she would either kill the old man within the year or see him through to old age. So, I reckon she's been good for him.'

As for the Common Room, Vanessa, without ever shunning it, never felt that she could embrace it with the same commitment as K. 'I think some of them thought me too flippant to be a second master's wife,' she conceded, 'So I didn't push myself.' Of course she never neglected her responsibilities and was always there at his side at official functions and social occasions. She was ever conscious that Malvern College was George's *raison d'être*, his second home, and she was much too loyal ever to let him down. But the school did not run through her veins like it did his. 'Too many ghosts,' she shivers. This I find a surprise. To any outsider, Vanessa has seemed a fixture, and a comfortable one at that, at George's side, at Malvern College and elsewhere. What she and George share above all is a sense of humour. Rather like I imagine life was like at the vicarage, there is a lot of laughter in the Chesterton household.

George was scheduled to retire in 1982 when he was sixty. Before a change of legislation moved the goalposts, it was mandatory for a public school teacher to hang up his gown at the end of the academic year that coincided with his sixtieth birthday. Some teachers feel that they still have more to give in the classroom beyond this date but teaching is a taxing occupation and most teachers, in boarding schools at any rate, are more than happy to chuck in the towel at sixty. George was no different. He was looking forward to spending more time with Vanessa and less time with the Remove. However, one more surprise in his professional career lay in store.

Martin Rogers had just been appointed as chief master of King Edward VI School in Birmingham. He was going to bow out from Malvern at the same time as George, both headmaster and second master riding off into the sunset together. It had been a surprisingly rewarding and satisfying partnership. They were two totally different characters but they worked together well and had developed a mutual respect. Rogers is in no doubt of the debt he owed to his second in command: 'My abiding memories of George will always be of a very civilised, broad minded and sensitive man. He was a superb schoolmaster and a very good friend of many Malvern staff, Old Malvernians and others. In the eleven years I was lucky enough to be at Malvern, I was very impressed by his very special qualities… George Chesterton is a very remarkable man.' How many teachers leave their school at the end of their career with such a heartfelt endorsement from their boss ringing in their ears?

One evening during that last summer term, George was telephoned by Sir Stephen Brown, lord justice of appeal and president of the Family Division of the High Court. Sir Stephen was also the chairman of the College Council and in the melodious tones of a high court judge, he explained to George that the man they had earmarked to succeed Martin Rogers had been unable to secure his release from his current headship at Glasgow Academy until after Christmas. 'Ye-es,' said George hesitantly, wondering what this had got to do with him. 'Well,' said Sir Stephen, 'it means there will be an awkward interregnum of one term until Roy Chapman can arrive.' 'Indeed,' agreed George, sympathetic but still unclear how he could help. He had plans to be on the golf course. Sir Stephen, well versed in handling obtuse and intransigent witnesses, gently outlined his proposition. Would George consider staying on for one more term and holding the fort as acting head?

Yet again, out of a clear blue sky, he had been made an offer that he did not seek but could not refuse. Any qualms he may have had about his suitability for the role were soon put aside. Vanessa encouraged him to accept and gave him confidence that he could do it, and do it well. In truth, there was no possibility of his declining the offer. The school was in a bit of a pickle and he, of all people, was unlikely to turn aside in its hour of need. Then a snag occurred to him. *His* successor, as second master, had already been announced. Shouldn't he take on the responsibility of running the school until Chapman arrived? George approached his colleague and broached the subject. I have spoken to Michael McNevin, the said appointee, and asked him about that conversation. 'Oh no,' he said breezily, 'There was *absolutely* no doubt in my mind that George should do it. Not for one second did I think otherwise.' George nodded appreciatively as he recollected the gesture 'That was jolly decent of him, don't you think?' However, McNevin did laugh long and loud at the memory of how he was outmanoeuvred by the wily old bird, in one respect anyway. 'We agreed that we should share some of the responsibilities. 'Oh, thank you so much, Michael,' George said to me, 'Why don't you do discipline and dances?' Discipline and dances! The two worst jobs in the school!' And he shook his head mournfully, yet another victim of George's silver tongue.

And so that September, George set up his command centre in the headmaster's study. As he took his seat behind the desk, his mind must have gone back all those years to when he was a young boy in that very room, as his father and mother reminisced with Frank Preston, the then headmaster, about the missing 2 inches of a rather tall man's grave. And now he was behind that desk, not in front. He reached for the phone. 'Can you get Andy Murtagh in here for me?' he asked his secretary. Nervously I presented myself. 'Now Andy, about that cricket match we discussed – all under control?' His first act as headmaster was to decree that a cricket match should take place on the Senior. Nothing unusual in that, you might think. Cricket matches at Malvern had been taking place for 120 years. But this was September, the beginning of the autumn term, the football season. 'Just want to annoy the footballers,' he told me with a wicked grin. 'Besides, the weather is often so balmy at this time of year.' Indeed it was, and the match did take place and it was a great success. Unfortunately, the tradition was not established.

George says that he greatly enjoyed his term in the saddle. The only aspect of the job which he did not take pleasure in was speaking in chapel every week. This will come as a surprise to those who have listened to him over the years giving a succession of assured and polished performances in front of a microphone, in church or out, but he was adamant that he 'hated it.' He does remember having a nasty row with one colleague, the reason for which escapes him, which upset him, even if it soon blew over. And one other regret that he had, a lesson that he would have learned from had his term been longer, was misjudging the tone of one of his reprimands. Not that he was too harsh but that he wasn't harsh enough. A very good junior colts football team had misbehaved during a match. The master in charge had been sufficiently alarmed to send them all to have their fortunes read by the headmaster in his study. 'I remember the look on their faces as I was speaking to them,' George said, 'as if I was some ineffectual old fart. On reflection, I should have punished them more severely. It doesn't do you any good if you're weak and feeble, does it?' Otherwise, it was plain sailing all the way. He sensed that the boys were not in any sort of mood to cause him grief and that the Common Room were supportive and anxious not to rock the boat during this tricky period. 'Marvellous, really. All I had to do were the best bits, the easy bits. All the difficult decisions I could put off until the new man arrived.'

There were the usual comical moments. He had a letter from the headmaster of one of Malvern's feeder prep schools, asking permission for 35 of his former pupils to attend the centenary celebrations of the school. George readily assented. The party was held in the brand-new squash court, built on the proceeds of their centenary fund. At the function, trays of drinks were circulating. As we have seen previously, it is never a good idea to present adolescent boys with any temptation where alcohol is concerned. One boy helped himself to six large sherries, downing them in swift succession. Inevitably, this had an unfortunate effect on his balance and, as he tripped and fell, he cut himself on the glass he had clutched in his hand. The blood spurted luridly and alarmingly all over the lily-white walls of the new court. George had to deal with the fall-out. The prep school headmaster was furious, blaming George and Malvern College for this boy's shocking behaviour. The implication was that he had been a little angel when he left prep school … and now look at him – totally out of control! George felt it was best to get on the front foot here and he berated the headmaster for being so foolish as to distribute drink to minors without proper supervision. The man took the point and no more was heard. But George still had to deal with the miscreant. He rusticated him for two weeks and banned him from any social functions for the rest of term.

One of George's good ideas was to invite all the new boys, in batches of a dozen or so, for tea with him and Vanessa at their home. At one of these gatherings, lo and behold, the sherry drinker presented himself. Obviously tea with the headmaster did not count, in his book at any rate, as a 'social function'. George laughed and allowed him to stay. The boy may have stayed for the jam cake but he did not stay at Malvern for long. 'I heard later,' said George with arched eyebrows, 'that he did not last the course.'

The weeks and months slipped by quickly, in a haze of pleasurable activity. *Did you do any teaching?* 'Good Lord no! That was the wonderful part about it. Makes being a teacher bearable!' If he had been required to take a few lessons, he would have been in trouble. His son Colin tells me that his father had painstakingly burnt all his teaching notes at the completion of each last lesson of each topic in the syllabus. Soon it was the end of term and once reports had all been signed off, Christmas suppers endured, carol services attended, there was only one remaining duty for George to perform. Final assembly. His speech was written. He checked that the bottle of Champagne, together with a glass, was safely hidden behind the lectern. He donned his gown, fixed the hood under his collar, checked his tie knot, smoothed down his hair, quitted his study, walked through the Toppin Room and out into the short corridor, paused, took a deep breath and pushed open the doors of Big School.

15

RETIREMENT

'Presidents are useless really but rally round, smile nicely and make the odd donation.'

George Chesterton

One can imagine George, on the first day of term in January 1983, allowing himself a wry smile, pouring himself another cup of coffee and turning to the sports pages of *The Daily Telegraph*. There must be that delicious moment for every recently retired worker when he realises that the irritating first customer does not have to be served, that the first item on the agenda of Monday's board meeting is no longer of any interest, that the hypochondriac scheduled for the first appointment is now the problem for someone else in the surgery, that the pesky bottom set in the Remove is another teacher's headache. From now on, thought George, taking an appreciative sip of his coffee, Period 1 on a Monday morning will no longer feature in my life.

And almost certainly, like every other man in his position, the thought must have crossed his mind … what now? Would he pace fretfully around the house, getting under Vanessa's feet, bored and restless, impatient to get his teeth into something meaningful? Or would he put his feet up, turn on the television and watch the golf? Without the benefit of hindsight, his friends and colleagues were pretty evenly split, I should say, between those who thought that he would take his sweater and toddle off down to third man for a breather and those who believed that his life's work was far from done. You can understand the variance in opinion. Even to those who know him, George can present a paradoxical figure. He swears that he has been blessed with enormous good fortune in his life, that a lot of what he has achieved has been the result of happy circumstance and good people keeping an eye out for him. As well as some smoke and mirrors on his part. Some of this self-deprecation can be ascribed to a natural modesty; he has always considered it bad form to brag. But a lot of it is genuinely felt. He was lucky to get into Malvern. His guardian angel worked overtime during the war. He would never have got into Oxford these days. The professionalism that is now part of the modern-day game of cricket would not have suited him. The thought of circuit training and ice baths makes him squirm. He doubts he would have enjoyed the current legislation and restrictions that afflict today's teacher and housemaster. Second master? They're deputy heads now and all have their eyes on promotion and headships. The evidence he assembles is compelling.

But then you consider that not *all* of what he has achieved can be put down to luck. Despite his protestations to the contrary, there must have been a lot of hard work involved, as well as no little talent. So how has he managed it, seemingly so effortlessly? The answer of course is that it has not been effortless at all. Like a swan, there has been much paddling going on below the surface. The impression of nonchalance is deceptive. He strove tirelessly to gain his pilot's wings. He bowled thousands and thousands of overs in the nets, often alone, to master accuracy and swing. He worked long hours to make No. 5 the success it was. And he expended far more nervous energy than he ever let on. The carpet of cigarette butts under the tree whenever the XI played bore testimony to that. But everyone was deceived, most likely because he was always fond of a nap. You see, falling asleep is perceived by some to be a symptom of an indolent nature; I do not believe it is.

George has always found it easy, nay irresistible, to nod off during the day. Speak to anyone who has ever known him and his fondness for forty winks is invariably mentioned. His old team-mate at Worcestershire, Roly Jenkins, always said of him, 'George could fall asleep on a clothes line.' His own son calls him 'King of the Kippers'.

That is why some people believed that, having bowled 30 overs uphill and into the wind, he would kick off his boots, put his feet up, take great draughts at his pint of beer and enjoy a long and well-earned rest. Well, how wrong can you be! What he has done and what he has achieved since he retired is astonishing. For example, I asked him once to list all the clubs and societies he has served as president. After half a dozen, he began to run out of steam, apologising for not remembering any more. I have done my best to unearth them all but I wouldn't be at all surprised if, between the two of us, we have missed something. He is typically unassuming about the impressive roll of honour. He says that he has no idea why people keep asking him to be chairman of this or president of that, other than that 'they probably think the old man needs something to do that isn't too taxing. After all,' he adds with a chuckle, 'presidents are useless really but rally round, smile nicely and make the odd donation.' There is no doubt that George fits the bill perfectly, on all three counts, but needless to say there is much more to his popularity as a front man than merely assuming the role of a figurehead.

What you first look for in a president is gravitas, someone with a certain amount of stature and eminence in his community. George has that in spades. Then you would hope that person has influence, contacts, friends in high places. George has plenty of them; if he hasn't taught them, he's bowled against them. You would expect that your president would have a genuine interest in the *raison d'être* of your club or society, its ethos, its identity. It will be seen that George has been in great demand as president of numerous cricket clubs, which is no great surprise, but what is a surprise perhaps is that his greatest and lengthiest contribution to his community has been at the helm of the Malvern Civic Society. 'What do they know of cricket,' wrote the great West Indian author and philosopher, C. L. R. James, 'who only cricket know?' George does possess a hinterland beyond the boundary. It helps too if your president can chair a meeting. George is a genius at this. Cordiality, concensus and conciseness are hallmarks of any meeting he's in charge of. A godsend would be someone who can put forward a case articulately, sum up a discussion succinctly and put together a few choice words off the cuff, perhaps cracking a joke or two along the way. George spent half a lifetime in front of a class and knows exactly how to pitch a lesson, or craft a speech. And the icing on the cake would be if you could secure the services of someone who knows how to say grace before dinner. George's graces, little vignettes of metric wit, are legendary. So there you have it. Even before George strode out of Big School in a gown for the last time, pens were busy putting his name at the top of the first page of handbooks, club manuals and fixture cards.

It is ironic therefore that the one job he did seek and hope for did not this time fall into his lap. The Malvernian Society is much more than a simple old boys' club. The society is wealthy in its own right, owning tracts of land and real estate around the College and jealously guards its independence and autonomy. It was set up as a foundation, administered by an elected committee, to forge closer links between the school and its alumni as well as providing financial help to the College in times of need. It is self-evident that its secretary, who is salaried and runs the show, ought to be someone in close contact with current and past Malvernians and members of staff. George would be the obvious candidate. And he thought so too. This was not arrogance on his part. He believed he was uniquely suited, as a recent member of the Common Room, an ex-housemaster and an OM himself, to shake up an institution that had become a little moribund in recent years. He wanted to do the job because he felt he could make a difference and because Malvern College had been such an important part of his life.

The stumbling block was a man named Cyril Lace. He was of course a former pupil, had taught some history in the school and was a powerful figure in the society. He had been secretary but had retired, though remaining on the committee and still wielding considerable influence. His successor lasted but a year owing to ill health. George, who had just left the teaching staff, let it be known that he was very keen to take on the role. He believed he had plenty of support amongst the OM fraternity and allowed himself to assume it was a done deal. But for reasons that he cannot fathom even to this day, Lace blocked the appointment and had the post advertised. In the end, someone else, Brian Jacomb was his name, was appointed. 'He was a very nice man,' George conceded, 'but not terribly *dynamic*.' To be frank, George was shocked and hugely disappointed at the snub. What hurt more than anything else was the discovery of the depth of Lace's hostility and the lengths he had gone to thwart George. It seemed personal yet George was at a loss as to the reason. He knew of no obvious cause for any antipathy; indeed he remembered Lace as a master when he was at school as a boy and had thought that he had got on reasonably well with him. Cyril Lace was a tricky customer and George wasn't the only one who thought so. He was a finicky and nit-picking man, quick to find fault and easily offended. Once you got on the wrong side of him, his enmity was implacable. George had obviously upset him and there was no way he was going to get the job of secretary of the society whilst Lace had any influence.

'Jealousy!' cries Vanessa, in her normal forthright manner, 'It was jealousy, pure and simple. Georgie had been successful in so many fields, especially cricket, and Cyril resented that.' George himself is inclined to agree. The trouble was, he explained, that Lace was locked in the 1920s, when he was a boy at school at a time he considered to be a golden era in Malvern's history. 'Games players were gods then, and though no sportsman himself, he worshipped them. And any change to the school since those halcyon days was never for the better.' Lace was indeed forever bemoaning new ideas and initiatives and did his best to block progress of any kind. The final straw for him came when Malvern went co-educational. He simply couldn't cope with the thought of his beloved school besmirched by the presence of *girls*, so he sold his house, left town and never returned. 'He was a resentful and bitter old man,' said George sadly, 'who seemed forever miserable and spiteful. What a waste of a life!'

In all the conversations and interviews I have had with George, I have only ever heard him speak ill of two people. One was Walter Robins, his captain on that ill-fated MCC tour to Canada in 1951. He it was who had challenged George's captaincy in a later MCC match against Ireland, following that up with an objectionable letter to the committee which George is convinced secured his removal from any further captaincy duties for the club. That rankled. So did Cyril Lace's hostile opposition to George's hopes of running the Society.

There are a couple of stories about Cyril Lace that say it all. After a rare holiday abroad in Australia (he infrequently strayed far from Malvern), he came back full of enthusiasm for the viniculture of the Antipodes. To illustrate his point, he came round to George's house with a bottle of Australian sherry, together with a couple of tiny glasses that George reckoned would not have looked out of place in a Wendy house. He poured some sherry into the two glasses and invited George to taste. Very nice, thought George, but a sip, for that is all it was, seemed barely enough to form an opinion. With that, Lace replaced the cork in the bottle, put it back into his case, retrieved the glasses and bade George g'day. His tight-fistedness was legendary. As was his tetchiness. Donald Lindsay, who was headmaster at the time when Lace was secretary of the OM Society and therefore had much to do with him and knew how difficult he could be, discovered one day that it was Lace's 70th birthday. He decided it was high time he ought to try to bury the hatchet. Accordingly, a bottle of wine in his hand, he knocked on Lace's door. 'Happy 70th birthday, Cyril,' he said, 'I know you and I have had our differences but please accept this bottle as a peace offering.' 'I'm 71!' snapped Lace and slammed the door in the headmaster's face.

George swallowed his pride and offered to help the new secretary, Brian Jacomb, in any way that he could. But Jacomb too soon fell ill and when it became clear that he could no longer continue, he resigned and George found himself once more back in the frame. But by now, the political landscape in the Society had changed. Geoffrey Levick, a keen supporter of George, was chairman and Cyril Lace's influence had started to wane. Despite making it as plain as a pikestaff that he thoroughly disapproved of George, his opinions were sidelined and George was duly elected. Better late than never, George thought, as he eagerly took hold of the reins and set about modernising the whole operation.

It amuses George, as he surveys the ranks of computers and secretaries that fill the current OM office. 'I only had dear old Joyce as secretarial help for two mornings a week,' he observes, with a smile. That cheerful good humour and dedication to the cause is why he is so popular with the young, why so many generations of OMs come up to greet him warmly and why he was such an obvious and successful choice as secretary. He may take a minute or two to remember the name (the most common surname in the Society's Register is 'Old Boy' and first name 'Hello') but the smile and easy laugh are never forced.

He remained at the helm for 15 years. He believed that the Society exercised its financial and political clout prudently, he developed closer links with the headmaster, Roy Chapman, and got on well with him, sensing that his help and advice were appreciated, and he put in train many new initiatives, such as a regular newsletter, that were deemed overdue and necessary. And, most of all, it kept him in touch. Every day, he was treading the same paths he had done as a schoolboy and a master, for most of his life in fact. *So, no withdrawal symptoms when you retired?* 'No, not really. The work in the OM office kept me busy. That and my job at *The Times*.' It was his friend, Denis Saunders, who had put him up to the latter. Saunders was the schools' sport correspondent for *The Daily Telegraph* and suggested that George could fill a similar role at *The Times*. Thus George found himself on the payroll of that venerable institution 'without ever, not even once, going to their offices in London,' reporting on schools' cricket and football, filing his copy down the phone line, 300 words of finely crafted prose, 'though sometimes a sub-editor would cruelly hack it apart a bit.'

Reading through cuttings of his match reports, meticulously preserved in scrapbooks, one is struck by the clear and urbane tone of his writing style. You feel that George would be incapable of inelegant expression, either spoken or written. He doesn't do ugly. How about this for a piece of purple prose? 'Sparkling football was played by both sides, there were short, crisp passes, excellent marking, fine handling in each goal and particularly skilful play from both No. 7s.' He often went to some length to describe the scene: 'In scorching weather on The Wilderness at Charterhouse, an ill-fitting name for a beautiful ground…' Or this: 'Repton beat Bolton yesterday on a beautiful surface that would have done Wembley no discredit.' As you would expect from a geographer, he usually made mention of the weather: 'The wind, which strengthened during the match, dictated territorial advantage.' And: 'In spring sunshine of scarcely believable warmth…' On one occasion, the match was so dull that he was hard-pressed to write anything of interest. So he penned some tosh about the school and its location in the depths of the country. In fact, it was situated only 12 miles from Marble Arch. 'And they printed it!' he hooted with laughter. As a former master in charge of cricket himself, he frequently went to pains to mention sympathetically the lot of the groundsman. For example: 'Agar's Plough was very wet after rain similar to that which curtailed play in the PGA golf championship.' Obviously the cricket that miserable afternoon did not greatly excite his attention, for the rest of the paragraph was devoted to the sterling work over the years of the Eton head groundsman.

George being George, he was careful to applaud the preservation of quirky little traditions. At Lord's, in the annual fixture between Eton and Harrow, 'there was a delay of 35 minutes but as the skies cleared, the fair sprinkling of toppers, the popping of Champagne corks and a few snatches of Harrow songs made the afternoon enjoyable.' And this: 'It was a pleasure to see the visitors wearing their traditional pink and something of a surprise to find the home team in red.' Tut tut. But the game went ahead despite this wardrobe faux-pas: 'Mr Ashby, the referee, found the contrast acceptable however.' And, par for the course, he somehow found room for the odd, comical observation. 'Both the Cheltenham and Malvern captains thought they had won the toss and both led their side out onto the field.' This one, however, takes the biscuit: 'We had the unlooked for and probably unique phenomenon of play being interrupted by a fish as the batsman was struck by a foot-long mackerel dropped by a passing seagull.'

For eight years, *The Times* readers were treated to George's little gems, if they had eyes to look. But sadly, the job began to contract. School sport, or at least the reporting of it, was falling out of favour with editors and George found himself more and more at the sharp end of a sub-editor's scalpel. Sometimes, his 300-word piece would be chopped down to 20. Slowly, he began to lose heart. Who wouldn't? It must be galling to labour over an article, taking pains to capture the moment and reflect accurately what has taken place, only to read the next morning a bland few lines with the score. 'Especially if you are being paid by the word,' he reminded me. In the end, he decided to jack it in. He wrote to his employers, whom he had never met, explaining his decision and thanking them for his employment. 'I had absolutely nothing but extreme courtesy from *The Times*,' he remarked, 'No matter whom I spoke to on the phone, they were always absolutely delightful.'

Did you dread or look forward to retirement? 'I think I welcomed it. I always knew it was coming so it was hardly a shock. Don't forget I was newly married, so the time

Vanessa and I had together was marvellous, immensely rewarding. And my involvement with the OMs and my reporting for *The Times* kept me from being idle. That is to say,' he added with a snort of the usual self-deprecating mirth, 'any more idle than I have always been!' And of course he had presidential credentials that could not possibly be squandered. Among the cricket clubs that sought his governorship, one that stands out for length of service is Malvern Ramblers Cricket Club. He was elected president at the club's inception and he remains in the saddle some forty years later. He remembers being invited for a drink at the Unicorn pub in Malvern by three senior members. After a pint or two, he cottoned on that he was being grilled as to his suitability for the post. He must have passed muster for he was invited to be their first president and no one has seen fit to challenge his position ever since. 'Probably forgotten I'm there. I'm going to resign next year. Getting too old.' That is, by the way, a familiar resolve, rarely carried out.

I am indebted to Mike Vockins for the following story about George and Malvern Ramblers Cricket Club. Mike was for 30 years the secretary, or chief executive these days, at Worcestershire CCC, and obviously knew George well through his association with the club. He is also a man of the cloth, rural dean of Ledbury and a prebendary of Hereford Cathedral, serving three parishes around the Malvern Hills. George pulled in a favour to get the reverend to speak at the annual dinner of Malvern Ramblers CC and he agreed. The event took place at The Railway Inn in Malvern Wells. Let me state straightaway that there is nothing wrong with The Railway Inn as a pub, though it has been under several different managements since then, but not even its most loyal customer would say that it ranks with the Long Room at Lord's as a venue for a cricket dinner. On arrival, both Mike and George were greeted by a gentleman with tattoos, earrings and an eye patch. He introduced himself as the MC for the night and enquired of them what they would like to drink. A gin and tonic would do nicely, they both agreed. The MC disappeared then came back with a *bottle* of gin. The tonic was less easily located.

The meal passed without incident though both president and guest speaker were vaguely aware of a gathering excitement among the diners that could scarcely be ascribed to anticipation of their speeches. Eventually, the cheese course having been dispensed with, the decks were cleared and George introduced Mike Vockins. He was listened to politely and sat down to a smattering of applause. George then said a few words in response, mentioning the season just passed and thanking the captain, the committee, the groundsman, the tea ladies, the bar staff, the umpires, the scorers, Uncle Tom Cobley and all. Knowing George, I doubt he left anyone out and I'm sure his speech was as witty and as diverting as always. He sat down with barely a single clap. Clearly his audience had their minds on something other than pretty speeches. With a bellow of approval, the bolts on the outside doors were rammed home as the MC with the eye patch announced the commencement of the night's entertainment. And in bounded a stripper dressed as a nurse. To the music of 'Goodness Gracious Me', made famous by Peter Sellers and Sophia Loren, she proceeded to act as no nurse ever should. One can picture the fixed smiles on the faces of president and reverend as the atmosphere in the room became steadily more raucous. Eventually, the nurse finished her shift … but worse was to follow. A comedian took centre stage and his material, to put it kindly, had only passing reference to the noble game of cricket. Finally, his lively and bawdy spell came to an end only for Eye Patch to stand up to announce that the second stripper had failed to turn up. The disappointment expressed by his audience was palpable. In fact, it threatened to turn mutinous. However Stripper Number One offered to do one of her 'specials' and her kind gesture was gratefully and noisily endorsed by one and all. That is except the gallant hero of our story and his loyal priest. They gave each other a quick glance and, making their excuses, they fled. 'To my dying day,' Mike Vockins told me, 'I shall never forget the look on George's face when the "special" was announced.' George said that he was all for staying but felt that he had to show solidarity with the Revd Vockins by leaving at the same time. 'And do you know what?' he said with a shake of the head, 'To this day, I have never met anyone who admits he was there to witness what was so special about the "special"!' To cap it all, the distinctly dodgy MC with the eye patch ran off with the evening's profit and was never seen again. Malvern Ramblers CC survived and George is still their president.

The great and the good of other cricket clubs beat a path to George's door to lure him into their president's chair, two of the most notable being The Gentlemen of Worcestershire and The Cryptics. But the most gratifying was the most unexpected. After he finished playing for Worcestershire in 1957, George was elected to serve on the committee and though not a regular fixture at meetings, he attended whenever he could, when school commitments allowed him. Mike Vockins, the secretary of the club at the time, takes up the story. 'We'd had a succession of presidents who, though very worthy in their own way, were hardly household names. It was my idea actually to invite former players to take on the role, people with stature who were known by the public at large for having made huge contributions to the club on the field of play. We didn't really need faceless committee men who had served their time. We wanted *names*!' His first choice was Don Kenyon and it was a popular decision. Kenyon was a prolific run-scorer, the heaviest in the county's history, and he had been a well-liked and successful captain, leading his team to successive championships in 1964 and 1965. Tom Graveney told me that Kenyon was the finest captain he had ever played under, 'and I played under a few in my time – including myself!' The move to appoint Kenyon as president was a clear success but then Vockins was left with the knotty problem of who was going to succeed him. 'To my mind, the obvious person was George. He was born to do it. And what an inspiring choice it turned out to be!'

The offer came as complete surprise to George but he was delighted to accept and hugely honoured. It was 1990 and he did it for four years. Originally, the term of office was two years but so good at it was he that they extended it for a further year, then another. It was a golden era at the club. The championship had been secured the year before and in George's tenure of office, the Benson and Hedges Cup, the Refuge Assurance Cup (both in 1991) and the NatWest Trophy (in 1993) were added to the trophy cabinet. In addition, the team finished second in the championship in 1993 and were runners-up in the Benson and Hedges cup final in 1994. There were some fine players on the staff: Phil Neale the captain, Graeme Hick, Ian Botham, Graham Dilley, Tom Moody, Neal Radford, Phil Newport, Steve Rhodes. It must have been heady times for George, who remembered the days when he was playing when Worcestershire were more used to finishing in the lower reaches of the championship table.

Duncan Fearnley (he of the bat-making and sports firm) was the chairman of the cricket committee and responsible for the playing side of things. Those who know Duncan, and he would probably agree himself, could never make the claim that he was a shadowy figure in the club. Someone who drove a white Rolls Royce around the country ('at breakneck speed,' George commented admiringly, 'and he was never pulled over by the cops!') was hardly a shrinking violet. He would stride up to Walter Hadlee, the manager of the touring New Zealand side, and address him thus: 'Let me introduce you to our president, George Chesterton. You won't know him but – ' Of course George and Hadlee had been old sparring partners when the Oxford side he was playing in beat the New Zealanders in 1949. And with Brian Close: 'You won't know our president, George Chesterton, so let me – ' Brian Close and George were old friends; they'd played against each other enough times. This happened on several occasions: George knows so many people, no more so than in the cricket world. He and Fearnley would attend as many of the away matches as they could and George would often be a passenger in the Rolls as it ate up the miles on England's motorways. 'George would often fall asleep in the passenger seat when I was driving,' Fearnley informed me, with some incredulity. 'Anyway, once we were travelling to Blackpool. We'd barely got out of Worcester before I noticed that George wasn't answering my questions. He was fast asleep! Just as we came in sight of the Blackpool Tower, George woke up. "Well, that was a bit of a boring journey, wasn't it?" he said. Bloody cheek!' George was listening to this account as Fearnley warmed to his theme wearing what you might call a beatified smile, as if allowing an excitable pupil his head as he tells his tall story. 'But I did enjoy those trips in the Rolls, I must admit,' George said, 'And wherever I went I would be greeted by "Good morning, Mr President" and "What can I get you to drink, Mr President?" Great for one's morale!'

His four years as president re-introduced him to the world of professional cricket and he loved it. He made sure that he got to know the players and their wives and enjoyed their company. 'Mind you,' he took pains to point out, 'I never got *too* close. That would never do.' He took pleasure in witnessing the action first-hand without ever feeling the urge to become *part* of what was going on. He just loved watching the game.

And where better to watch it than on the balcony of the committee room? When he could tear himself away from the action, his opinions were constantly sought and his advice valued. He was made chairman of the Centenary Committee and 'many good things that happened that year were down to George,' Mike Vockins swears. 'He has such a warm personality and people respect him. Great at getting people to work together. He was a brilliant president. And his little speeches off the cuff… And the graces, too. Priceless!' Norman Whiting, a former team-mate, who latterly became president as well, told me that George set the pattern which others strove to follow: 'He was a natural. Everybody liked him and had great respect for him.' Tom Graveney was another huge fan. How much George was responsible for Tom's being nominated to succeed him as president in 1994 is a matter of speculation but Tom is in no doubt whose fingerprints were all over the decision. And he was immensely grateful. 'I got to know him well during those years. It's true he had bowled me out all that time ago in the Parks but it wasn't until he became president that we became firm friends.' He listed the reasons for George's success in the role. 'First, he was good company. He could talk to anyone and make that person somehow feel special. He was level-headed, he remained calm at all times and he suggested, quietly and without fuss, the most sensible course of action. People listened to him. He had an aura about him. And of course, he had been a mighty fine player in his own right. He brought wisdom to the presidency. He also had a great sense of humour; there were these little barbs of wit that you had to listen out for. There was never a dull conversation when George was in the room. But he was strong too. He was nobody's fool and you underestimated him at your peril.' And how about this for a tribute from one of the greatest living figures in English cricket? Graveney finished his assessment thus: 'There has never been a nicer man in the game. George is a gentleman to the core.'

Mind you, it wasn't all gin and tonic and idle chat on the committee balcony. There was one episode when all of George's powers of diplomacy and conciliation were tested to the limit. Phil Neale had been captain since 1982, and a very fine one too. He had led the side to successive championships in 1988 and 1989, so one would have imagined his position at the helm to be reasonably secure. But in the 1991 season, the results had been poor and the cricket committee became jittery. They voted to sack him mid-season. George was horrified. He felt that it was grossly unfair, that Neale deserved more time and, in any case, to change jockeys halfway through a race would only unsettle the horse. But the president had no vote on the cricket committee so he was powerless to do anything about it. Neale got the chop. Tim Curtis replaced him and of course George did all he could to support the new captain taking over in difficult circumstances. But he believed it was the wrong choice. 'It was an unhappy chapter,' was his verdict.

That chapter may have been an unhappy one but the rest of his time as president of his old club was a thoroughly enjoyable interlude in his life. He still maintains close contact with old players and friends. Indeed, the Worcestershire Old Players Association (WOPA) was his idea. They meet once a year, at the New Road ground, during a county game, for food, drink and reminiscence, providing at the same time blessed opportunity for autograph hunters. George is now the second oldest surviving player, Norman Whiting edging him out by one year, and still he keeps the photo album immaculately up to date.

That he was invited to become president of a cricket club, even one as prestigious as Worcestershire, will be a source of wonder to none of his acquaintances. But his involvement in the Malvern Civic Society would not have been so readily predicted. The realisation of what the Civic Society is and what it purports to do rather crept up on me over a period of time. Like many people, I glance through the local rag each week, sometimes more closely than other times.

Slowly, I became aware that George's photograph appeared more frequently than that of anyone else I knew, either by name or by sight. He would be extending a guiding hand to some dignitary or smiling benignly in the midst of a group of important personages or welcoming a VIP with a chain of office or pointing out an artefact of great interest or unveiling a blue plaque on a building. Mr George Chesterton, president of the Malvern Civic Society, was obviously in great demand for photo opportunities. So I thought I had better do some homework. George was pretty hopeless with my investigative endeavours. 'Oh, they're very nice to me,' he said airily, 'but I'm useless really.' Fortunately I was put in touch with a lovely lady, Katherine Barber, who was only too happy to give the lie to George's assessment of his contributions, providing me with chapter and verse on George's involvement with the Civic Society and how much was owed by them to his patronage.

The Malvern Civic Society is a pressure group set up to preserve what is best in the historic town of Malvern and to encourage improvements in appearance, amenities and facilities. Much of the significant Victorian architecture would have been lost if the society had not put its oar in and thwarted misguided building plans by unscrupulous developers. Many a shop front and dwelling façade has been restored, several old buildings have been saved, the heritage of the water cure, the wells and the spas, so inextricably bound up in the history of the town, have been preserved and often given a facelift. Weekly planning applications are scrutinised and blueprints for new housing estates are carefully monitored in an attempt to stop Malvern from sprawling, a fate that has befallen too many of our English towns. Those of us who are lucky enough to live in Malvern and who appreciate its particular charm, nestling as it does on the slopes of the beautiful Malvern Hills, clearly owe the Civic Society a debt of gratitude.

George was involved from the outset. A redoubtable lady, Mabel Varley, who was well known in the town, had the idea and soon persuaded George to climb aboard. This was way back in 1958. He had just retired from county cricket and clearly needed occupying in the holidays. At the time, it was known as the Friends of Malvern and he continued to take an active interest in its affairs whenever duties at the College permitted. After finishing with teaching, he was able to become more involved and in 1985, he was elected chairman of the newly named Malvern Civic Society. He was an effective chairman and kept on getting re-elected year after year, despite his protestations and expressed wishes to resign. Eventually, he got his own way and stood aside in 1992. So they made him president, determined that his expertise would not be lost to them, and so he remains to this day.

Notable successes on his watch have been the restoration of the old bandstand in Priory Park, saving and renovating the war memorial in Barnards Green, marking the 150th anniversary of the water cure by commissioning and unveiling numerous plaques around the town on the significant sites and salvaging many other small but important features in the area. His knowledge of local history is encyclopaedic. He has conducted guided town walks and is a most informative chaperone. His ghost tours are great fun, I'm told, and no one dare ask him if they are lost because he is of course a geographer and knows his maps. He is always in great demand at annual dinners and other functions. Mrs Barber related that he once made a cake in the shape of the bandstand, which is the society's logo, and presented it at a celebratory picnic in the park. I hope they recognised it and didn't mistake it for the ayatollah's hat.

All this I discovered from Mrs Barber. George's account of his contributions naturally differs from hers. 'I do nothing but unveil plaques.' *Any plaque in particular you remember?* 'Er ... oh yes. I do remember the one outside Lloyds Bank.' And he started to giggle and soon he had me going, before I'd even heard the story. As the bank was on the main road, he felt that it would be advisable to warn the police so that they could set up the necessary traffic controls. It so happened that he had a descendant of one of the famous Foster brothers (six of them played for Worcestershire at the turn of the 20th century) as a guest in his house. There was a county match on the next day and they were going to watch the cricket. George prevailed upon his houseguest to come along 'as rentacrowd.' It was just as well. No one else turned up. The traffic on the Malvern to Ledbury road was held up for three people: Foster, George and the bank manager. Unfortunately, the plaque had to be situated 8 feet up, to prevent vandalism. And the bank manager, who was to pull the toggle, was barely 5 feet tall. They got a chair from inside the bank. What the motorists, held up by the men in blue, thought of it all is not recorded.

I asked him about a photo of him in the *Malvern Gazette* in front of yet another blue plaque, this time in the company of some wild-looking Rastafarians with colourful beads and shaggy dreadlocks. 'You know,' he said, 'you couldn't meet a nicer bunch of fellows. They were simply delightful.' *No doubt, but what were you doing posing with Rastas in front of the Abbey Hotel in Malvern?* He was playing for time. And then he remembered. 'Haile Selassie!' he cried, 'Ah, I remember now. Haile Selassie apparently came to Malvern and stayed in the Abbey Hotel. Quite what his connection was with these ... chaps with their long hair, I haven't a clue. But they were great fun. It was a splendid little occasion.'

RETIREMENT

It wasn't all blue plaques. Of course it wasn't. There was one episode where all George's skills as a steadying influence were called into play. Waitrose wanted to build a store in Malvern, in an area called Back Lane. In many people's opinion, Back Lane was an appropriate name for a scruffy and neglected part of town and a brand new supermarket was just what the place needed. George was all for it. 'Why on earth would anyone want to object to a nice supermarket like Waitrose, especially on such a seedy piece of land? In any case, Malvern didn't have a supermarket.' But to his surprise, the planned development ran into violent opposition and the Civic Society, to his mortification, was split down the middle over the issue. Passions were stirred, some very unpleasant meetings were held and the chairman resigned. As president, George had to steer a tricky middle course, attempting to prevent the society from tearing itself apart. Membership dropped alarmingly; at one stage, they were down to a bare 150. Katherine Barber stepped into the breach as chairman, even though she had little or no experience of the job. George is full of praise for her. He felt she was a brave leader, with unquenchable enthusiasm and optimism, and she quickly proved to be a woman of substance. Under her leadership, the society was saved and went from strength to strength. Numbers are now up to a creditable 400 and the society is flourishing. She is rather more inclined to praise George for his calm guidance in a time of crisis, saying that without his charisma and strength of character, they would have been sunk. 'And he's still there,' she says, 'contributing immensely to the society and to Malvern.' Waitrose built their supermarket, by the way, and it's still there too, contributing immensely to Malvern, or not, depending on your point of view.

At a recent AGM of the Civic Society, he decided to make more of an effort than usual for his annual report, so for inspiration, he delved into the minutes of the meeting some forty years previously. Solemnly, he informed the members of the three most pressing local concerns at that time. 'One: the gas lamps along the Wells Road. Two: the disgraceful state of disrepair of the Tudor Hotel. Three: what to do with the "Worm", the passage that used to link the railway station to the big hotel opposite, now the Girls' College! In other words, not much has changed in forty years. *Plus ça change...*'

Well George, you have convinced me that life is very busy in your retirement but not every day can be filled with meetings, guided tours and cricket matches. I reminded him that I used to walk home for lunch when I was teaching and pass his house. On my way back for the first period of the afternoon, I would cast a glance in through the French windows of his sitting room and see a pair of feet up on the armrest of the sofa. Often, at the end of the day, trudging wearily uphill towards home, I would see the same pair of feet still perched on the armrest. He laughed. 'Power nap,' he assured me. Apart from the odd nap, I wondered, what else does he do on those days when he has not much on? He is proud that, in his ninetieth year, he still manages the odd round of golf. He has a large extended family and he is a great hit with the new generation, now growing up fast. I motioned at the army of little porcelain boxes lined up on the mantelpiece. 'I am a bit of a collector,' he admitted, 'Nothing serious. Mainly cricket memorabilia.' He and Vanessa keep a house in Devon, which provides a welcome bolthole for them every so often. And, encouraged by his stepdaughter Tamsin, he wrote a book. Originally, he had been putting down, in the form of letters to her, memories of his wartime experiences in the RAF. Most veterans of conflict are reluctant to go back over old ground, claiming that it can be of no interest to the younger generation. In addition, it is likely that some memories are just too painful. And if we are not careful, it will be too late and all that valuable, primary, verbal history will be lost. You can understand their reluctance, however, and that is why we should be immensely grateful to Tamsin. She persuaded George to gather all the material contained in his letters and to publish it as a book. The result is *Also Flew*. The inscription within the cover says it all: 'This book is dedicated to all those who were not able to queue for their demob suits.' I found the account of his life in the RAF riveting ... and somehow humbling. Such understated courage and unswerving sense of duty. It contributed to my determination to write my own book about George and, needless to say, I have drawn on it heavily in the chapter on his wartime experiences. He writes well, he has a felicitous turn of phrase and his subject matter is absorbing. I have little doubt that much time and effort were expended on its publication. George always takes the trouble to get things *right*.

And then he disclosed, almost as an afterthought, that the great love of his latter years has been the Cricketer Cup. I remembered that chance meeting years ago we had on the balcony of the pavilion when he was nervously watching his old boys' team in action. The last rites of an easy victory were being enacted but he was as jumpy as a kitten in a dogs' home. Clearly, the match meant a great deal to him. Or, not so much the match itself, but the *result*. 'Come on,' he was muttering testily, 'Stop messing around and get on with it!' Someone had played an airy-fairy shot. It mattered little. Malvern were cantering home. 'We've got to wrap it up now!' The passion in his voice was as plain as a pikestaff. George always likes to win, we know that. But this was special. This was the Cricketer Cup.

The concept was born in 1966, over a few glasses of port, with Tony Winlaw and Jim Swanton, journalists both, and Ben Brocklehurst, editor of *The Cricketer* magazine, in attendance. The idea was that the old boys of the sixteen major cricket-playing public schools would play each year in a knock-out format. Malvern was one of those selected. As it happened, Malvern against Winchester was the very first match played in the fledgling competition. George captained the Old Malvernians and his old friend and contemporary, Hubert Doggart, captained the Old Wykehamists. George had played against Doggart in school matches, RAF v the army, Oxford v Cambridge and Worcestershire v Sussex. And now they were to renew their rivalry in the Cricketer Cup. Malvern won. They lost in the semi-final to Radley, a match George remembers well. 'I used to bowl my 12 overs straight off. I'd seize up if I had to come back for a second spell. I got someone out. In strode Ted Dexter. Just as I was about to bowl, he pulled away, announcing in that drawl of his that he had forgotten to put on his box! He then said, "Oh, never mind. I'll get it at the end of this over." The insult! But I bowled him first ball. So he didn't have to bother!' Notwithstanding the cheap dismissal of the great man, Malvern batted badly and succumbed meekly.

They made no mistake the following year, beating Harrow in the final. There is a lovely photo of George, in his blazer, walking forward, arms outstretched, to receive the winner's pennant from the chairman of the MCC, Gubby Allen. What strikes me is the expression on George's face. It is something akin to ecstatic. It transcends the joy of victory or the satisfaction of a job well done. It obviously meant a great deal to him. And so it has remained to this very day. The passion has not dimmed, not by a single watt, over the years. It is a wretchedly glum Chesterton household when Malvern have just been knocked out.

To be fair, that happens far less frequently than you might imagine. Malvern's record in the cup is second only to Tonbridge (they had won 8 to Tonbridge's 14 by 2011). I say 'cup' but in fact for several years there was no cup at all. So incensed was Ian MacLaurin at the perceived slight of there being 'no cup' when Malvern won it that first time that he continued the furious diatribe long into the evening's celebrations. In the end, the barmaid at the pub where the merrymaking was taking place got so fed up with him that she seized a tiny pewter cup, 'the size of an eggcup', and presented it to him to shut him up. Ian MacLaurin did get his way though. He usually does. There is now a fine trophy for the winners.

They won it again three years later but the next decade was fallow. By now, the competition had been extended to 32 schools. Each of the original 16 was asked to nominate another school to join. Because Malvern had a close affinity with Eastbourne College, they recommended them, only to have the choice rejected unilaterally by E. W. Swanton. 'Too many schools from the south,' he declared, 'What about Ampleforth? They do a good lunch there!' Typical Swanton, those who knew him would say. But he was the self-appointed supreme being of all things cricket and his word went. Then came a golden era in OM cricket. Their record up until the present day has been outstanding and is a source of great pride to their spiritual leader. That is, if they can negotiate the first round. 'That's true,' agreed George, 'We normally give a good account of ourselves once we get over that hurdle. Malvernians are invariably slow off the mark. Not early risers, you might say.'

I wondered aloud at the reason for Malvern's success. It's not as if Malvern has had a monopoly of all the promising young cricketers passing through its doors. But the good players come from far and wide to play. Their loyalty to their old school is commendable but they wouldn't do it if they didn't enjoy it. George must take a lot of the credit for fostering this relaxed yet focussed team spirit. Cricket is more of an individualistic game than most team sports but the best sides are invariably the most united. Although he was all for playing down his contribution, George did acknowledge that his constant presence as player, captain and latterly team manager has had a beneficial and stabilising influence on the club. Is it any surprise, to draw a parallel with, say, football, that Manchester United are so successful when they have kept faith with the same manager for 30 years when other clubs seem to change theirs season by season? The acid test will come when George is no longer able to fulfil his all-encompassing role. It's probably the same at Old Trafford; everyone gives a shudder and puts that unwelcome problem firmly on the back burner.

I then spent some time in deliberation as to why the Cricketer Cup means so much to George. There is no one, simple answer, I concluded. It is part and parcel of the very fabric of his being and as such is interesting to unravel. First and foremost, his love of cricket and Malvern, the two great pillars of his life, find their continued expression in the OM Cricket Club. Second, he is mixing with people whom he has known and liked over so many years. Then there is the reputation of the school to care about; there is no doubt that Malvern's success in the Cricketer Cup has kept the name of the school at the forefront of national consciousness. And of course it keeps him in touch with generation after generation of boys. Photographs of the teams with thinning hair and increased girth might give the lie to their description as 'boys' but to him they are still his boys. And they repay this loyalty with unashamed affection. He is known as Mr Malvern and there is no more popular figure on the boundary's edge. There is not the slightest hint of condescension in their regard. They really do respect him. Of course they do. He's done it all anyway in his career and, in any case, he makes them laugh with his humorous anecdotes. If any one of them has a funny story to tell, George can always trump it.

But all this would count for little if the cricket were not competitive. There is no doubt that the standard of the Cricketer Cup is high enough to satisfy his exacting standards. Just take a look at a snapshot of the players who have represented their schools in the competition: Peter May (Charterhouse); Colin Cowdrey (Tonbridge); Trevor Bailey (Dulwich); Ramon Subba Row (Whitgift); Ted Dexter (Radley); Nawab of Pataudi (Winchester); Graham Roope (Bradfield); Roger Tolchard (Malvern); Vic Marks (Blundells); Derek Pringle (Felsted); Phil Tufnell (Highgate); Nick Knight (Felsted); Andrew Strauss (Radley); Matt Prior (Brighton). And let us not forget Clare Connor (Brighton), the England women's captain who, in 2002, became the first old girl to play in the Cricketer Cup. Test match players all. Not to mention a host of county, minor county and good club players as well. You can be assured that the standard of cricket, and the level of intensity in which it is played, is hot enough. George tells a story, as usual, to illustrate the point. Malvern were playing Whitgift. Ramon Subba Row came out to bat. It so happened that Subba Row had just had a successful time opening the batting for England but on this occasion he found the middle of his bat hard to locate and, after scratching around ineffectually for a while, he was dismissed. On his return to the pavilion, he complained about being 'sledged'. Now, I am not sure that in the early 1960s, the verb 'to sledge' had been invented, at least not when it pertained to anything that wasn't snow related. But I am equally sure that then, as now, if your opponents took exception to the cut of your jib or the brittleness of your technique, someone would tell you. In any event, Subba Row felt that, as an England player, he should have been accorded a little more respect out there, in the middle. George offered no moral judgement in his telling of the story but I saw Bryan Richardson quietly smirking in the background and as he used to field at short-leg, it didn't need much to put two and two together to guess the culprit. No, Cricketer Cup matches are definitely not genial affairs between the clergy and the local pub team on the village green.

Oh, and by the way, George is president of the Cricketer Cup.

❋ ❋ ❋ ❋ ❋

The problem for anyone writing a biography is how to end your story. This is particularly acute when your subject is still alive. There may be yet a chapter to tell, a twist in the tail, a last-minute equaliser. I am always faintly amused by those so-called biographies, usually of footballers, anxious to get their story into print even when they are still playing so that they can maximise their earnings before their star starts to wane.

Obviously that is not the purpose of this book. Although his three careers have ended, George is still very much alive and kicking and no one would dare to suggest his star is on the wane. Besides, stars can be seen to burn bright long after they've ceased to exist, I'm told. I've no doubt that, in years to come, when Malvernians refer affectionately to 'George', they won't be talking about the statue of the warrior saint standing guard at the top of the steps, with his hands on the hilt of his sword, looking down over the school grounds and out over the Severn Valley.

But the problem remained; how to bring George's story to a fitting conclusion. Then I remembered a conversation with his son, Colin. He told me how worried he had been on the occasion of George's 70th birthday and what sort of suitable present he should get him. It transpired that he was friendly with an artist who had been in the RAF and over a jar or two of ale in their Devon local, they discussed the possibility of commissioning a painting of George's Stirling when he was in 190 Squadron during the war. The idea took hold, and with Posy's support, both emotional and financial, they ran with it. Employing a certain amount of subterfuge, Colin got Vanessa to 'borrow' George's logbook and proper and exhaustive research was undertaken. The result was better than anyone could have expected and helped to establish the artist's reputation in this particular military niche. The painting was of George's Stirling, at 1400 hours on 18th September 1944, towing a Horsa glider through fierce enemy flak at the battle of Arnhem. Great care had been taken over the authenticity of the scene, the bridge shrouded in smoke on the ground, the wind direction, the right tactical air support, the precise markings and correct class of the Spitfires in the background. Anyone looking at this painting could not possibly be unaffected by its powerful depiction of conflict in the air.

But would George like it? Was it true to life? Were there any howlers of inaccuracy? Was it as he remembered it? Nervously Colin drew up outside his father's house, unloaded the painting, swathed in wrapping paper, from the boot of his car, and carried it inside. Solemnly, the present was unveiled. George looked at it and said nothing. Eventually Colin could no longer bear the silence. 'Is it all right, Dad?' he enquired anxiously, 'Is it … is it OK?' Still George stared at it wordlessly. Eventually, he said, in a voice not entirely in control of itself, 'All I can remember is the noise and the smell.'

It was an emotional moment. Even if, God forbid, George had been unable *to queue for his demob suit,* and the rest of his life, all those overs, all those lessons, all those people whose lives have been touched, all those stories and anecdotes, had never happened, the representation on canvas of one moment of one aircraft in one sortie in one battle of a titanic struggle for freedom is deserving of our admiration and gratitude.

INDEX

References to illustrations are shown in *roman italics*. Subheadings under George Chesterton appear in approximate chronological order, while others appear alphabetically.

Aircraft: Airspeed Oxford 78–9; Avro York 102; Boeing Stearman 77, 78; English Electric Canberra 226; Focke-Wulf FW190 76, 82; Glider towing 83–4, 86, 87, 95, 264, *x–xi*; Lockheed Ventura 81, 82, 83–4, 92–3; North American Mitchell 83; Short Stirling 13, 14–16, 84–5, 86–7, 88, 91, 92, 93–4, 95, 96–7, 98–9, 101, 102, 137, 157, 264
Akhtar, Shoib 161
Alberta, Canada 77–9
Allen, David 153
Allen, Gubby 113, 261, *xxii*
Also Flew 260
Anderson, Lord 216
Anton, Hamish *xiv*
Archer, Ken 160
Ardennes counter-offensive 101
Arnhem, 1944 13–16, 18, 94–100, 102, 157, 264, *x–xi*
Atomic bombs 102
Austen, Jane 26
Australian cricket team 159, 160, 165–8, *xvi*

Bailey, David 195–6, 198, 199, 200, 203, 208
Bailey, Trevor 72, 120, 143, 159–60, 175, 176, 263, *xvii*
Bannister, Roger 111
Barbados cricket tour 230–1, 232
Barber, Katherine 257, 258, 259
Barnards Green knock-out cup 136
Barrington, Ken 153, 161
Bath and Wells, Bishop of 238–9, *xxiv*
Beckenn, David 196–7
Bedser, Alec 120, 148, 153, 159, 161, 175
Bedser, Eric 120, 161
Benaud, Richie 160, 166, 167
Bennett, Don 173, 174
Benson and Hedges Cup 254
Bentley car 189–92, 200, 217, 218, *xxiii*
Berlin 104
Berry, Bob 164, 169
Beveridge, Bob 51–2, 125, 128, 136
Bird, Ronnie 137, 145, 156, 161–2, *xiv, xvi*

Blackpool, Stanley Park 174
Blackshaw, John 227, 238
Blenheim Palace 54–5, 56–61, 187, 233, *iv, v*; Great Park 61: South Lawn 59–60, *iv*
Bletchley Park 76
Blumenau, Ralph 46, 55, 56, 57, 67, 70
Boobyer, Brian 119, *xiv*
Booth, Roy 173–4, *xvii, xviii–xix*
Boscombe Down airfield 88
Botham, Ian 177, 254
Bournemouth 82; Dean Park cricket ground 156
Bowlers, fast 160–1
Boycott, Geoff 139
Brasenose College, Oxford 105–10; cricket team 110; Mods (first-year exams) debacle 109–10; scout Ernest 107; Heath Harrison Exhibition 64–5, 69, 106
Brennan, Don 159–60, *xvii*
British Army: 1st Airborne Division 13, 14, 15, 16, 87; 6th Airborne Division 90, 91; Dorset Regiment 95; Home Guard 61, 72; Special Air Service (SAS) 93, 94, 100
British Expeditionary Force 60
Brize Norton RAF station 217, 218
Broadbent, Bob 172, 173, 174, *xvi, xvii, xviii–xix*
Brocklehurst, Ben 197, 261
Brooks, David 78
Brown, Freddie 177, *xix*
Brown, Sir Stephen 241
Buccaneers cricket club 110
Bulge, Battle of the, 1944–5 101
Burke, Jim 166
Burnett, Bruce 217, 218

Cambridge, Old Malvernians dinner 214–15
Cambridge University cricket team 110–11, 117–18
Campbell, Ian 119, *xiv*
Canada: MCC tour 138, 148, 149–50, 151, 152, 154, *xv*; RAF training in 76–9, 80–1
Canadian Army 61
Canterbury, Archbishop of *ii, see also* Runcie, Robert
Carr, Donald 103, 114, 115, 116, 177, *xiv*
Carter, Alan 190, 193–4, 199–200, 206, 214–15
Carter, Sarah 220–1
Cartwright, Tom 176
Chamberlain, Neville 55

INDEX